KAFKA AND PINTER: SHADOW-BOXING

Kafka and Pinter Shadow-Boxing

The Struggle between Father and Son

Raymond Armstrong

First published in Great Britain 1999 by
MACMILLAN PRESS LTD
Houndmills, Basingstoke, Hampshire RG21 6XS and London
Companies and representatives throughout the world

A catalogue record for this book is available from the British Library.

ISBN 0–333–63116–1

First published in the United States of America 1999 by
ST. MARTIN'S PRESS, INC.,
Scholarly and Reference Division,
175 Fifth Avenue, New York, N.Y. 10010

ISBN 0–312–21541–X

Library of Congress Cataloging-in-Publication Data
Armstrong, Raymond.
Kafka and Pinter: shadow-boxing : the struggle between father and son / Raymond Armstrong.
p. cm.
Includes bibliographical references and index.
ISBN 0–312–21541–X (cloth)
1. Pinter, Harold, 1930– —Criticism and interpretation. 2. Domestic drama, English—History and criticism. 3. Pinter, Harold, 1930– —Knowledge—Literature. 4. Kafka, Franz, 1883–1924—Influence. 5. Fathers and sons in literature. 6. Drama–Psychological aspects. I. Title.
PR6066.I53Z594 1998
822'.914—dc21 98–3711
CIP

---

10 9 8 7 6 5 4 3 2 1
08 07 06 05 04 03 02 01 00 99

Printed and bound in Great Britain by
Antony Rowe Ltd, Chippenham, Wiltshire

To my mother
Dolores Armstrong

Contents

Acknowledgements

I would like to thank my family, friends and others who have supported and encouraged me throughout the writing of this book. I am especially grateful for the assistance I received from Graham Armstrong (my brother), Ronnie Bailie, Martin McGuinness, Andrew O'Kane and Adrian Rice.

Acknowledgements are also due to the undermentioned copyright-holders for granting me permission to use the following material:

Extracts from 'Letter to his Father':
From *Dearest Father: Stories and Other Writings* by Franz Kafka, translated by Ernst Kaiser and Eithne Wilkins. English translation (US) copyright © 1954, renewed 1982 by Schocken Books, Inc. Reprinted by permission of Schocken Books, distributed by Pantheon Books, a division of Random House, Inc.

From *Wedding Preparations in the Country, and Other Posthumous Prose Writings* by Franz Kafka, translated by Ernst Kaiser and Eithne Wilkins. English translation (UK) copyright © 1954 by Martin Secker and Warburg Ltd. Reprinted by permission of Reed Consumer Books Ltd.

'Home-Coming':
From *Description of a Struggle* by Franz Kafka, translated by Tania and James Stern. English translation (US) copyright © 1958 by Schocken Books, Inc. Reprinted by permission of Schocken Books, distributed by Pantheon Books, a division of Random House, Inc. English translation (UK) copyright © 1960 by Martin Secker and Warburg Ltd. Reprinted by permission of Reed Consumer Books Ltd.

Extracts from the plays of Harold Pinter are reprinted by kind permission of Grove/Atlantic, Inc. and Faber and Faber Ltd:
A Night Out, copyright © 1961, 1966, 1968 by Harold Pinter; *The Dwarfs*, copyright © 1961, 1966, 1968 by Harold Pinter; *The Homecoming*, copyright © 1965, 1966, 1967 by H. Pinter Ltd; *No Man's*

Land, copyright © 1975 by H. Pinter Ltd; *Betrayal,* copyright © 1980 by H. Pinter Ltd; *Family Voices,* copyright © 1981 by Neabar Investments Ltd; *Victoria Station,* copyright © 1982 by Askerdale Ltd; *One for the Road,* copyright © 1984 by Harold Pinter; *Moonlight,* copyright © 1993 by Harold Pinter; *Ashes to Ashes,* copyright © 1996 by Harold Pinter.

List of Abbreviations

The following abbreviations appear (with the relevant page numbers) throughout the text and notes:

A	*America*, Franz Kafka
AA	*Ashes to Ashes*, Harold Pinter
C	*The Castle*, Franz Kafka
CK	*Conversations with Kafka*, Gustav Janouch
CP	*Conversations with Pinter*, Mel Gussow
CS	*The Comfort of Strangers and Other Screenplays*, Harold Pinter
CSS	*The Complete Short Stories*, Franz Kafka
D	*The Dwarfs* (a novel), Harold Pinter
DI	*Diaries, 1910–1913*, Franz Kafka
DII	*Diaries, 1914–1923*, Franz Kafka
FEL	*Letters to Felice*, Franz Kafka
FFE	*Letters to Friends, Family and Editors*, Franz Kafka
GWC	*The Great Wall of China and Other Short Works*, Franz Kafka
I	*Plays One*, Harold Pinter
II	*Plays Two*, Harold Pinter
III	*Plays Three*, Harold Pinter
IV	*Plays Four*, Harold Pinter
M	*Moonlight*, Harold Pinter
MIL	*Letters to Milena*, Franz Kafka
PT	*Party Time*, Harold Pinter
T	*The Trial* (definitive edition), Franz Kafka
TOS	*The Transformation and Other Stories*, Franz Kafka
WPC	*Wedding Preparations in the Country, and Other Posthumous Prose Writings*, Franz Kafka

Full publication details are given in Works Cited.

Where words have been deleted from quotations, an ellipsis in square brackets ([. . .]) is used, in order to distinguish such omissions from other ellipses in the original text.

All quotations from stage directions appear in italics.

Biblical quotations are from the Authorized Version, unless otherwise indicated.

1

Descriptions of a Struggle: 'The Judgement' and 'The Metamorphosis'

> [A]s a little child I had been defeated by my father and because of ambition have never been able to quit the battlefield all these years despite the perpetual defeats I suffer. (DII 200)

'The revolt of the son against the father is', as Franz Kafka once said, 'one of the primeval themes of literature, and an even older problem in the world' (CK 68). Indeed, with the obvious exception of romantic love, the patri–filial struggle is at once the most personal and the most universal of literary motifs, transcending as it does all social, temporal and geographical frontiers. Writers down through the ages and across the globe have been fascinated by this archetypal conflict, as evidenced by its predominance in such diverse texts as *Oedipus Rex, The Brothers Karamazov, Death of a Salesman, Le Morte D'Arthur, The Playboy of the Western World* and, of course, the Bible. Nowhere, however, has this classic pattern been expressed with more desperate lucidity than in the writings of Kafka himself. Kafka was in fact convinced that his *cacoethes scribendi* had resulted directly from his disastrous relationship with his own father – a relationship which he documented so incisively in the unique and monumental 'Letter to his Father':

> My writing was all about you; all I did there, after all, was to bemoan what I could not bemoan upon your breast. It was an intentionally long-drawn-out leave-taking from you, only although it was brought about by force on your part, it did take its course in the direction determined by me. (WPC 197)

As fate would have it, this 'gigantic letter' (MIL 67) – written in November 1919, when Kafka was thirty-six years old – fell short of its purpose, because, like those which comprise Pinter's *Family Voices*, it was never received by the person to whom it was addressed. The author had certainly intended to have the missive delivered to his father; characteristically, though, he chose not to hand it to the old man himself, relying instead on the good offices of his mother, who, no doubt worried about its potentially explosive contents, prudently decided to withhold it from her husband. In the letter, which has been called 'the most comprehensive attempt at an autobiography that he ever made',[1] Kafka gives a painful and circumstantial account of virtually every aspect of his troubled existence – including his memories of childhood, his relations with his mother and sisters, his Jewish heritage, his education and choice of career, his antipathy to the family business, his attitude to writing, and his 'superhuman' (WPC 199) desire for marriage – all of which converge, like the spokes of a wheel, in the pivotal connection with his father.

The author's father, Hermann Kafka (1852–1931), was a successful merchant, who, in his formative years, as he never ceased to remind his son, had suffered great privation, but through hard work and perseverance had pulled himself up out of the ghetto and established a thriving wholesale business. This impressive *curriculum vitae*, coupled with his position as a happily married man and the head of a family, made Herr Kafka such a paragon of individual prestige and intrepid vitality that his son despaired of ever being able to emulate him. Franz was even depressed by his father's physical presence (WPC 163); since he recognized in the form of this Titan everything that he himself (supposedly) lacked:

> that is to say, strength, and scorn of the other, health and a certain immoderation, eloquence and inadequacy, self-confidence and dissatisfaction with everyone else, a superior attitude to the world and tyranny, knowledge of human nature and mistrust of most people, then also good qualities without any drawback, such as industry, endurance, presence of mind, and fearlessness. (WPC 213–14)

Although the eldest of six children born to his parents, Franz was a very lonely little boy. His two brothers both died in babyhood, and the first of his three sisters did not arrive until he was six years old. Much of his infancy was spent in the company of various domestic servants, since his mother was frequently busy helping her husband in the warehouse. There was, for the most part, little direct contact between father and son. The pair normally saw each other only at meal times. It was on these occasions that the father, who did not hold with displays of paternal affection (WPC 158), chose to lay down the strict code of conduct that he expected the lad to follow. Hermann's attitude to his son was comparable to that of a Draconian legislator: as far as he was concerned, Franz was simply a potential transgressor who had to be kept in check by threats, humiliation and fear. In the face of the father's censorious tirades and sarcastic asides, it seemed as if the boy could do absolutely nothing right. Matters were complicated, moreover, by the fact that the father would often quite blatantly contravene his own edicts. This was especially evident in the area of table manners. While the father always insisted on the highest standards of etiquette at the dinner-table from his son, he himself would crack bones with his teeth, slurp vinegar, cut the bread crookedly with a gravy-stained knife, drop scraps on the floor, clip his fingernails, sharpen pencils, and even use a toothpick to clean out his ears (WPC 167). Such behaviour was totally incomprehensible to the child, for whom the father – having assumed that enigmatic quality of all autocrats, whose prerogatives are based not on reason, but on the strength of their own personality (WPC 164) – came to resemble a throw-back to some mythical race of 'gods and kings' (WPC 176). Indeed it was from observing the patriarch clench his teeth and gurgle with malicious laughter that the boy had formed his 'first notions of hell' (WPC 174). Years later, with the agonies of his upbringing still fresh in his mind, Kafka hinted that it might almost have been kinder if the old man had chewed him up and swallowed him, just as Kronos – 'the most honest of fathers' (FFE 295) – had done with his sons.

The author's dread of the paternal ogre was accentuated by a rather disturbing incident which occurred when he was about four years old. It was late at night and young Franz, instead of going to sleep, decided that he would have some fun at his parents expense by importunately crying out for a drink of water. After several stern warnings went unheeded, an exasperated Hermann stormed into the boy's room, seized him from his cot and carried him out on to the *pavlatche*,[2] leaving him to stand there – alone, in his nightshirt, outside the locked door.[3] The son was forever haunted by this experience, which he maintained had done him 'inner harm' (WPC 162). The problem was that the infantile delinquent could not really see the connection between his mischievous whimpering for water and the blood-curdling horror of being carried off into the darkness, as if by the Erl-king:[4]

> Even years afterwards I suffered from the tormenting fancy that the huge man, my father, the ultimate authority, would come almost for no reason at all and take me out of bed in the night and carry me out on to the *pavlatche*, and that therefore I was such a mere nothing for him. (WPC 162)

In the apparent absence of a specific charge, the bewildered youngster was left to suppose that guilt was somehow ingrained in his own person. Accordingly, the traditional Romantic conception of the child as the embodiment of innocence[5] came to be inverted in Kafka's psyche, where the very fact of being a tiny tot had seemed enough to warrant his summary exclusion.

Crushed in spirit and presumed culpable of sins unknown and unnumbered, little Franz was given to believe that his high and mighty father actually ruled the world from his armchair (WPC 164);[6] and indeed everything the patriarch shouted at the boy from that arbitrary throne was received as 'positively a heavenly commandment' (WPC 167):

> the world was for me divided into three parts: one in which I, the slave, lived under laws that had been invented only for me and which I could, I did not know why, never completely comply with; then a second world, which was infinitely remote from mine, in which you lived, concerned with government, with the issuing of orders and with annoyance about their not being obeyed; and finally a third world where everybody else lived happily and free from orders and from having to obey. I was continually in disgrace, either I obeyed your orders, and that was a disgrace, for they applied, after all, only to me, or I was defiant, and that was a disgrace too, for how could I presume to defy you, or I could not obey because for instance I had not your strength, your appetite, your skill, in spite of which you expected it of me as a matter of course; this was the greatest disgrace of all. (WPC 167–8)

In the light of such a forbidding cosmography, it is hardly surprising that the future novelist should have turned inward for asylum, burrowing deep into the fertile soil of his own imagination. In point of fact, Kafka's *oeuvre* consists almost entirely of a series of excavations of this same existential nightmare. Whether he is a Dickensian urchin transported half-way across the globe to a vast neoteric jungle (as in *America*), a bank clerk unaccountably trapped in a dark labyrinth of legalism (as in *The Trial*), or a land surveyor summoned to an inhospitable village by an opaque bureaucracy (as in *The Castle*), the Kafkan hero is wont to find himself on the wrong side of the 'perpetually shifting frontier that lies between ordinary life and the terror that would seem to be more real' (DII 225).

* * *

According to Max Brod, Kafka's closest friend and chosen literary executor/executioner,[7] the author had wanted to lump all his writings together under the banner – 'attempt to get away from my father'.[8] Remarkably, though, only two of his multifarious fictional works – namely, 'The Judgement' and 'The Metamorphosis' – actually 'describe a war' (FEL 265) between father and son: *ipso facto*, it is this pair of stories, especially when read alongside 'Letter to his Father', which provide the most vivid and compelling testimony of the battle that was fought without respite in the theatre of Kafka's mind. Superficially absurd yet secretly autobiographical, both these narratives centre on a filial character whose name (while not distinguished by the 'offensive, almost disgusting' (DII 34) letter K, as would later be the case with the hero in each of the novels) is a half-acknowledged cryptogram of that of the author – a tell-tale sign of Kafka's psycho-dramatic identification with his proxy-like protagonists, through whose trials and torments he evidently hoped to win for himself a measure of cathartic justification.

'The Judgement' and 'The Metamorphosis' were written within three months of each other in the latter part of 1912. Arguably the two most important of Kafka's works to have been published during his lifetime, they made their respective débuts in the periodicals *Arkadia* (June 1913) and *Die weissen Blätter* (October 1915). However, the author felt quite strongly that the stories, having been cast in the same mould, should appear side by side in the same collection. He twice sought to have them printed together as two-thirds of a designated trilogy: first (with 'The Stoker') in a volume entitled *The Sons* (FFE 96–7), and then (with 'In the Penal Colony') in a volume entitled *Punishments* (FFE 113; 118 ff.). Although neither of these proposed editions ever actually rolled off the presses,[9] it is in the synthesis of their titles that we find Kafka's most telling allusion to the thematic affinity between 'The Judgement' and 'The Metamorphosis'. Thus, it may be inferred that – from the author's own point of view – both tales are about filial chastisement.

To all appearances, Georg Bendemann in 'The Judgement' and Gregor Samsa in 'The Metamorphosis' would both seem to be hard-working, conscientious and loving sons. What is it about these young men that could posssibly justify the terrible and exemplary punishments that are meted out to them? The answer is not to be found on the surface of either narrative, but resides – as we shall see – in their almost subliminal figurations of religious imagery and authorial angst.

'THE JUDGEMENT'

A landmark in the development of Kafka's art, and his personal favourite of all his works (FFE 126), 'The Judgement' (*Das Urteil*) was once described by its author as 'the spectre of a night' (CK 31):

> Each sentence in this story, each word, each – if I may say so – music is connected with 'fear'. On this occasion the wound broke open for the first time during one long night [. . . .] (MIL 191)

The night in question was that of 22–3 September 1912. It had been a Sunday and he was feeling so dejected that he could have screamed (FEL 265). Around ten o'clock (DI 275; cf. FEL 265), he sat down at his desk and opened up his diary. Almost automatically, he started writing like a man possessed. Many emotions stirred within his palpitating heart, as the elements of a narrative came together through a spellbinding chemistry of water and fire (DI 276). After eight hours, the story was finished. It had come out of him 'like a real birth', covered with ectoplasmic 'filth and slime' (DI 278). He put down his pen with the sense that he had undergone a 'complete exorcism' (CK 31). Even though his legs were extremely stiff from sitting so long, he remained clear-eyed and alert, exulting in what was manifestly a major creative breakthrough: 'Only *in this way* can writing be done, only with such coherence, with such a complete opening out of the body and the soul' (DI 276). The next day, he read the story to one of his sisters. She was convinced that its domestic setting had been modelled on their own parental home. Purportedly 'astonished at how mistaken she was' (DI 280), Kafka responded by cracking a joke, which, in its spontaneous subversiveness, appears to have been catapulted straight from the *oubliette* of his unconscious: 'In that case, then, Father would have to be living in the toilet' (DI 276; 280).

The action of 'The Judgement' is as terse as it is terrifying. The story begins with Georg Bendemann, a young entrepreneur, preparing to send a letter to a friend in Russia with news of his impending marriage to a certain Fräulein Frieda Brandenfeld. Before leaving the house for the post-box, Georg decides to look in on his elderly father. There follows a bizarre see-saw encounter between Georg and the old man, which climaxes with the son being sentenced to death by drowning. Without further ado, Georg rushes out and throws himself into a nearby river.

Shortly after completing 'The Judgement', Kafka inserted the following words of dedication beneath the title – 'To Fräulein Felice B.' (FEL 12; 192–3).[10] This elliptical tribute pertained to Felice Bauer, the young woman to whom he was subsequently twice engaged to be married. He had been introduced to Fräulein Bauer in August 1912,[11] and had penned the first of innumerable epistles to her just two days before writing the story. He initially proposed to her in June 1913, the same month that 'The Judgement' was published. It was perhaps inevitable that their relationship, which was so intricately connected with this 'very doubtful creation' (FEL 87), would never quite make it to the altar. Indeed Kafka himself had noted – first in his diary (DI 279), and then in a letter to Felice (FEL 265) – how the names of the star-crossed couple in the story even bore an uncanny resemblance to those of himself and his future fiancée.[12]

In another diary entry, written immediately after the full draft of 'The Judgement', Kafka acknowledged that the story had partly derived from 'The Urban World' (DI 276), a fragmentary tale which he wrote – also in his journal – sometime between February and March 1911 (DI 47–54). Striking parallels abound between the two works. In both cases:

(1) the drama begins with a young man entering a room occupied by his father;
(2) the father is initially seated but then stands up, revealing his prodigious size;[13]
(3) the old man condemns his son for leading a wayward and wanton existence;

(4) the son tries to appease his father by announcing that he is determined to be more assiduous in future;
(5) the lad is confounded by a sudden and unsettling change in the patriarch's character;
(6) the son has a rather odd relationship with a male friend, to whom he has allegedly been showing precious little courtesy.[14]

This catalogue of affinities confirms that in many respects 'The Urban World' was something of a dry run for 'The Judgement'. There are, however, just as many differences between the pair. Very much an embryonic effort, the earlier piece is by comparison stylistically jagged and thematically unfocused; it consists mainly of dialogue, lacks tension and promises little in the way of a resolution. In short, there is nothing here to match the mystical chiaroscuro or the fearsome musicality of 'The Judgement'. But then, as Kafka pointed out, 'The Judgement' 'is more a poem than a story' (FFE 125).

* * *

The author told Felice that even though 'The Judgement' was 'somewhat wild and meaningless' (FEL 86–7), it did possess a certain internal logic, the relevance of which could 'never be universally established, but [had] to be accepted or denied every time by each reader or listener in turn' (FEL 87). It is the opinion of this reader that, what Kafka called, the 'inner truth' (FEL 87) of the story derives in no small measure from its dynamic assimilation of biblical types. In the next two sections, I shall offer both an exposition of and an explanation for these key symbolic elements, beginning with those which relate to the Old Testament patriarchs – Abraham, Isaac and Jacob – and then moving on to those which allude to the figure of Jesus Christ.

* * *

The first stage of the encounter between Georg Bendemann and his father follows the pattern of Genesis 27, with its account of how Jacob tricked Isaac into granting him the blessing that had been reserved for his brother, Esau. On entering his father's sanctum sanctorum, Georg finds the old man sitting near the window in a corner surrounded with various mementoes of his late lamented wife. Although the room is inordinately dark, Bendemann

Snr holds an 'enormous newspaper' (CSS 82), at which he squints through a pair of spectacles. Despite his defective eyesight, the patriarch proves to have extraordinary powers of perception, and – in contrast to the purblind Isaac – 'doesn't need to be taught how to see through his son' (CSS 85). Georg cowers beneath the paternal gaze, apprehending 'the pupils, over-large, fixedly looking at him from the corners of the eyes' (CSS 83). Even while he is informing his father of his intentions, he admits semi-consciously that the old man is aware of these already. His repeated use of the phrase 'you know' is neither simply a rhetorical stratagem nor an idiomatic habit; rather it is an involuntary acknowledgement of the father's precognition. And sure enough, Mr Bendemann instantly registers that Georg has not been relating 'the whole truth', and entreats the boy not to 'deceive' him (CSS 82).

Although somewhat embarrassed, Georg fleetly evades this challenge to his *bona fides* by insinuating that the aged parent is starting to lose his faculties. Ostensibly concerned at the fact that the old man has not been eating properly or getting nearly enough sunlight or fresh air, he declares that 'a radical change' (CSS 83) will have to be made to Mr Bendemann's mode of living. The son proposes that he himself should take the room currently occupied by his father, and that the old fellow, and all his belongings, should be moved into the front room.[15] He insists on putting his father to bed straight away – despite the fact that it is just a little after breakfast-time. By lifting the old man up and then lowering him down again, Georg contrives to remove most of his father's clothes, relegating him in the process to a state of infantile dependence. This dramatic change in roles is duly reflected in the Old Testament subtext: Mr Bendemann retains his identification with Isaac, only now the part has also regressed to that of a child; Georg, on the other hand, having established himself *in loco parentis*, recasts himself as Abraham, the father of Isaac. Effectively, therefore, the child has become the father of the man. In their new roles, the two principals perform a sinister pantomime of the narrowly averted sacrifice of the son as described in Genesis 22. Georg carries the toothless dotard to bed in his arms, during which operation the elder Bendemann childishly toys with his 'father's' watch-chain. Symbolically, the bed corresponds to the altar – a parallel which is drawn much more explicitly in the infernal machine in 'In the Penal Colony'. Having laid the old-timer on the bed, Georg attempts to quell him by tucking the blankets closely around him. (The ominous dialogue which accompanies this 'covering up' will be examined in detail later with respect to a remarkably similar exchange between Lenny and Max in Pinter's *The Homecoming*.)

Just when Georg thought that 'all seemed well' (CSS 84), the aged parent is suddenly and miraculously transformed into a theanthropic vision of the Almighty Himself. As a number of critics – notably Heinz Politzer and Herbert Tauber – have already pointed out, the key to this apotheosis of the old man lies in the Kafkan equation: 'father–Father–God'.[16] Still, what we have here is not merely some household deity or, as Tauber claims, a neological 'God of Justice',[17] but an apparent manifestation of the Lord God of Israel. In 'The Judgement', the familiar confusion of the father and God finds perfect thematic expression in El-Shaddai – 'the God of [the] father, the God of Abraham, the God of Isaac and the God of Jacob' (Exodus 3:6). Moreover, the transfiguration of the patriarch is precisely timed within the metaphorical framework of the story to simulate the moment when the Lord had rewarded Abraham's trust and intervened to save the life of Isaac. In Kafka's version, though, it is not paternal meekness, but filial presumption which stirs the hand of Providence.

In an explosive display of indignation, Mr Bendemann throws off the blankets and springs erect on the bed, reaffirming the potency of his prime. He touches the ceiling with his hand, as if to emphasize his tremendous stature and majesty. Antithetically, Georg shrinks into a corner, fearing 'a pounce from behind or above' (CSS 85), rather like the petrified mouse in 'A Little Fable'. All his fatuous attempts to ridicule 'the bogey conjured up by his father' (CSS 85) boomerang as a whirlwind of jumbled thoughts rages through his mind. He fancies that the sire is not really supreme and expects him to topple and smash like some derelict pagan idol. Nonetheless, the ancient one stands sure and steadfast, and only reinforces his towering strength when he ecstatically asserts that he is much the stronger of the two. As a result, the lad finds himself compelled to kneel before the paternal numen in deference to his ultimate authority. Georg evidently 'doesn't see the ordinary man' anymore, just 'this monstrous Abraham in the clouds' (FFE 200).[18] The ritual sacrifice of the son now proceeds in 'deadly earnest' (CSS 87), the roles having been irrevocably transposed. The judgement of the father must be implemented. There is no question of a last minute reprieve: no sign of an angel, or a ram caught in a thicket.

Like most Jews, Kafka would have been introduced to the mysterious world of the Old Testament at a very early age. Later, as a writer, he came to regard the various books of the Bible as part of his literary heritage and often made reference to them throughout his work. The account of Abraham's intended sacrifice of Isaac was one which held a particular fascination for him, not least because it seemed to enlarge upon his deepest anxieties about his relationship with his own father. The story told in Genesis 22 is in essence an apologue of twofold submission to paternal authority: not only does Abraham faithfully comply with the instructions of his Heavenly Father, but Isaac also dutifully yields to the knife of Abraham. The old man becomes the point at which child and Creator meet – a righteous demigod apparently invested with full power to translate divine will into executive action. Obedience to the Almighty, therefore, is predicated on submission to the father – His earthly representative. In human terms, Abraham is the father-figure *par excellence*. Down through the ages, he has been revered as the foremost of the Old Testament patriarchs, the progenitor of both the Hebrew and Islamic nations, and the father of all those who believe in Christ (Romans 4:9–16). Abraham's paternal pre-eminence was established by divine decree and sealed in the covenant between himself and the Lord (Genesis 17). Indeed the name 'Abraham', which was conferred on him during the making of this covenant, literally means 'father of many' and derives from his former name 'Abram', which itself means 'exalted father'. Accordingly, in 'The Judgement', when Georg Bendemann begins to 'sham Abraham' in a bid to usurp his father's sovereignty, he wilfully tarnishes the divinely imputed lustre of the patriarch, and thereby commits sacrilege of the highest order.

A preoccupation with the story of Abraham and Isaac had loomed even larger in the *oeuvre* of one of Kafka's literary heroes – the great Danish thinker and theologian, Søren Kierkegaard. In *Fear and Trembling*, perhaps the most famous of his studies of religious psychology, Kierkegaard, who was himself the son of a domineering father, presents a masterly exegesis of the personal and philosophical dilemmas involved in Genesis 22. In August 1913, after reading an anthology of Kierkegaard's writings, Kafka reflected in his diary: 'As I suspected, his case, despite essential differences, is very similar to mine, at least he is on the same side of the world. He bears me out like a friend' (DI 298). (The last sentence is of course especially ironic given the situation in 'The Judgement'.) Some years later, in one of several rather capricious glosses on *Fear and Trembling*,[19] Kafka hypothesized that Abraham's filicidal mission to Mount Moriah was potentially a universal predicament: in other words, every man, regardless of social position or parental status, was liable to receive the same command to step out in faith as if he himself were in Abraham's shoes. The novelist distinguishes two types of inchoate Abraham. Bearing in mind how the Scripture says that Abraham had 'put his house in order' (FFE 285) before he was given the assignment, Kafka reckons that a first group of men – 'who, to be sure, would not make it all the way to patriarch, not even to old-clothes dealer' (FFE 285) – 'stand on their building sites' (FFE 285) and deliberately choose not to finish their houses so that they might exempt themselves from the call. Then there is a second breed of Abraham, 'who certainly wants to carry out the sacrifice properly and in general correctly senses what the whole thing is about' (FFE 285), but, while waiting in anticipation for the signal, constantly runs the risk of overstepping the mark and becoming a laughing-stock in the eyes of the world. It could be argued that Georg Bendemann belongs to this latter category, since he too is, what Kafka terms, 'An Abraham who comes unsummoned!' (FFE 286) – an ignoble upstart who chances his arm and is suitably punished for his hubris.

* * *

Perhaps the most tantalizing of all the imponderables in 'The Judgement' is the matter of the friend in Russia. Although he never actually appears in the flesh and is never identified by name, this elusive fellow certainly cannot be dismissed as a man of straw. On the contrary, his shadowy figure colours the proceedings to such an extent that he might even be said to have catalyzed the conflict between Georg and his father. Indeed, on the evidence of Kafka's own attempts to elucidate 'The Judgement', it would seem that an appraisal of the friend must be the corner-stone of any valid interpretation of its oneiric machinery:

> The story is full of abstractions, though they are never admitted. The friend is hardly a real person, perhaps he is more whatever the father and Georg have in common. The story may be a journey around father

and son, and the friend's changing shape may be a change in perspective in the relationship between father and son. (FEL 267)

In their efforts to solve the riddle of the protean friend, most commentators have either overlooked or underestimated the significance of the silky threads of Christian symbolism that have been deftly woven into the fabric of the narrative. If examined in isolation, each of these allusions could easily be discounted as dust in the balance: nevertheless, their cumulative weight is indicative of something much more substantial.

The comparatively obvious symbol of the cross of blood is perhaps the most useful starting-point for an exposition of the New Testament sequence in 'The Judgement'. On his visits to the Bendemanns' home, the friend, according to Georg, used to recount amazing tales of his experiences during the Russian Revolution. One of the most memorable concerned a street riot in Kiev, where he 'saw a priest on a balcony who cut a broad cross in blood on the palm of his hand and held the hand up and appealed to the mob' (CSS 83). Through this quasi-parabolical yarn, a very telling connection is established between the friend and the concept of Christian martyrdom – and, by extension, the figure of the Saviour Himself. That is not to say that the friend is Jesus Christ, but simply that he is given to reflect the traits of the Nazarene which have a direct reference to the world of 'The Judgement'. The image of the sanguineous cross itself brings to mind the mark of the paschal lamb, which had shielded the Israelites from the holy wrath of Jehovah when He slew the first-born of all Egypt (Exodus 12); and, significantly, it was during the commemorative feast of the Passover that the Lamb of God was Himself betrayed by Judas Iscariot. The cross of blood is therefore doubly important; since it anticipates both Georg's betrayal of the friend, and the protection which the latter receives from the father.

The city of St Petersburg, in which Georg's friend has settled, takes its name from the disciple who insistently pledged his loyalty to Jesus, yet famously perjured himself in this regard on three occasions (Matthew 26; Mark 14; Luke 22; John 13; 18). This idea of denial is echoed quite explicitly in the original German text of 'The Judgement', when Georg confesses that several years earlier he had repeatedly lied to his father about the whereabouts of the friend: '*Wenigstens zweimal habe ich vor dir verleugnet, trotzdem er gerade bei mir im Zimmer saß*'. The verb *verleugnen* – 'to deny' –

which Kafka employs here is also used in German language editions of the New Testament with respect to Peter's disownment of Christ. Unfortunately, this nuance is lost in the 'definitive' English translation of 'The Judgement', where the usually admirable Willa and Edwin Muir render the above sentence thus: 'At least twice I kept you from seeing him, although he was actually sitting with me in my room' (CSS 83). On this particular point, the more recent translation by Malcolm Pasley is appreciably closer to the flavour of Kafka's original: 'At least twice when you asked after him I denied his presence, though in fact he was sitting with me in my room all the time' (TOS 43). Having solved the linguistic problem, we must now address the numerical discrepancy. In the New Testament, all four of the evangelists state very clearly that Peter disavowed Jesus *thrice*; yet, strictly speaking, Georg only admits to disclaiming his friend 'At least twice'. Be that as it may, if we turn back a few pages in 'The Judgement', we can find the voice of the narrator testifying to another – and indeed triple – instance of prevarication on the part of the protagonist. Rather than inform the friend directly about his own relationship with Frieda Brandenfeld, Georg had opted to tell him

> three times in three fairly widely separated letters [. . .] about the engagement of an unimportant man to an equally unimportant girl, until indeed, quite contrary to his intentions, his friend began to show some interest in this notable event. (CSS 79)

These are what the father later calls Georg's 'lying little letters to Russia' (CSS 85); and one begins to suspect that the friend only abides in the bleak isolation of that wintry land because Georg has chosen to banish him from his society. 'How could you have a friend out there!' (CSS 83) exclaims Mr Bendemann incredulously to his son. The paradoxical statements made by the father which both negate and confirm the existence of the friend are indeed symptomatic of Georg's treacherous attitude to his distant comrade. Moreover, such apparent contradictions bear witness to the baffling infallibility of the Kafkan patriarch, who has 'no need to be consistent at all and yet never cease[s] to be in the right' (WPC 164). The fact of the matter is that Georg has repudiated his friend by 'playing him false' (CSS 85); therefore, as a friend, he can no longer be said to exist.[20]

In the most elaborate of his diaristic rubrics on 'The Judgement', Kafka submits that the friend is a kind of umbilical cord linking Georg and his father – 'the circle of blood' (DI 279) which binds the patri–filial pair together and insulates them from objective reality. Even though Georg's fiancée exists outside this haematic orbit, it is she who comes closest to explaining its jealous inviolability: 'Since your friends are like that, Georg, you shouldn't ever have got engaged at all' (CSS 80). The hero evidently hopes that by getting married he will be able to extricate himself from 'the inmost, strictest, strangling ring of [paternal] influence' (WPC 189), and thus be in a position to assert his own independent existence. It was indeed this same aspiration which would later induce each of Kafka's own 'attempts at marriage' (WPC 209). On an anagogic level, however, Georg's plan to assume the role of bridegroom could be interpreted as a profane imitation of the returning Christ (Matthew 22:1–14; 25:1–13; Luke 5:34; 12:36; John 3:29; Revelation 19:7–9). (Interestingly, the Hebrew words for 'friend' which are used in the Old Testament – *rēa', rē'eh* and *mērēa'* – can sometimes have the special connotation 'friend of the bridegroom'.)

As the story unfolds, the father, according to Kafka, 'uses the common bond of the friend to set himself up as Georg's antagonist' (DI 278). Whereas Georg is wont to regard the friend as something of a millstone hung about his neck, the old man proclaims: 'He would have been a son after my own heart' [*Er wäre ein Sohn nach meinem Herzen*] (CSS 85). This asseveration proves strangely prophetic – in both senses of that word. In the first instance, it clearly echoes the rebuke which the wayward King Saul had received from the prophet Samuel:

> Thou hast done foolishly: thou hast not kept the commandment of the LORD thy God, which he commanded thee: for now would the LORD have established thy kingdom upon Israel for ever. But now thy kingdom shall not continue: the LORD hath sought him a man after his own heart, and the LORD hath commanded him to be captain over his people, because thou hast not kept that which the LORD commanded thee. (1 Samuel 13:13–14)

The 'man after his own heart' here refers to David, himself an anointed figure and the ancestral father of the human nature of Jesus Christ – 'the son of David, the son of Abraham' (Matthew 1:1). Indeed the compact which God made with David, promising victory over death and succession to an exalted throne, was fulfilled in the Resurrection and Ascension of the Son (Luke 1:32–3; Acts 2:22–36). In the second instance, Kafka would use a very similar expression when talking about himself some seven years later in 'Letter to his Father':

> It is indeed quite possible that even if I had grown up entirely free from your influence I still could not have become a person after your own heart [. . . *doch kein Mensch nach Deinem Herzen hätte werden können*]. (WPC 159)

The scar on the elder Bendemann's thigh, while reportedly the remnant of a war wound, is emblematic of his secret affiliation with the Christ-like friend; since it replicates the lesion inflicted on Jacob when he had wrestled in prayerful union with the Godman at Peniel (Genesis 32:24–32) – widely interpreted as a manifestation of the pre-incarnate Logos. (Incidentally, this means that Georg and his father are both identified with all three of the patriarchs – Abraham, Isaac and Jacob – in the course of the biblical tableaux.)

As we saw earlier, the dénouement of the Genesis-inspired sequence is preceded by a decisive turning of the tables. A similar phenomenon also occurs in the Christian arena, only this time it is not the positions of the father and the son that are dramatically interchanged, but those of Georg and the friend. In what amounts to a righteous inversion of the moment when Pontius Pilate sanctioned the release of a notorious insurrectionist (Barabbas) in place of Jesus (Matthew 27:16–26; Mark 15:6–15; Luke 23:18–25; John 18:40), the apotheosized Mr Bendemann intervenes to ensure the preservation of the faithful friend at the expense of the deceitful Georg. The Scriptures relate how the Sanhedrin had earlier convicted Jesus for (allegedly) committing blasphemy by avowing Himself 'the Christ, the Son of the Blessed' (Mark 14:60–4; cf. Matthew 26:62–6); and, in the reversal of roles in 'The Judgement', this 'guilt' is transferred on to Georg, who, having been indicted as an arrogant schemer and spurious heir, effectively blasphemes by calling the exalted father a 'comedian' (CSS 86).

Announcing his verdict *in camera*, the paternal judge all but dons the black cap:

> An innocent child, yes, that you were, truly, but still more truly have you been a devilish human being! – And therefore take note: I sentence you now to death by drowning! (CSS 87)

The oxymoronic logic of this decree insinuates that the son is being damned not for any personal transgressions, but because he exemplifies the satanically-induced depravity of the whole human race. The effect is to further underscore Georg's *ad hoc* affinity with Christ, who, although entirely blameless Himself, came to embody the sins of the world in the eyes of His Father, and was cursed accordingly (2 Corinthians 5:21). (It is worth noting that 'The Judgement' was written just one day after Yom Kippur – the Day of Atonement – the most holy date in the Jewish calendar, on which an impeccable substitute had traditionally been sacrificed to Jehovah in order to expiate the iniquities of Israel (Leviticus 16).)

No doubt there are some who would contend that Georg's demise should really be regarded as suicide; because not only does he meekly accept the sentence handed down by his father, but he also takes responsibility for its execution. Still, this is either too simplistic or – given that Kafka himself once defined suicide as 'a form of egotism raised to the point of absurdity' (CK 45) – too perverse a reading of Georg's compulsive act of self-destruction. In any case, it could be argued that the son is merely adopting (not to say adapting) the quietistic attitude of all martyrs, who are – perforce – 'at one with their antagonists' (WPC 41). More precisely, though, Georg's irresistible urge to be 'odedient unto death' (Philippians 2:8) is, to all intents and purposes, a fanatical travesty of the example of Christ Himself. The prevailing concern of the condemned man in 'The Judgement' is neatly epitomized by Bonario in Ben Jonson's *Volpone*: 'rather wish my innocence should suffer, / Than I resist the authority of a father'.[21] Indeed, as Kafka points out:

> only because [Georg] himself has lost everything except his awareness of the father does the judgement, which closes off his father from him completely, have so strong an effect on him. (DI 279)

Hurtling down the stairs on his dolorous way to the scaffold, Georg bumps into the charwoman, who – obviously flabbergasted by his appearance – cries, 'Jesus!' (CSS 87) and covers her face with her apron.[22] From the son's point of view, this pregnant expletive is tantamount to an acknowledgement of his Messianic vocation.

We are referred back to the opening paragraph of the story, which, in the light of subsequent events, contains two rather intriguing phrases. Firstly, the action occurs on 'a Sunday morning in the very height of spring' (CSS 77), and thus by implication coincides with the festival of Easter. Moreover, the fact that it is Sunday, and not Friday, suggests that a resurrection will never take place; the execution having been postponed deliberately to guarantee its finality. Secondly, we are told that Georg sits at his desk, 'gazing out of the window at [. . .] the hills on the farther bank with their tender green' (CSS 77). This detail insinuates a theme which will be amplified in Kafka's subsequent work – the failure of the hero, both physically and spiritually, to scale the heights of a Christ. (The most exquisite treatment of this motif occurs in 'In the Penal Colony'; and the most expressionistic in the final chapter of *The Trial*.) Significantly, Georg is not raised upon a tree on some suburban hill, but instead experiences a 'fall' (CSS 88); and, because he is not truly the Son of God, no angels are summoned to bear him up to safety (Psalms 91:11–12; Matthew 4:6; Luke 4:9–11).

The sentence of 'death by drowning' has itself a multiple appropriateness. On a broad canvas, this punishment recalls the deluge that God sent to purge the earth of the reprobate human race at the time of Noah (Genesis 6–8). More immediately, it demonstrates that Georg is a Christ *manqué*, since he is unable to walk on water without the blessing of his father (Matthew 14:25; Mark 6:48; John 6:19). Perhaps most surprising, though, is the fact that there is a physiological link between *noyade* and crucifixion. Once a person is pinned up on a cross, he is no longer able to expand or empty his lungs properly, and so the organs gradually fill up with water. To some extent, therefore, death by crucifixion could be compared to a very slow form of drowning. It is worth noting that when Jesus's side was punctured by the spear of a Roman soldier, water, as well as blood, gushed out (John 19:34). The figure of Georg dangling from the bridge is indeed reminiscent of the Man of Sorrows hanging on the Rood. However, unlike Jesus, whose last breath was marked by all manner of cataclysmic signs and wonders (Matthew 27:51–4), Georg plunges into Lethean obscurity under the humdrum rhythm of 'an unending stream of traffic' (CSS 88). For the rest of the world, Georg's fall from grace is as unnoticed and as inconsequential as the splash-down of Icarus – another son with ideas above his station who did not heed his father – appears to be to those going about their everyday business in Pieter Brueghel's celebrated painting of that incident.[23]

By subtly merging the twin narratives of Genesis and the Gospel, 'The Judgement' taps into a whole network of scriptural cross-references:

(1) Abraham's willingness to offer up 'his only begotten son' (Hebrews 11:17)[24] obviously foreshadows the ultimate filial sacrifice made by God the Father.
(2) There is, moreover, a geographic link between these two events – Mount Moriah, where Abraham built his altar, is itself only a short distance away from the scene of the Crucifixion on Mount Calvary.
(3) After sparing the life of Isaac, the Angel of the Lord had ratified the covenant with Abraham: 'in thy seed shall all the nations of the earth be blessed; because thou hast obeyed my voice' (Genesis 22:18). St Paul, in his epistle to the Galatians, makes it clear that Christ Himself is the Seed of Abraham and the singular consummation of the promises spoken in Genesis (Galatians 3:16).
(4) As well as being descended from the same earthly father, Isaac and Jesus were both born of the power of the Holy Spirit (Galatians 4:29; Luke 1:35), in the barren and virgin wombs of Sarah and Mary, respectively.
(5) The question of fidelity to a hallowed friend is conspicuously related to both Abraham and Jesus. A man of unwavering faith and fervent devotion, Abraham enjoyed especially close fellowship with his Creator, and because of this came to be known as 'the Friend of God' (2 Chronicles 20:7; Isaiah 41:8; James 2:23). Correlatively, in the New Testament, Jesus vows that anyone who trusts in Him will be called His friend (John 15:13–15).

While choreographing the symphonic *danse macabre* in 'The Judgement', Kafka was actually experiencing something of a spiritual crisis in his own life. In July 1912, two months before he wrote the story, he had stayed at a natural therapy sanitorium in Jungborn, where he had met a member of a 'Christian Community' who had witnessed to him at some length and presented him with various evangelical pamphlets (DII 305–7).[25] During his sojourn there, he had also been reading the Bible regularly after every meal (DII 306). In a letter to Felice Bauer that November, two months after the penning of 'The Judgement', he intimated that he was still very much preoccupied with the Person of Jesus, having 'decided quite definitely' that his 'only salvation' was to contact the man who had befriended him during the summer and tried to convert him to Christ (FEL 49). Years later, Kafka – despite having more or less reconciled himself to his Jewish heritage – was to say of the Sun of Righteousness: 'He is an abyss filled with light. One must close one's eyes if one is not to fall into it' (CK 166).

Bearing in mind how the Saviour had announced that He had come to divide father against son and son against father (Luke 12:53), it is entirely appropriate that the key moment in Kafka's struggle to come to terms with Christianity should have apparently coincided with the writing of the boldest of his fictional explorations of patri–filial strife. The author's ambivalence about putting his faith in Jesus is indeed spectacularly illustrated in the attitude of the numinous father in 'The Judgement', whose conflicting opinions of the friend and Georg reflect the diametrical opposition between Christian and Judaic orthodoxies with respect to the character and claims of the Nazarene. On the one hand, the friend is embraced as Jesus, the suffering Servant and true Son of the living God; and on the other, Georg is rejected as Jesus, the blaspheming bastard and false Messiah.

'THE METAMORPHOSIS'

On Sunday 17 November 1912, Kafka mentioned in a letter to Felice that an idea for a short story had occurred to him that morning as he lay in bed feeling miserable. He added that the story – which he would later call 'The Metamorphosis' (*Die Verwandlung*) – troubled him, but that it demanded to be written (FEL 47). Unlike 'The Judgement', which was the product of a single apocalyptic night, 'The Metamorphosis' was to have a difficult and protracted genesis. Ideally, Kafka would have preferred to have composed the entire story in a couple of marathon sittings (FEL 64); however, his job at the Workers' Accident Insurance Institute meant that he could not avail himself of 'the fire of consecutive hours' (FEL 84), and so the writing had to be done in a piecemeal fashion in the evenings after work. The creative process was further stalled when, with the tale roughly half-finished, he was obliged to travel to Kratzau on official business. The author felt that the various interruptions – which were compounded by other extraneous concerns – had grievously affected the spontaneous flow and integrity of what was, after all, supposed to be a dreamlike narrative (FEL 64; 89). (One is reminded here of how Coleridge's transcription of his laudanum-orientated rhapsody 'Kubla Khan, or A Vision in a Dream' had been stymied by the untimely intervention of a visitor from Porlock.[26]) As a result, Kafka was left with a 'Great antipathy' to 'The Metamorphosis', which, in his estimation, was 'Imperfect almost to its very marrow' (DII 12). He was especially dissatisfied with the quality of 'the more tender passages' (FEL 89) and with the 'Unreadable ending' (DII 12).

'The Metamorphosis' begins with what is probably the most famous opening sentence in all of modern fiction: 'As Gregor Samsa awoke one morning from uneasy dreams he found himself transformed in his bed into a gigantic insect' (CSS 89). This basic premise had in fact been adumbrated some five years earlier in Kafka's abandoned novel 'Wedding Preparations in the Country'. Anxious to escape from the pressures and responsibilities of human society, Eduard Raban, the hero of that fragmentary text, had dreamed of undergoing a transformation very similar to the one experienced by Gregor Samsa:

> 'As I lie in bed I assume the shape of a big beetle, a stag-beetle or a cock-chafer, I think.' [. . .]
> 'The form of a large beetle, yes. Then I would pretend it was a matter of hibernating, and I would press my little legs to my bulging belly. And I whisper a small number of words, instructions to my sad body, which stands close beside me, bent. Soon I have done – it bows, it goes swiftly, and it will manage everything efficiently while I rest.' (WPC 12; CSS 56)

Still, as a devotee of ancient Chinese literature and philosophy (CK 152–5),[27] Kafka would perhaps have known the Taoist proverb which says that a man should be careful what he wishes for; and when the fantasy of Raban is fulfilled in the life of Samsa, it turns out to be a nightmare rather than a nostrum. (Notwithstanding the charwoman's scarcely scientific classification of Gregor as an 'old dung beetle' (CSS 127), the species of the insect in 'The Metamorphosis' is less certain than that of its conceptual antecedent. Kafka was evidently keen to maintain an air of mystery about the animal nature of the protagonist. Indeed, shortly before the story was due to appear in book form, he wrote a letter to his publisher in which he stipulated that the insect itself should under no circumstances be depicted on the front cover, not even from a distance (FFE 114–15).)

As Kafka explained to the inquisitive Gustav Janouch, 'The Metamorphosis' 'is not a confession, although it is – in a certain sense – an indiscretion'; since it could be considered 'bad manners' to talk so freely 'about the bugs in one's own family' (CK 32). Sure enough, the autobiographical elements are there in the story for anyone with an eye to see them. In the first instance, there is, as Janouch rather tactlessly spelt out, a striking affinity between the surname of the protagonist and that of the author: 'Five letters in each word. The S in the word Samsa has the same position as the K in the word Kafka. The A . . .' (CK 32). Secondly, it is no coincidence that Kafka, when he came to write 'Letter to his Father', should have chosen to characterize himself as an entomic creature. Towards the end of that epic epistle, the filial correspondent – in a mimetic anticipation of the patriarch's reply – is labelled as a specimen of the genus of 'vermin, which not only sting but, at the same time, suck the blood, too, to sustain their own life' (WPC 216). Moreover, Janouch records how his mentor had subsequently claimed to be a chrysalis 'caught in an iron-hard web, without the slightest hope that one day a butterfly [might] fly out of [his] cocoon' (CK 142). Thirdly, as an indecorous discourse on domestic affairs, 'The Metamorphosis' speaks not only of Kafka's hostilities with his father, but also of his relations with both his mother and his favourite sister. How fitting, then, that the very layout of the Samsas' flat should duplicate that of Kafka's family home – where the son's room was likewise sandwiched between the living-room and the parental bedroom (FEL 54).

* * *

'The Metamorphosis' is unusual among Kafka's works insofar as the religious affiliation of its characters is clearly indicated. Surprisingly perhaps, the Samsa family belong not to the Jewish faith, but to a branch of Christianity. This allegiance is highlighted several times in the story. First, we are told that Gregor's sister, Grete, was inclined to utter 'an occasional appeal to the saints' (CSS 109) whenever she entered his room. Next, it emerges that the family celebrate the feast of the Nativity, since Gregor had intended to announce 'with due solemnity on Christmas Day' (CSS 111) his plan to send Grete to the Conservatorium to study music. Lastly, at the sight of Gregor's carcass, Mr Samsa sanctifies himself by making the sign of the cross, whereupon his wife, daughter and the charwoman all follow suit (CSS 136).

Like 'The Judgement', 'The Metamorphosis' is illuminated with a vibrant array of synchronous symbolic allusions to both the Old and New Testaments. In the latter fable, the author goes right back to the start of the book of Genesis, and in particular to the story of the Fall of man. Kafka was in fact convinced that he understood the Fall better than anyone else (MIL 178). This was neither an idle conceit nor a passing fancy. Throughout his various writings, there are indeed many remarkable tracts and aphorisms which seem to confirm his unique insight into both the circumstances and the consequences of that catastrophic episode in Eden.

'The Metamorphosis', like the narrative of the Fall, is set in a rare horticultural milieu. Gregor Samsa's bedroom – where the bulk of the action takes place – is decorated with flowered wallpaper, and thus borders on a pastiche of, what Milton calls, the 'blissful bower'[28] in Paradise:

> it was a place
> Chos'n by the sovran Planter, when he framed
> All things to man's delightful use; the roof
> Of thickest covert was inwoven shade,
> Laurel and myrtle, and what higher grew
> Of firm and fragrant leaf; on either side
> Acanthus, and each odorous bushy shrub
> Fenced up the verdant wall; each beauteous flow'r,
> Iris all hues, roses, and jessamine
> Reared high their flourished heads between, and wrought
> Mosaic; under foot the violet,
> Crocus, and hyacinth with rich inlay
> Broidered the ground, more colored than with stone
> Of costliest emblem. Other Creature here,
> Beast, bird, insect, or worm durst enter none;
> Such was their awe of man.[29]

After creating Adam and placing him in the Garden of Eden, the Lord declared that it was not good for the man to be alone. Accordingly, He put Adam to sleep and – in what amounted to the first operation under general anaesthesia – extracted one of the man's ribs in order to fashion a helpmate for him. When Adam regained consciousness, he discovered Eve by his side (Genesis 2:18–23). In 'The Metamorphosis', Gregor, having dwelt as a bachelor in his blossomy sanctum for the last five years, has recently presumed to take matters into his own hands. It is reported that he spent several evenings before the start of the story making a gilt frame for a picture that he had cut out of an illustrated magazine. The picture in question

> showed a lady, with a fur cap on and a fur stole, sitting upright and holding out to the spectator a huge fur muff into which the whole of her forearm had vanished! (CSS 89)

This *bella donna* would seem to be Gregor's Eve. When he wakes up on the morning of his transformation, he briefly inspects the place where his ribs ought to be, and then looks up to see the woman of his dreams gazing at him from the wall opposite his bed. The fact that the lady is pictured in such an alluring pose is suggestive of the role played by Eve in the temptation of Adam. Perhaps Gregor was attracted to this voluptuous cover-girl because she excited his lower instincts. In any event, she certainly seems to have brought out the beast in him. Moreover, since she is swaddlingly clad in animal skins, the cockroach-teaser appears to be less than entirely human herself.

Some commentators have sought to explain the offence of Adam and Eve by linking it with the getting of carnal knowledge. This view – although contradicted three times in the text of Genesis itself (Genesis 1:28; 2:24; 4:1) – has a peculiar relevance to Kafka's teratological version of the Fall. The dramatic climax of the biblical pageant in 'The Metamorphosis' comes when the mother and daughter start to remove various articles of furniture from Gregor's den. Initially, Gregor looks forward to having the extra space to crawl about in. However, he soon begins to resent the fact that his room is being stripped of all vestiges of his former existence, and determines to 'rescue' (CSS 118) some of these precious mementoes from the two women. It is no coincidence that his immediate priority should be to save the portrait of 'the lady muffled in so much fur' (CSS 118). He franticly scurries up the wall and presses himself against it, concealing the entire frame with his body. At this juncture, Gregor would appear to care more for the picture than he does for his own family. He is even prepared to fly in his sister's face rather than relinquish it. At first, he finds that the coolness of the glass comforts 'his hot belly' (CSS 118). Nevertheless, it quickly becomes apparent that this material is in fact an icy barrier which separates him from the true object of his desire. He remains tantalizingly close to his furry mate, yet cannot lay hold of her. The grotesquerie of this unconsummated marriage between the creepy-crawly and his bestial bride is starkly contrasted with the 'complete union' (CSS 122) of Mr and Mrs Samsa.

At the sight of the beetle on the wall, Mrs Samsa screams, 'Oh God, oh God!' (CSS 119), and collapses. When Grete rushes to find some medicine for her mother, Gregor follows her into the living-room. As she makes her way back to the patient, the daughter slams the door of Gregor's bedroom in his face, excluding him temporarily from his demi-paradise. Distracted with worry and remorse, Gregor proceeds to crawl all over the furniture, walls and ceiling, and eventually falls down on to the large table. This idea of falling has featured prominently from the beginning of the story. For example, on the morning of his transformation, Gregor knew that he would have to 'fall' out of bed, but, perhaps because of his bad conscience, was anxious about making a 'loud crash' (CSS 94) and thereby drawing attention to himself. Subsequently, however, the insect seemed quite oblivious to all such inhibitions, since he was wont to amuse himself by hanging suspended from the ceiling of his bedroom, and often crash-landed on the floor with the blithe conviction that 'such a big fall did him no harm' (CSS 115). Gregor's complacency about the law of gravity mirrors the attitude of Adam and Eve, who evidently believed that they could flout the law of God without having to suffer the consequences. Incidentally, we should remember that Georg Bendemann literally fell to his death in 'The Judgement', and that he too had (first) fallen under the spell of an Eve-like seductress.

As if in response to the mother's call for divine intervention, the door-bell rings, signifying that Mr Samsa has arrived home from his new job at the bank. This is not the first time that the patriarch has answered such a plea from his wife. When Gregor had emerged from his room on the morning of his transformation, the old lady had issued a similar appeal – 'Help, for God's sake, help!' (CSS 103). The father, although heartbroken at what had become of his son, immediately rose to the occasion and, brandishing a walking-stick with one hand and a newspaper with the other, drove the insect back into the bedroom. Interestingly, these same two 'weapons' also feature very prominently in the patri–filial skirmish at the start of Pinter's *The Homecoming*.

Gregor is astounded at the appearance of the old man: 'Truly, this was not the father he had imagined to himself [. . .]' (CSS 120). The suspicion that someone, or something, else may have assumed the shape of the father is also shared by the filial heroes of both 'The Urban World' and 'The Judgement'. Gregor is inclined to see the patriarch as a ferocious ogre, whose 'black eyes [dart] fresh and penetrating glances' (CSS 121) from under his bushy eyebrows. Nevertheless, Mr Samsa – as his name might suggest – is actually more like the blinded Samson in Gaza, stumbling helplessly through a maze of tormentors, his mane shorn and his providential strength defunct (Judges 16). This analogy is reinforced when we learn that the father's 'onetime tangled white hair [has] been combed flat on either side of a shining and carefully exact parting' (CSS 121).

From Gregor's point of view, the 'smart blue uniform with gold buttons' (CSS 121) which the old man wears only enhances his aura of terrible majesty. In reality, however, this uniform – like all uniforms – is a badge not of supremacy, but of service: and for all his sartorial splendour, Mr Samsa is just a glorified errand boy.[30] In the evenings, after coming home from work, the father is apt to fall asleep fully dressed in his armchair, 'as if he were ready for service at any moment and even here only at the beck and call of his superior' (CSS 123).[31] As a result, his celestial costume (which is, incidentally, second-hand) soon becomes covered with patches of dirt and grease. Kafka's treatment of this vestiary motif prefigures F.W. Murnau's classic silent film *The Last Laugh,* in which the great German director exposes his fellow countrymen's obsession with fancy regimentals, through the tale of an elderly hotel doorman who loses his job and with it the impressive outfit which gave him status in his neighbourhood.

In 'Letter to his Father', the author submits that the disparity between himself and his own progenitor was such that a student of biomathematics would probably have expected Kafka Snr to simply trample the filial runt underfoot so that nothing was left of him (WPC 160). Ominously, in 'The Metamorphosis', Mr Samsa roars 'in a tone that [sounds] at once angry and exultant' (CSS 120) and lifts his feet 'uncommonly high' (CSS 121) as he chases his son around the living-room. Gregor is utterly 'dumbfounded at the enormous size of his [father's] shoe soles' (CSS 121), and clearly petrified that one of them will crush him into the ground like some common or garden pest – but then isn't that what he is? (This sequence is echoed in the finale of Pinter's first play,

The Room, where Bert sounds the war-cry 'Lice!' (I 110), before knocking Riley down and repeatedly putting the boot into him as he lies on the floor.) During their run-in in the previous chapter, Mr Samsa had stamped his feet loudly on the floor and, as if to emphasize the serpentine nature of his son's aspirations, made an 'unbearable hissing noise' (CSS 104). To Gregor's mind, it scarcely seemed possible that such a stentorian sibilation could simply be 'the voice of one single father' (CSS 104). It is indeed fitting that the jittery bug should be so intimidated by the combined effect of his sire's vocals and gait; because the shamefaced Adam and Eve had been equally alarmed when 'they heard the voice of the LORD God walking in the garden' (Genesis 3:8). To make matters worse, Gregor can say nothing in his defence. Whenever he tries to speak, he can hardly recognize his own voice for

> a persistent horrible twittering squeak behind it like an undertone, that left the words in their clear shape only for the first moment and then rose up reverberating round them to destroy their sense [. . . .] (CSS 91)

This confusion of the son's linguistic faculties is distinctly reminiscent of another episode in Genesis – the story of man's hubristic bid to reach heaven itself through the building of the Tower of Babel, and of the punishment that resulted therefrom (Genesis 11).

Panic-stricken and disorientated, Gregor starts to feel quite breathless, and recalls that his lungs had been less than reliable even in his former life – a tragically ironic presage of Kafka's fatal tuberculosis. The hero's respiratory problems are further symptomatic of his identification with Adam. Genesis describes how the Lord had breathed life into the nostrils of the first man, who thereupon became a living soul (Genesis 2:7). However, when Adam broke the divine injunction and ate the forbidden fruit, he forfeited his claim to immortality. Correspondingly, Gregor, in choosing to rebel against his (pro)creator, loses his right to breathe and the life it affords him.

Hanging on one of the walls of the living-room is a photograph of Gregor, as he was before his transformation, in which he looks for all the world like a prelapsarian Adam. Taken during his days of military service, it depicts the protagonist 'as a lieutenant, hand on sword, a carefree smile on his face, inviting one to respect his uniform and military bearing' (CSS 101). Interestingly, Hermann Kafka had himself served for several years in the Austro-Hungarian Army, and had been greatly invigorated by the experience: even in later life, he never tired of relating anecdotes about his time as a man-at-arms. When Franz was a young boy, the paternal veteran did his best to make a regular little soldier out of him, by teaching him to march and salute and by encouraging him to drink beer and sing patriotic songs (WPC 162–3). Accordingly, in 'The Metamorphosis', the photograph of Gregor could be regarded as a representation of the Kafkan son fashioned in the image and likeness of the father, just as Adam had been created in the image and likeness of God (Genesis 1:27). The fact that the portrait is given pride of place in the family home indicates that this is how the Samsas wish to remember Gregor. Yet from the insect's point of view, this illustrious avatar of his former self must now resemble a sardonic evocation of the cherubim and the fiery sword which were posted to prevent man from returning to Eden (Genesis 3:24).

Perhaps the single most evocative incident in 'The Metamorphosis' is that in which Mr Samsa bombards the beetle with small red apples. The majority of these fruity missiles miss their target and roll about the floor like wayward billiard balls. With one of the apples, however, the old man manages to score a direct hit. This astonishing image of the lofty father hurling an apple into the back of the cowering creature vividly conjures up the drama of the original sin. It is as if God, in His holy wrath, were chastising the primordial trespassers with the object of their offence. The book of Genesis does not actually specify the type of fruit that was borne by the tree of knowledge of good and evil; nevertheless, throughout the history of Western art and literature, the forbidden fruit has customarily been represented as an apple. Kafka and Pinter have both used the image of an apple being eaten in circumstances which allude to man's ultimate frailty: in the opening chapter of *The Trial,* the doomed Joseph K. furtively devours an apple after his breakfast has been intercepted by the arresting officers (T 14); while in *Moonlight,* the dying Andy – himself something of an Adamic figure – is promised an apple by his wife (M 34).

According to Genesis, the serpent had assured Eve that if she and Adam were to ignore the Maker's instructions and eat the prohibited pome then they would become like God Himself, being both omniscient and immortal (Genesis 3:4–5). By succumbing to this temptation, the primeval couple proved themselves to be guilty of the sin of pride. The hero of 'The Metamorphosis' is culpable of a similar kind of vanity. Gregor, who had assumed the role of breadwinner after his father's business went bankrupt, took 'great pride in the fact that he had been able to provide' such a comfortable and carefree lifestyle for his family (CSS 106). When it came to putting money on the table, the son obviously considered himself more than a match for his old man. Even though Samsa Snr remained the nominal head of the household, Gregor appears to have exercised executive control over all of the more important areas of domestic life. It was the son who, for example, had insisted on choosing the apartment in which the family resides. What is more, he obviously did not take their needs into account when he made his choice; because the apartment is too big, too expensive, poorly situated and difficult to run. As soon as the insect dies, the surviving Samsas unanimously agree that the 'greatest immediate improvement in their condition would of course arise from moving to another house' (CSS 139).

By attempting to usurp the position of paternal authority, Gregor had been following in the presumptuous footsteps of Georg Bendemann, who, not content simply to be about his father's business, had all but taken over the business himself, and even asserted his right to shut it down if he saw fit (CSS 82). Samsa *père*, however, like his opposite number in 'The Judgement', did not put all his faith in the activities of his son. It emerges that Mr Samsa had prudently invested a small amount of money which had been left over from the collapse of his business. Significantly, Gregor had not been informed about the existence of this sum, 'and of course he had not asked [his father] directly' (CSS 110). The selfish side of the son's nature is revealed when he reflects that he would rather have used this nest-egg to offset the debt owed to the chief clerk – thus bringing forward the moment when he could quit his job. However, in deference to his father's 'thrift and foresight' (CSS 111), he is forced to concede that it was doubtless better the way the old man had arranged things (CSS 112). The fact that the father has kept this money in reserve not only suggests that he knows better than his son, it also indicates that he may have possessed a quasi-divine foreknowledge of Gregor's fall.

Genesis records how God was satisfied that He had put the finishing touch to His Creation with the making of mankind. On the following day, He decided to rest, trusting that the world and everything in it would be safe in the stewardship of Adam.

But when the man lapsed into disgrace, the Lord had to step in and take control Himself in order to salvage the situation. Correlatively, in 'The Metamorphosis', Mr Samsa – who, after a lifetime of labour, had long since settled into retirement – is forced to start work again when Gregor takes his turn for the worse.

In 'In the Penal Colony', the officer tells the explorer that, as a general rule, 'Guilt is never to be doubted' (CSS 145). To attempt to deny one's guilt, therefore, is merely to draw attention to one's iniquity. This principle tallies with the author's own particular gloss on the doctrine of the original sin. In one of his aphorisms, Kafka likens the fundamental instance of all peccancy to the incessant bleating of a self-proclaimed scapegoat, whose protestations of innocence are in fact being uttered *in flagrante delicto*:

> Original sin, the ancient wrong committed by man, consists in the complaint which man makes and never ceases making, that a wrong has been done to him, that it was upon him that the original sin was committed. (GWC 110)

All this is especially pertinent to 'The Metamorphosis', in which the Adamic protagonist is also determined to see himself as one more sinned against than sinning – a victim rather than a violator.

The sad history of Gregor Samsa may well have many striking affinities with the Fall, but the hero himself is more inclined to highlight parallels with the Atonement. In typological terms, Adam represents the exact opposite of Jesus Christ. The former was the capricious creature who impudently aspired to place himself on a par with the Almighty: whereas the latter, who was in His very nature divine, did not consider equality with God something to be grasped, but humbly lowered Himself to take the form of a creature and remained obedient unto death (Philippians 2:6–8). Moreover, just as sin and condemnation came into the world through the wanton insubordination of the first man, so righteousness and reconciliation were effectuated through the perfect submission of his counterpart (Romans 5). Jesus Christ has therefore come to be known as 'the Second Adam' – since He signified a new beginning for the human race. In 'The Metamorphosis', Gregor appears to acknowledge his identification with Adam, but persuades himself that he is the all-sufficient substitute rather than the disappointing prototype.

From the very beginning of the story, the son has been presented in a quasi-Christological light. As a commercial traveller,

Gregor was constantly having to live out of a suitcase. This meant that he had to forgo the simple domestic comforts that other men take for granted. Seldom could he have been sure where he would be eating or sleeping from one night to the next. And even though he may have met many people on his way, these were invariably casual acquaintances with whom he could never have become intimate. In some respects, therefore, the lifestyle of Kafka's travelling salesman was not unlike the peripatetic existence of the Nazarene. Jesus once said to a certain scribe who talked about following Him: 'The foxes have holes, and the birds of the air have nests; but the Son of man hath not where to lay his head' (Matthew 8:20). And, on one level, Gregor's zoological transformation may be viewed as a misconceived attempt to secure his own place of rest. This, after all, had been the motive for the entomic escape fantasy in 'Wedding Preparations in the Country'. Alternatively, Gregor's metamorphosis could be regarded as a bizarre analogue of Christ's Transfiguration; since it appears to confirm both the supernatural importance of the son's mission and the imminence of his passion. Incidentally, even when he was not on the road, Gregor had occupied his time by pursuing a Christ-like activity. His only hobby was fretwork, which is of course a kind of carpentry, and thus recalls the trade that Jesus had plied before taking up His ministry.[32]

On the morning of his miraculous awakening, Gregor is overcome with gloom as he lies in bed contemplating the onerous nature of his vocation. Twice he invokes the Almighty – 'Oh God' (CSS 89) and 'Heavenly Father!' (CSS 90) – wishing, as Jesus had done in the garden of Gethsemane (Luke 22:42), that it might be possible for him to be relieved of this bitter cup. (However, with the exclamation, 'The devil take it all!' (CSS 90), Gregor lets slip that his attitude to the Tempter is more characteristic of Adam than Christ.) Gregor's sole reason for enduring this tribulation is to earn enough money to pay off the debt that his parents owe to his employer. The son is therefore apt to see himself as the saviour of his family. He has offered himself as a vicarious sacrifice in order to procure their redemption.

Far from being the original sinner, Gregor reckons that he is more akin to the sin-bearing Servant whose sufferings had been described by the prophet Isaiah:

> He is despised and rejected of men; a man of sorrows, and acquainted with grief: and we hid as it were our faces from him; he was despised,

> and we esteemed him not. Surely he hath borne our griefs, and carried our sorrows: yet we did esteem him stricken, smitten of God, and afflicted. But he was wounded for our transgressions, he was bruised for our iniquities: the chastisement of our peace was upon him; and with his stripes we are healed. All we like sheep have gone astray; we have turned every one to his own way; and the LORD hath laid on him the iniquity of us all. He was oppressed, and he was afflicted, yet he opened not his mouth: he is brought as a lamb to the slaughter, and as a sheep before her shearers is dumb, so he openeth not his mouth. (Isaiah 53:3–7)

Like the Lamb, the insect takes it upon himself 'to propitiate his father' (CSS 120). Just as Jesus had borne the sins of humanity in His body on the Cross (1 Peter 2:24), so Gregor plays host to an apple – the emblem of man's innate depravity – which festers in his back until the hour of his death. The analogy with Calvary is hammered home when we are told that Gregor felt as if he had been 'nailed to the spot' (CSS 122). Furthermore, it is worth remembering that when he had sustained an earlier injury to his flank, ichor had flowed freely from the wound (CSS 105), just as it had done from the spear-pierced side of the crucified Christ.

Only the intercession of the mother – who has in the meantime been resuscitated by her daughter – prevents the rampant father from exterminating Gregor there and then. In a kind of parodic inversion of Salome's death-demanding dance of the seven veils, Mrs Samsa discards her loosened petticoats one after another, as she rushes to plead 'for her son's life' (CSS 122).[33] Her husband relents and grants the creature a further stay of execution; but ultimately Gregor, like the first man, must return to the dust from which he emerged (Genesis 3:19).

This image of Mrs Samsa as a type of Marian mediatrix, stationed midway between the almighty father and the child of wrath, prefigures to some extent Kafka's characterization of his own mother in 'Letter to his Father'. Julie Kafka (*née* Löwy) represented a spirit of grace, moderation and reason in 'the maze and chaos' of the author's childhood (WPC 176–7). She too was wont to plead on behalf of her wretched son and did her best to shield him from the worst excesses of his father's fiery temper. However, in retrospect, Kafka felt that his mother, for all her good intentions, had 'unconsciously played the part of a beater during a hunt' (WPC 176), and that he, as the quarry, was always being driven back into the path of the paternal Nimrod (WPC 177). This irony is echoed and exaggerated in 'The Metamorphosis', where the burden of the Stabat Mater has something of a hollow ring to it. After all, there is no escaping the fact that on the two occasions that Mr Samsa advances towards Gregor with the 'grim visage' (CSS 121) of vengeance, he does so only at the instigation of his wife. Remarkably, a similar *casus belli* is also implied in 'The Judgement', even though the maternal figure in that story has been dead for two years. Indeed Mr Bendemann, who had apparently been less aggressive and less dictatorial after the demise of his spouse (CSS 78), claims that it is she who has given him the necessary strength to deal with their son (CSS 86).

One of the most intriguing aspects of 'The Metamorphosis' is the relationship between the hero and his teenage sister. The extraordinary devotion which Grete initially demonstrates towards her misshapen brother – she quickly comes to accept the reality of his transformation and assumes responsibility for feeding him and cleaning his room – can no doubt be attributed to the fact that she and Gregor had previously enjoyed a singularly 'intimate' (CSS 111) rapport. This sympathetic sibship adumbrates the very loving alliance between Kafka himself and Ottla, the youngest of his three sisters (and the only one of them who was neither married nor betrothed when he was writing 'The Metamorphosis'). However, unlike Grete – who, 'when the agony becomes too great, [. . .] withdraws, embarks on a life of her own, and leaves the one who needs her' (FEL 395) – Ottla never stopped caring for her fraternal mate, and indeed continued to attend to him even after she got married and had a child. It sometimes seemed to Kafka as if his angelic little sister were 'literally bearing [him] up on her wings through the difficult world' (FFE 137).

The last time that Gregor ventures out of his lair is when his sister agrees to entertain the lodgers by playing the violin. Despite the disappointment that is registered in the conduct of the paying-guests, the beetle is beguiled by Grete's performance. As he proceeds into the living-room, Gregor feels 'as if the way [is] opening before him to the unknown nourishment he crave[s]' (CSS 130–1). He is struck with such a profound affection for the virginal virtuoso that he becomes oblivious to those around her. Rapt in a sentimental reverie, he aspires to tug at the girl's skirt, and to lead her (violin in tow) back with him into his flowery bower, so that they might live there together in consummate bliss.

He imagines how Grete would sit beside him on the sofa and how he would whisper tenderly in her ear and kiss the nakedness of her neck (CSS 131). Another kind of forbidden fruit, this undeniably incestuous variation on the theme of 'Beauty and the Beast' elaborates on a rather unsettling equation of fraternal and marital devotion which appeared in the author's diary several weeks prior to the writing of 'The Metamorphosis': 'Love between brother and sister – the repeating of the love between mother and father' (DI 273).

His Christomania notwithstanding, Gregor now appears to regard his sister as the true embodiment of Eve. The fur-clad woman in the picture has been put out of his mind altogether, as if she were Lilith, the vixenish first wife of Adam.[34] Just as God, in creating Eve, had blessed Adam with a companion of whom he could say, 'This is now bone of my bone, and flesh of my flesh' (Genesis 2:23), so Gregor's father, in begetting Grete, has furnished him with a perfect genetic match. This elemental compatibility of the Samsa siblings is even insinuated in their curiously alliterative forenames.

Gregor's fata morgana of a paradisical existence with his sister is echoed by a postcard which Kafka sent to Felice in the autumn of 1916. The postcard describes how he and Ottla had visited two secluded beauty spots near Prague, which were 'as silent as the Garden of Eden after the expulsion of Man' (FEL 497). As they relaxed together in these idyllic environs, he read Plato aloud to her and she taught him to sing. Incidentally, the following year, after his tuberculosis was diagnosed, he went to stay with Ottla, who was managing their brother-in-law's farm in Zürau. He thrived in the atmosphere of pastoral geniality, and remained there for eight months in 'a good minor marriage' (FFE 141) with his darling sister.

The concord of Gregor's Edenic rhapsody is abruptly shattered when he is spotted by one of the lodgers. Amid the resultant pandemonium, the outraged boarders give notice of their intention to quit the premises and are prompted to take refuge behind the *cordon sanitaire* of their bedroom door. Mr Samsa then experiences a mild seizure and, with Mrs Samsa choking helplessly for breath, Grete is compelled to take the initiative herself. With an air of judicial finality, the daughter thumps the table and, refusing to utter her brother's name in the presence of the *bête noire*, declares: 'We must try to get rid of it' [*Wir müssen es loszuwerden suchen*] (CSS 133). By applying the neuter pronoun to Gregor, Grete effectively negates both his masculinity and his membership of the human race. Having shocked her parents out of their stupor, the girl continues:

> You must just try to get rid of the idea that this is Gregor. The fact that we've believed it for so long is the root of all our trouble. But how can it be Gregor? If this were Gregor, he would have realized long ago that human beings can't live with such a creature, and he'd have gone away on his own accord. (CSS 134)

Thus Grete proleptically endorses the verdict of the paternal stooge in 'Letter to his Father' and pronounces the parasitic son 'unfit for life' (WPC 216). Significantly, then, it is not his father, but his sister, who sounds the death-knell for Gregor. He would seem to have been condemned by the one he has cherished most of all. The fact of the matter is, though, that – as in 'Letter to his Father' – this is a self-condemnation on the part of the son; since the unsuspecting Grete is merely voicing Gregor's own determination to beetle off: 'The decision that he must disappear was one that he held to even more strongly than his sister [. . .]' (CSS 135). As he makes his slow and painful retreat into his room, the others remain silent and motionless. But once he is inside, Grete sees to it that the door is suddenly 'pushed shut, bolted and locked' (CSS 135). The scarab has now been sealed alive in its mastaba.

* * *

In 'The Metamorphosis', the struggle with the father ends, as it had done in 'The Judgement', with the death of the son. Death was perhaps the only dénouement that ever truly satisfied Kafka.[35] A fascination with this ultimate happy ending pervades and underpins all of his work. And even though *The Trial* – which closes with Joseph K. succumbing to the grim reaper's blade – is the only one of his three novels to actually reach a conclusion, both *America* and *The Castle* were likewise meant to finish with the poignant exit of the principal character.[36] The author himself had noted how he always experienced a tremendous sense of rapture when dealing with the subject of death. In 'these fine and very convincing passages' – which he considered among the best things he had written – Kafka would not only 'calculatingly exploit' the reader's sympathy for the moribund hero, but would also 'rejoice' vicariously in the whole process of dying, as if he were himself *in extremis* (DII 102).[37] The rationale for this secret game was, he supposed, a special capacity on his own part 'to meet death with contentment' (DII 102). In September 1917, he wrote in his diary: 'I would put myself in death's hands, though. Remnant of a faith. Return to a father. Great Day of Atonement' (DII 187).[38] As mentioned earlier, 'The Judgement' was penned one day after the Day of Atonement; and the analogy here, as in both that story and 'The Metamorphosis', again appears to be with Jesus Christ, whose 'once for all' sacrifice had effectively rendered that annual ceremony of expiation null and void (Hebrews 10:10). As St Paul points out in his epistle to the Romans, it is only through the death of the Son that man can be reconciled with the Father (Romans 5:10). However, blinded by his own Messianic paranoia, the Kafkan protagonist fails to appreciate the unique and universal nature of Christ's intercession, and -- since his concept of the Almighty is based on the imago of his own father – perversely believes that by offering up his own life he will be made right with God. Accordingly, in both 'The Judgement' and 'The Metamorphosis', the hero acquiesces in his own demise with thoughts of filial devotion: just before he drops off the bridge, Georg Bendemann professes his lifelong affection for his parents (CSS 88); while Gregor Samsa contemplates 'his family with tenderness and love' as his head sinks to the floor 'of its own accord' (CSS 135),[39] and so dies 'peacefully enough and reconciled to all' (FEL 89). Furthermore, it is interesting that these aspiring Christs should both choose to give up the ghost around the time of Easter: Georg drowns himself at 'the very height of spring' (CSS 77), while Gregor takes his last breath at 'the end of March' (CSS 137). The quasi-religious ecstasy that Kafka felt in killing off such fictional *alter egos* strongly implies an element of wish-fulfilling propitiation of his own father. Death was celebrated as the supreme ordinance through which the fallen son could repair the breach with the exalted patriarch and thus restore fellowship. The journey unto Abraham's bosom represented a cessation of hostilities, an end to separation – a final homecoming.

2

Return to a Father: *The Homecoming*

It is once again the old fight with the old giant. True, he does not fight, only I fight, he only sprawls over me as a labourer does on the tavern table, crosses his arms on the upper part of my chest and presses his chin on his arms. Shall I be able to endure this load? (WPC 286)

In 1966, during an interview for *The Paris Review*, Harold Pinter revealed that, though he left school at sixteen, he had been an enthusiastic student of literature from an early age:

PINTER: The only thing that interested me at school was English language and literature, but I didn't have Latin and so couldn't go on to university. So I went to a few drama schools, not studying seriously [. . . .] And then I was reading, for years, a great deal of modern literature, mostly novels.

INTERVIEWER: No playwrights – Brecht, Pirandello . . .

PINTER: Oh certainly not, not for years. I read Hemingway, Dostoevski, Joyce and Henry Miller at a very early age, and Kafka. I'd read Beckett's novels, too, but I'd never heard of Ionesco until after I'd written the first few plays.[1]

When asked whether any of these authors had particularly influenced his own writing, Pinter confessed:

Beckett and Kafka stayed with me the most – I think Beckett is the best prose writer living. My world is still bound up by other writers – that's one of the best things in it.[2]

Six years earlier, in an interview for the BBC European Service, Pinter had also acknowledged the same two writers as kindred spirits who had made the most profound and lasting impression on him and his approach to literature. He declared that when he read the work of Beckett and Kafka, 'it rang a bell' within him: 'I thought: something is going on here which is going on in me too'.[3]

At once manifest and irrefutable, the affinity between Pinter's *oeuvre* and that of Beckett has already generated considerable and widespread debate. Pinter himself has been remarkably forthcoming about both his admiration for and his indebtedness to the Irish writer. For example, in 1967, he contributed a staggeringly effusive eulogy to the *Festschrift, Beckett at Sixty*;[4] and in December 1971, he announced to *The New York Times* that for some years he had actually been sending his plays in manuscript form (that is, before they appeared in performance or print) to Beckett, who would graciously respond with 'the most *suc-cinct* observations' (CP 28).[5] All the same, such statements, however laudable in their frankness and generosity, inevitably gave ammunition to Pinter's detractors, who throughout his career – from the early 'comedies of menace'[6] to the later studies of memory – have accused his work of being overly derivative of that of his Hibernian mentor. It is somewhat ironic therefore that, as Ronald Hayman points out, the words 'Pinterish' and 'Pinteresque' should have been absorbed into the language long before the term 'Beckettian' was coined.[7]

By total contrast, the influence of Kafka on Pinter's work has – or at least had until quite recently[8] – received only nominal attention from the critical establishment. Even Hayman, who has published creditable monographs on both writers individually, makes virtually nothing of the connection between them. Other commentators, while taking cognizance of Pinter's avowed debt to Kafka, have tended to satisfy themselves with facile observations about a reciprocal atmosphere of nightmarish uncertainty, or with vague assumptions about a common philosophical purpose. In reality, though, Kafka's influence is much more concrete and much less woolly than such glosses would have us believe.

There are two obvious reasons why the legacy of Kafka has seemed more difficult to quantify than that of Beckett. Firstly, Kafka was not a dramatist;[9] whereas Beckett – whose star was very much in the ascendant when Pinter first appeared on the literary scene – was celebrated as much for his plays as his prose fiction. Secondly, Kafka was not a native anglophone; and while most of Beckett's work was originally written in French, he himself translated it into his mother tongue. Nevertheless, both these 'problems' are in fact complete red herrings. Intractable only because of their specious prominence, they represent no practical obstruction to serious inquiry. In any case, Kafka's bequest to Pinter must be appreciated not in terms of dramaturgy or linguistics, but as an essentially thematic phenomenon. The overriding factor is one of content rather than form; one of substance rather than style.

The true kidney of Kafka's influence is perhaps nowhere more tellingly illustrated than in *The Homecoming* – the play in which Pinter deals explicitly for the first time with the relationship between father and son. Now this of course is what Kafka himself had claimed his own writing 'was all about' (WPC 197). It is scarcely conceivable therefore that Pinter, having asserted his filiation from Kafka so emphatically, could compose a drama on this most pregnant of subjects devoid of reference to his Czech forbear. What is so astonishing, however, is that such allusions should be so fundamental and far-reaching as to constitute the very pith and marrow of *The Homecoming*. Indeed Kafka's shadow hangs over almost every aspect of the play – its characters, imagery and milieu – giving shape and colour, register and resonance to what might otherwise have been a fairly obscure domestic farce. And yet, having said that, *The Homecoming* remains incontrovertibly Pinter's own creation – an elegantly crafted and electrifying piece of theatre, which bears the unmistakable stamp of his own artistic genius.

Pinter's knowledge of German notwithstanding, English language editions of Kafka's works had been appearing steadily since the first publication of *The Castle* in 1930. By 1954, three years before Pinter penned his first play, the vast majority of Kafka's writings – including all three novels, the complete diaries, the notebooks, *Letters to Milena*, 'Letter to his Father' and most of the short stories; but excluding the selection of pieces in *Description of a Struggle* (US 1958; GB 1960)[10] and the volumes of correspondence to Felice (US 1973; GB 1974), friends, family and editors (US 1977; GB 1978) and Ottla (US 1982) – had been translated and were freely available in Great Britain. Pinter therefore would certainly have had the opportunity and, judging from his own remarks, the inclination to obtain and digest the lion's share of the Kafkan canon long before he came to write *The Homecoming* (1964). At the same time, he would also have had access to the essential biographical information about Kafka contained in the memoirs of both Max Brod and Gustav Janouch.

The Homecoming was Pinter's fourth full-length play and is, in the opinion of many critics, his masterpiece. The setting is an old house in North London, where Max, a seventy-year-old widower and retired butcher, lives with Lenny and Joey, the younger two of his three grown-up sons, and Sam, his slightly prissy sexagenarian brother. The action takes place over a period of two days in summer, during which Teddy – Max's eldest son, who had emigrated to America some six years earlier – arrives unexpectedly with Ruth, his enigmatic wife, about whom he has hitherto neglected to tell the family. On these basic premises, Pinter works his special alchemy to conjure up a monumental and multi-faceted representation of patri–filial rivalry.

We have already seen how Kafka's treatment of the father–son conflict was largely determined by the peculiar oppressiveness of his own domestic situation – a fact supported by the wealth of documentary evidence preserved in his sundry personal writings. It must be stated from the outset, however, that there is really nothing to suggest that Pinter had experienced similar persecution at the hands of his father. From what he has said in various interviews over the years, the playwright would seem to have enjoyed a comparatively happy childhood, even if he was, by his own admission, 'quite a morose little boy'.[11] Young Harold, an only child, was evidently the apple of his parents' eye; and he hated being separated from them when, at the outbreak of the Second World War, he was sent away from his home in Hackney to Cornwall as a nine-year-old evacuee. Intriguingly, though, Pinter has revealed that he 'got on very badly'[12] with his father during his adolescence and early adulthood:

> My father was a man of considerable authority [... and] I was a pretty rebellious young man. [...] There was a considerable tension in my own youth. There's no question about that. (CP 103)

He has mentioned, for example, how much he resented the old man's rather regimental insistence that he should be smartly dressed and well groomed:

> He always wanted me to have my shoes immaculate, and wanted me to wear a shirt and tie at all times ... hair precise ... no untidiness and so on. I objected strongly to all this.[13]

The two issues which appear to have caused the most friction in the Pinter household were: (1) the son's stance – and subsequent prosecution – as a conscientious objector,[14] and (2) his decision to marry out of the family's religion (CP 103).[15] Still, in later years, the dramatist claims to have had 'the most wonderful relations' (CP 102) with both his parents.

While the family circumstances of Pinter and Kafka were by no means identical, they did have a number of salient similarities. Both families were Jewish – the roots of the Pinter family tree can also be traced back to a Hebraic strain in Eastern Europe[16] – and the bread-winner in each case exemplified that community's customary aptitude for private enterprise. Pinter's father, like that of Kafka, earned his living as a shopkeeper. Moreover, both men specialized in ladies clothing. But whereas the more prosperous Hermann Kafka merely sold ready-made garments, together with a range of fancy goods, Jack Pinter (1902–) was a skilled tailor and actually fashioned his own wares. The two fathers worked very long hours in their respective stores; yet, for various reasons, neither was able to pass the business on to his only son. As a youngster growing up in the East End of London, Harold (like Franz) never really had any cause for material worries. Thanks to his father's tireless industry and his mother's careful thrift, the Pinters 'lived very well'.[17] Implicit in some of the playwright's remarks about this period is a residual feeling of indebtedness to both his parents, and to his father in particular. Consequently, there can be little doubt that, on reading Kafka's 'Letter to his Father', Pinter would have been struck by the exaggerated sense of obligation which Hermann had so rigorously sought to impress upon his son:

> You have always reproached me [. . .] for living in peace and quiet, warmth, and abundance, lacking for nothing, thanks to your hard work. I think here of remarks that must positively have worn grooves in my brain, like: 'When I was only seven I had to push the barrow from village to village.' 'We all had to sleep in one room.' 'We were glad when we got potatoes.' 'For years I had open sores on my legs from not having enough clothes to wear in winter.' 'I was only a little boy when I was sent away to Pisek to go into business.' 'I got nothing from home, not even when I was in the army, even then I was sending money home.' 'But for all that, for all that – Father was always Father to me. Ah, nobody knows what that means these days! What do these children know of things? Nobody's been through that! Is there any child that understands such things today?' (WPC 177–8)

Although the dramatist may well have seen several other aspects of his own background magnified and distorted through the lens of Kafka's epistolary memoir, this parallel is especially interesting, because it may also have provided him with the template for one of the speeches of the patriarch in *The Homecoming*. Indeed Pinter draws in the pivotal figure of Max a grotesque and wicked caricature of a father who has had to make many sacrifices for the sake of his dependants. Never one to hide his light under a bushel, Max stridently boasts about what he had to endure and how hard he had to struggle to guarantee the welfare and comfort of not just one but

> Two families! My mother was bedridden, my brothers were all invalids. I had to earn the money for the leading psychiatrists. I had to read books! I had to study the disease, so that I could cope with an emergency at every stage. A crippled family, three bastard sons, a slutbitch of a wife – don't talk to me about the pain of childbirth – I suffered the pain, I've still got the pangs – when I give a little cough my back collapses [. . . .] (III 55)

On a more personal note, the 'twelve-hour day'[18] which Pinter claimed his own father had clocked up is mischievously doubled in the sometime routine of Max, who, we are told, 'was busy working twenty-four hours a day in [his] shop' (III 54).

* * *

Proudest of all Max's achievements is that he has walked in the ways of his own father, whose memory he has sanctified by maintaining both the family tradition and bloodline:

> I respected my father not only as a man but as a number one butcher! And to prove it I followed him into the shop. I learned to carve a carcass at his knee. I commemorated his name in blood. I gave birth to three grown men! All on my own bat. (III 47–8)

Pinter's decision to assign this occupation to the *paterfamilias* in *The Homecoming* must surely have been taken in the knowledge that the Kafka gens was also steeped in the same sanguinary mores. Certainly, the fact that Hermann Kafka was the son of a kosher village butcher has been well documented, and not least because Franz himself had exhibited a morbid fascination for the stock-in-trade of his paternal ancestor. The image of a butcher's knife cutting into the flesh loomed large in Kafka's nightmares, and recurs with alarming frequency throughout his multifarious writings; nowhere more graphically perhaps than in the celebrated climax of *The Trial*, where the lethal implement is thrust into the heart of Joseph K. and turned twice. Sometimes Kafka even pictured himself in the blood-stained robes of the *schochet*,[19] wielding the 'long, thin, double-edged' (T 254) blade:

> Between throat and chin would seem to be the most rewarding place to stab. Lift the chin and stick the knife into the tensed muscles. But this spot is probably rewarding only in one's imagination. You expect to see a magnificent gush of blood and a network of sinews and little bones like you find in the leg of a roast turkey. (DII 130)

At other times, he imagined that he himself was being carved up like an animal carcass:

> Always the image of a pork butcher's broad knife that quickly and with mechanical regularity chops into me from the side and cuts off very thin slices which fly off almost like shavings because of the speed of the action. (DI 286–7)

As the author of the story 'A Crossbreed' ['A Sport'] – which centres on a family mascot, 'half kitten, half lamb' (CSS 426) – he identifies simultaneously with both willing victim and reluctant executioner:

> Perhaps the knife of the butcher would be a release for this animal; but as it is a legacy [from my father] I must deny it that. So it must wait until the breath voluntarily leaves its body, even though it sometimes gazes at me with a look of human understanding, challenging me to do the thing of which both of us are thinking. (CSS 427)

In general, however, his sympathies lay with the animals. Time and again, in fable after fable, he would transform himself into all manner of dumb beast (mouse, ape, beetle, dog, mole, and so on), experience the world from their point of view and, invariably, articulate their sense of uncomprehending anguish. Indeed, on one level, the purgatorial quality of these tales would seem to suggest that Kafka believed it incumbent upon himself to expiate the sins which his father's father had committed against the animal kingdom. Worst of all, though, was the fear that he might have to 'eat as much meat as [his paternal grandfather had] slaughtered'.[20] In terrible flights of gastronomic fancy, he conceived how he would franticly 'shove the long slabs of rib meat unbitten into [his] mouth, and then pull them out again from behind, tearing through stomach and intestines' (DI 122). Appalled at the prospect of such monstrous and machine-like gluttony, the novelist sought refuge in the *Weltanschauung* of vegetarianism. As he once quipped to Gustav Janouch: '[. . .] I'm a vegetarian. We only live on our own flesh' (CK 169). (Kafka apparently thought that vegetarian food was not only more palatable, but also more spiritually nutritious. He compared the scorn that the world meted out to vegetarians to the persecution of the early Christian saints.[21] And, on one occasion, he even submitted himself to a 'medical' examination by a naturopathic 'magician' who gave a vegetarian exegesis of both the Old and New Testaments.[22]) As a rule, Kafka would not eat meat or anything that had to be killed, and even the merest trace of blood would fill him with revulsion. It was perhaps this rejection of the carnivorous that inspired him to write such stories as 'A Hunger Artist' – where a circus freak starves himself in a cage before an audience headed by a permanent triumvirate of butchers – and 'An Old Manuscript' – in which a timorous butcher tries to 'spare himself the trouble of slaughtering' (CSS 417) an ox, only to witness the creature being eaten alive by an army of ravenous nomads. The unsavoury ethos of 'the chopper and the slab' (III 55) is similarly, if less spectacularly, repudiated by all three of Max's sons in *The Homecoming*, who have, it seems, neither the stomach nor the deference to follow their father into the family business. The individual pursuits of the young men further conspire to banish the stigma of this red-handed heritage through a process of sublimation: Joey carries the lust for blood over into the square ring; Teddy, instead of cutting up the bodies of dead animals, dissects metaphysical suppositions in his 'critical works' (III 69); while Lenny sets up his stall, not in the meat markets of Smithfield, but in the flesh-pots of Soho.

Images of butchery are not confined to *The Homecoming*, but infuse much of Pinter's other work besides. At the end of *The Dwarfs*, for example, Len, in a passage bulging with emetic detail, paints a grisly yet strangely nostalgic picture of a knacker's yard

> littered with scraps of cat's meat, pig bollocks, tin cans, bird brains, spare parts of all the little animals, a squelching, squealing carpet, all the dwarfs' leavings spittled in the muck, worms stuck in the poisoned shit heaps, the alleys a whirlpool of piss, slime, blood, and fruit juice. (II 105; cf. D 183)

In *That's All*, a revue sketch for two women (written in 1959, but not performed until 1964, around which time Pinter was working on *The Homecoming*), the word 'butcher' occurs no less than ten times within a page and a half of dialogue (III 223–4). The overall effect is strongly reminiscent of the famous breakfast-table sequence in Alfred Hitchcock's *Blackmail* (the first 'talkie' to be made in England), during which the word 'knife' is repeatedly and menacingly ejaculated. Indeed knives, a trademark of Kafka's literature, are drawn in anger in the course of several of Pinter's plays – namely, *The Caretaker*, *The Collection*, and *The Hothouse*, where it is subsequently reported that Roote and the aptly named Miss Cutts have both been stabbed to death as they lay together in bed (I 323): moreover, in *The Homecoming* itself, Max fears at one point that Lenny has 'got a knife stuck in him' (III 43). However, the most telling of Pinter's allusions to the butcher's trade – at least so far as Kafka is concerned – is to be found in *Victoria Station*, where the splenetic Controller threatens to torture and kill Driver 274:

> Well, it'll be nice to meet you in the morning. I'm really looking forward to it. I'll be sitting here with my cat o'nine tails, son. And you know what I'm going to do with it? I'm going to tie you up bollock naked to a butcher's table and I'm going to flog you to death all the way to Crystal Palace. (IV 354)

The crucial point here is not the mode of execution (a sadistic hybrid of the punitive measures exercised in 'The Whipper' chapter of *The Trial* and 'In the Penal Colony'), but rather the fact that the vindictive 'butcher' should cast himself in the paternal role by calling his victim 'son'. A further thematic twist is added in *Moonlight*, where Jake claims that his legendary father, who rejoiced in the hieratic appellation 'The Incumbent', had kept a 'butcher's hook' in order to deal with 'troublemakers' (M 62).[23] This dynamic (con)fusion of the roles of patriarch and butcher not only relates directly to the story of Abraham and Isaac in Genesis 22, but, on a broader canvas, brings into sharp focus the whole issue of blood sacrifice – a practice which is alluded to in *A Kind Of Alaska*, when Deborah emerges from her cataleptic trance with the suspicion that her doctor is in fact a latter-day Moloch, to whom she has been immolated by her parents (IV 313–14). Katherine H. Burkham has observed quite correctly that a sacrifical element is also at work in *The Homecoming*; yet her assumption that this has its basis in pagan fertility rites is somewhat at odds with the ethno-theological subtext of the play. For Pinter, like Kafka, locates each of his paternal figures within the very specific cosmos of the Hebrew Scriptures. Striking confirmation of this pattern comes in *One for the Road*, when Nicolas, the Fascist Grand Inquisitor and sworn defender of patriarchal values, informs his captive: 'God speaks through me. I'm referring to the Old Testament God, by the way, although I'm a long way from being Jewish' (IV 374). (It is interesting that the Old Testament should also be cited as the 'sole and only constitution' of the misogynistic dystopia in *The Handmaid's Tale*, Pinter's screen adaptation of the novel by Margaret Atwood.[24]) Thus the dramatist deliberately exploits the supposed disparity between the God of the Old Testament – the Law, wrath and retribution – and the God of the New Testament – grace, peace and mercy. The emphasis here is very much on Jehovah (the God of the fathers, the God of Abraham, Isaac and Jacob), just as it had been in Kafka's work, where even the phrase 'God the Son' would have seemed a contradiction in terms. By the same token, it is surely no coincidence that the father and all three sons in *The Homecoming* should refuse to acknowledge the divinity of Jesus: Max and Joey both (mis)use the name 'Christ' as an expletive (III 24; 66); and when Lenny badgers Teddy about 'a certain logical incoherence in the central affirmations of Christian theism' (III 59), the scholarly brother replies that this matter does not fall within his province. Indeed, despite Nicolas's gentile disclaimer, the Semitic character of the family in *The Homecoming* – albeit implied rather than stated – is never really in question. A fairly obvious clue is provided by the names of the *dramatis personae* which, as various commentators – notably William Baker and Stephen E. Tabachnik – have already pointed out, either derive from the Hebrew Bible (Joey, Ruth, Sam), or are traditionally popular among Western Jews (Max, Lenny, Teddy). It is, however, Barry Supple, a contemporary from Pinter's schooldays at Hackney Downs Grammar, who has captured most succinctly the quintessential Jewishness of the play:

> [. . .] Pinter uses no direct words or references which would 'place' the characters. But anyone with a knowledge of the social patterns and habits, the speech tones and vocabulary, of North London working class Jewry, let alone a knowledge of Pinter's own background, can be left in no doubt.[25]

Supple's remarks have been echoed by Paul Rogers, the actor who portrayed Max in both the original stage production and the subsequent film version of *The Homecoming*. Moreover, according to Rogers, it was tacitly understood by everyone involved with the play that the family were Jewish.[26]

Having been brought up in the Jewish faith, Pinter, like Kafka, would almost certainly have been well acquainted with the teachings of the Torah. Of particular relevance to the world of *The Homecoming* are the sacrifical procedures of the Law, as expounded in the book of Leviticus. These observances had existed in some form or other for many generations, yet it was during the ministry of Moses that they received their fullest definition. There were in fact four main types of sacrifice: (1) the burnt offering, (2) the peace offering, (3) the sin offering and (4) the guilt offering. Each had a special purpose and was governed by different regulations: however, the common denominator in all of them was the ritual shedding of blood. Blood alone had the sacred elixir-like properties which could secure forgiveness, bring about reconciliation and restore fellowship:

> For the life of the flesh is in the blood: and I have given it to you upon the altar to make atonement for your souls: for it is the blood that maketh an atonement for the soul. (Leviticus 17:11)

The blood sacrifice was therefore a divine provision which signified that a price had to be paid for man's redemption. The crux of this propitiation was the idea of a substitutionary death. In the first instance, the contrite supplicant would symbolically transfer his guilt on to a choice animal – usually a young ox, sheep or goat, though sometimes certain birds (for example, a pigeon or a turtle-dove) would also be permitted – by laying his hands on its head and confessing his sins. The animal would then be slain, whereupon the High Priest – initially Aaron or one of his sons, though later one of the tribe of Levi – would take some of the blood and sprinkle it against the altar in the Tent of Meeting, towards the veil of the Holy of Holies or, in the case of the Day of Atonement, upon the mercy-seat of the Ark of the Covenant itself. Thus God would graciously accept the lifeblood of the creature in place of that of the human offender.

The sacramental power of such ancient ceremonial blood-letting was by no means lost on Kafka, whose imagination, already primed with the symbolism of the abattoir, would often vent itself through a kind of lustral haemophilia. And so it is that blood runs thick and fast across the pages of Kafka's work: from the self-inflicted stab-wound in 'Description of a Struggle' to the maggot-infested ulcer in 'A Country Doctor'; from the irrigated mutilation of the racked bodies in 'In the Penal Colony' to the stinking pools around a dead camel in 'Jackals and Arabs'; from the nitty-gritty of a less than hygienic circumcision (DI 196) to the author's own tubercular sputum. Perhaps most revealing, though, is the orgiastic frenzy of 'A Fratricide', where Schmar, the knife-wielding assassin, exults in the 'relief, the soaring ecstasy from the shedding of another's blood!', regretting only that his victim is not 'simply a bladder of blood', which, when stamped upon, would 'vanish into nothingness' (CSS 403). Correspondingly, in *The Homecoming*, it is Max who asserts the mysterious solemnity of this motif, not only by his ensanguined commemoration of his father's name, but also through his incessant, emphatic, almost incantatory use of the word 'blood' and its derivatives – 'bloody' and 'bleeding'.

The sacrifical rites of the Old Testament confirm that man, even in his fallen state, is still superior to all other creatures. Originally a sinless being fashioned in the image and likeness of God, man is the consummate act of Creation and the most exalted of all earthly bodies; entirely distinct from every other form of organic life, over which he has been given dominion. Hamlet, in one of his famous soliloquies, puts it thus:

> What a piece of work is a man! How noble in reason, how infinite in faculty, in form and moving how express and admirable, in action how like an angel, in apprehension how like a god [. . . .][27]

It is this uniquely divine image which permeates human nature and gives rise to all of those qualities – moral, rational and spiritual – that distinguish mankind from the animal kingdom. Nevertheless, as a result of Adam's disobedience to the will of the Almighty, the numinous aspect of man's character became tarnished and debased, if not totally obliterated. Man forfeited his spiritual union with the Creator and degenerated to the level of the beasts. He became mere 'flesh': mortal, frail, corruptible – a slave to his lower nature. Nowhere is this consequence of the Fall more brutally illustrated than in the handiwork and raw material of the butchery. (It is interesting that the word used for 'flesh' in German translations of the Bible should also provide the root for the word 'butcher': *das Fleisch/der Fleischer*.) Paradoxically, though, it was through the office of the butcher that man was able to raise himself – albeit temporarily – above the beasts. For what indeed was the Aaronic priesthood, but a patrilineal order of butchers consecrated to serve in the Tabernacle of the Lord? (Moreover, like all butchers, the sacrificial slaughterer enjoyed the perquisite of keeping some of the choicest cuts of meat for himself and his family.) By far the most solemn of these sacerdotal duties took place once every year on the aforementioned Day of Atonement, when the High Priest would be permitted to enter the normally inviolable Holy of Holies with the blood sacrifice of a ritually clean substitute to expiate the accumulated sins of the Children of Israel. Before doing so, however, he first had to bathe himself, put on his sacred linen vestments and offer an atoning sacrifice for his own transgressions. Provisionally the least sinful person on earth, he was thus singularly eligible to approach the awesome glory of God's presence. At the moment of truth, the High Priest, having become judge and executioner of his victim, briefly restored the lustre of the divine righteousness to mankind; while the animal in turn came to represent all that was wicked, profane, base and unclean. Nevertheless, there was perhaps always a danger that, given his peerless position and lethal authority, this kosher shaman might be tempted to look upon the rest of the human race as inferior creatures, parasitically dependent on his bloody ministrations. Such megalomania would appear to have taken hold of both Hermann Kafka and his counterpart in *The Homecoming* – themselves the sons of Jewish butchers, and therefore heirs to an ancestral tradition which is in many respects a rough-hewn equivalent to that of the Old Testament priesthood – who characteristically regard other people as lower forms of life.

'Letter to his Father' features quite a number of examples of Hermann Kafka's perversely theriomorphic caricatures. We are told, for instance, that it was typical of Herr Kafka's methods of upbringing to chasten his impressionable son with such monstrous threats as 'I'll tear you apart like a fish' (WPC 171). Moreover, while the father himself displayed the most deplorable table-manners, anyone else whom he found wanting in this department – including the young Franz, his daughter Elli's husband Karl Hermann, and grandson Felix – was roundly condemned as 'a swine' (WPC 168). Referring to an employee who was suffering from TB (the disease that would later claim the life of his own son), he regularly scoffed: 'Sooner he dies the better, the mangey dog' (WPC 181). On another occasion, he compared Kafka's thespian friend Yitzhak Löwy to vermin, and in a such 'a dreadful way' (WPC 166) that the novelist later could not even bring himself to remember the exact details. Indeed, when speaking about people of whom his son was fond, the old man would automatically recite the proverb: 'Whoever lies down with dogs gets up with fleas' (DI 131; WPC 166).

In *The Homecoming*, Max complains that the other members of his clan have turned his home into a shambles: 'They walk in here every time of the day and night like bloody animals' (III 24). What is more, like all domestic livestock, they expect to be fed and watered. Fortunately, however, the versatile Max possesses not only 'an instinctive understanding of animals' (III 18), but also a 'special understanding of food' (III 25). It is not surprising therefore that the unique brand of cuisine which he serves up to his brood should reflect his zoomorphic perception of them. Yet the prescribed bill of fare is not to everyone's taste, and Lenny in particular is less than complimentary about his father's culinary credentials: 'Why don't you buy a dog? You're a dog cook. Honest. You think you're cooking for a lot of dogs' (III 19). This dietetic suspicion is duly confirmed when Max – displaying the same confused notion of gender as the father of Stephen Daedalus in *A Portrait of the Artist as a Young Man*[28] – denounces the vituperative Lenny as a 'bitch' (III 19). The same word, having been used earlier to describe Jessie (III 17), is also applied to Sam, when he confesses to feeling a bit hungry (III 24), and then to Teddy, after he inquires, 'What's for breakfast?' (III 48–50). Elsewhere Max classifies his demure brother generically as 'just an old grub' (III 26), and then more specifically as 'a maggot' (III 27); while Teddy is subsequently reviled as a 'lousy stinkpig' (III 79) for refusing to pay anything towards Ruth's running costs.

It should be noted that almost all of the animal images evoked by both Hermann Kafka and Max refer to creatures which are expressly tabooed under Mosaic Law. The book of Leviticus makes it clear that, in addition to such traditional *bêtes noires* as the dog and the pig, creatures of a lowly posture are particularly detestable in the sight of God:

> Whatsoever goeth upon the belly, and whatsoever goeth upon all four, or whatsoever hath more feet among all creeping things that creep upon the earth, them ye shall not eat; for they are an abomination. Ye shall not make yourselves abominable with any creeping thing

> that creepeth, neither shall ye make yourselves unclean with them, that ye should be defiled thereby. (Leviticus 11:42–3)

Significantly, though, it was with these very creatures – noxious insects, verminous rodents and low-bred curs – that Kafka most often chose to identify himself. In his dreams, as he confided to Felice Bauer, the novelist always felt most at ease when 'lying on the ground among the animals'; so much so that he became convinced that he 'wouldn't have survived the terror of standing upright' (FEL 447). (We may remember how Gregor Samsa had also experienced a tremendous 'sense of physical comfort' (CSS 102) when he first began to crawl about on the floor, and that later he was too frightened even 'to make the circumstantial preparations for standing up on end' (CSS 104).) Conversely, whenever Hermann Kafka appeared in these filial fantasies, he invariably took the form of a quasi-divine figure – immense in stature, imperious in bearing, and immaculate in character. Indeed, even in the sober light of day, the author was inclined to view his father as 'so huge, a giant in every respect' (WPC 174).[29] This perception was in turn mirrored in the oneiric world of Kafka's fiction. For example, in 'The Judgement', Mr Bendemann, although senile and infirm, 'is still a giant of a man' (CSS 81) in the eyes of his son; and, in 'The Metamorphosis', the entomic protagonist is astounded at the 'enormous size' (CSS 121) of his father's shoe soles. Similar apprehensions also lurk just beneath the surface of *The Homecoming*. Having sneaked into the parental home under cover of darkness, Teddy tries to reassure the 'nervous' Ruth (and also perhaps himself) that his family are 'not ogres' (III 31); yet a few moments earlier, in the scene which immediately preceded their arrival, Max had hinted at just such a prodigious pedigree, by recalling how he, as a small child, was often playfully manhandled by his gigantic father:

> He used to come over to me and look down at me. My old man did. He'd bend right over me, then he'd pick me up. I was only that big. Then he'd dandle me. Give me the bottle. Wipe me clean. Give me a smile. Pat me on the bum. Pass me around, pass me from hand to hand. Toss me up in the air. Catch me coming down. I remember my father. (III 27)

This picture of the tiny boy falling into the hands of a paternal superman also brings to mind the traumatic episode in which the infant Franz was snatched from his bed and carried out on to the *pavlatche* (WPC 161–2). (Incidentally, the name 'Max' is itself a token of the patriarch's supreme transcendence, insofar as it echoes the abbreviated form of the Latin *maximus* – 'greatest'.)

As far as Kafka was concerned, his father was not just the high one, but also the holy one – a *nonpareil* of moral, spiritual and physical excellence upon whom 'there was almost no smudge of earthly filth' (WPC 206). By contrast, the son tended to believe that he himself was fundamentally soiled – an impression which was vividly captured in a quintessential Freudian nightmare that he had during the spring of 1912:

> I was riding with my father through Berlin in a trolley. [. . .] We came to a gate, got out without any sense of getting out, stepped through the gate. On the other side of the gate a sheer wall rose up, which my father ascended almost in a dance, his legs flew out as he climbed, so easy was it for him. There was certainly also some inconsiderateness in the fact that he did not help me one bit, for I got to the top only with the utmost effort, on all fours, often sliding back again, as though the wall had become steeper under me. At the same time it was also distressing that [the wall] was covered with human excrement so that flakes of it clung to me, chiefly to my breast. I looked down at the flakes with bowed head and ran my hand over them. (DI 260)

Notwithstanding his own intrinsic perfection, the father still has to contend with the wallowing excesses and fetid excretions of those around him. In *The Homecoming*, Max, who is reputed to be 'obsessed with order and clarity' (III 41), finds himself confronted at every turn by seemingly inexhaustible supplies of faecal and purulent matter: 'Look what I'm lumbered with. One cast-iron bunch of crap after another. One flow of stinking pus after another' (III 27). Nonetheless, the odour of sanctity which emanates from the patriarch is apparently so overpowering that the reprobate cannot abide for long in his temple. After spending just one night in his father's house, Teddy, the dubious prodigal son,[30] begins to imagine that he would feel 'cleaner' (III 63) if he were to go back to America – and this despite, or possibly because of, there being 'lots of insects there' (III 61). Kafka *fils* had attributed his own preoccupation with cleanliness to the fact that he himself was 'infinitely dirty' (MIL 185) and thus liable to contaminate a place simply by being there (MIL 199). Correlatively, if England is, as Teddy rather fastidiously suggests, less clean than America, then it is perhaps his very presence that makes it so. This antithesis of paternal purity and filial filth (which we shall encounter again later when we attempt to unravel the knotty problem of Teddy's marriage) finds its *locus classicus* in *One for the Road,* where the despotic Nicolas fulminates with fire and brimstone after Gila has presumed to take the hallowed name of the father in vain:

> Your *father*? How dare you? Fuckpig.
>
> *Pause.*
>
> Your father was a wonderful man. His country is proud of him. He's dead. He was a man of honour. He's dead. Are you prepared to insult the memory of your father?
>
> *Pause.*
>
> Are you prepared to defame, to debase, the memory of your father? Your father fought for his country. I knew him. I revered him. Everyone did. He believed in God. He didn't *think*, like you shitbags. He *lived*. He lived. He was iron and gold. He would die, he would die, he would die, for his country, for his God. And he did die, he died, he died, for his God. You turd. To spawn such a daughter. What a fate. Oh, poor, perturbed spirit, to be haunted forever by such scum and spittle. How do you dare speak of your father to me? I loved him, as if he were my own father. (IV 389)

Shortly after this searing philippic, Nicolas – whom Pinter may have modelled on the character of O'Brien in George Orwell's *Nineteen Eighty-Four* (and *One for the Road* was in fact premièred during that ominous year) – announces that he has enlisted an entire army of 'daddies' to help him 'keep the world clean for God' (IV 394). Nicolas's 'business' (IV 394) is also the *métier* of Disson in *Tea Party*. Himself the father of two teenage boys, Disson has established a thriving commercial empire through the manufacture and installation of sanitary ware. Moreover, he too regards this work as a kind of divine calling. As he explains to his future secretary: 'It's almost by way of being a mission' (III 96).

'Woman is natural, therefore abominable',[31] according to Baudelaire. And indeed the patriarch in *The Homecoming* recognizes a natural enemy in the womanly shape of Ruth – a sensual temptress whose pernicious influence threatens to deprave and brutalize himself as well as his family: 'Where's the whore? Still in bed? She'll make animals of us all' (III 76). It is both ironic and appropriate that Max should deliver this warning at a time when – unbeknown to him – his sons are arguing about which of them can 'go the whole hog' (III 76) with 'the whore'. (Incidentally, the book of Leviticus decrees that, if they are to remain holy unto the Lord, the priestly descendants of Aaron 'shall not take a wife that is a whore, or profane; neither shall they take a woman put away from her husband' (Leviticus 21:7).) Women are also prone to bring out the beast in Kafka's protagonists. In *The Castle*, for example, a moment of intimacy between K. and Frieda is described thus:

> like dogs desperately tearing up the ground they tore at each other's bodies, and often, helplessly baffled, in a final effort to attain happiness they nuzzled and tongued each other's face. (C 64)

Correspondingly, in *The Trial*, we are told that Joseph K. had seized Fräulein Bürstner 'and kissed her first on the lips, then all over the face, like some thirsty animal lapping greedily at a spring of long-sought fresh water' (T 38). And later in the same novel, the hero, while admiring Leni's 'pretty little paw' (T 124), is pulled down on to the carpet by the girl, who immediately declares, 'You belong to me now' (T 125). A similar tactic is deployed in *The Homecoming* by Ruth, who contrives to 'make animals' of her conquests by literally flooring them – that is, getting them to adopt a submissive posture by kneeling or lying down on the floor. During their initial clash of wills, Ruth nonplusses Lenny by suggesting that he should lie on the floor so that she can pour water down his throat (III 42). This invitation both parallels and inverts the dramatic climax of the book of Ruth, where the eponymous Old Testament heroine slips into the threshing room late at night and lies down at the feet of Boaz, her dead husband's near kinsman, in order to betroth herself to him (Ruth 3). However, unlike Boaz, Lenny rejects his sister-in-law's 'proposal' (III 42), and later, when the opportunity arises, pointedly threatens to bring her to heel:

> JOEY *and* RUTH *roll off the sofa on to the floor.*
> JOEY *clasps her.* LENNY *moves to stand above them. He looks down on them. He touches* RUTH *gently with his foot.*
> RUTH *suddenly pushes* JOEY *away.*
> *She stands up.*
> JOEY *gets to his feet, stares at her.* (III 68)

Indeed, at the close of the play, the sure-footed Lenny is the only one of the male characters who manages to stand on his dignity. We are reminded of how Odysseus had stood firm against the spell of the sorceress on the island of Aeaea, while all about him his companions were being transformed into pigs:

> Who knows not Circe,
> The daughter of the Sun? whose charmèd cup
> Whoever tasted, lost his upright shape,
> And downward fell into a grovelling swine.[32]

With Teddy having left for the airport, and Sam out for the count, the paternal prophecy of bestialization is all but fulfilled when Max himself falls from on high and kneels, with Joey, beside the figure of Ruth, who sits – irresistible and serene – on what was once the patriarch's throne.[33]

* * *

The very fact that Max has sired a *troika* of male children means that Pinter is able to present us in *The Homecoming* with three quite distinct and highly contrasting versions of the relationship between father and son. What is most remarkable, however, is that these 'Three fine grown-up lads' (III 53), while differing greatly in terms of both outlook and demeanour, should ultimately be united in their atavistic identification with Franz Kafka. That is not to say that any of the young men represents an out-and-out clone of Kafka, but rather that all three complement one another insofar as they each reflect and illuminate several of the various elements of the Czech writer's persona. This idea of a filial subject being portrayed from a multiplicity of angles is curiously reminiscent of the technique employed by Kafka himself in 'Eleven Sons'. In the course of that story, the paternal narrator supplies the reader with a series of thumb-nail sketches of ostensibly unique individuals: by the end, though, the assorted vignettes seem to have merged almost subliminally to form a single composite figure. Nonetheless, in the context of *The Homecoming*, Pinter's decision to restrict the scope of his study to a triptych really could not have been more inspired. For it just so happens that his literary model was himself one of three sons born to Hermann and Julie Kafka. Franz was actually the eldest of this fraternal trio – and, tragically, the only one of them to survive infancy. The other two Kafka boys, Georg and Heinrich, died before their second and first birthdays, respectively. Accordingly, the lot fell upon the future novelist, 'a weakly, timid, hesitant, restless' (WPC 159) child, who (notwithstanding the subsequent arrival of his three sisters) 'had to bear the whole brunt' (WPC 159) of his father's reign of terror alone. The seeds of despair sown during these formative years brought forth a bitter harvest which Kafka reaped in adult life, leaving him with a profound mistrust of himself and a perpetual anxiety in relation to everything else. By contrast, each of the sons in *The Homecoming* would seem to be surrounded with an air of relative self-assurance. Still, this can probably be attributed to the fact that the paternal threat against them has for the most part been diminished by a factor of three. To that extent, Pinter's play – having also split the personality of Kafka *fils* into three separate sons – offers a possible scenario as to what the situation in the Kafka household might have been like if both of the younger brothers had reached maturity. The result is a vengeful proliferation of the Kafkan struggle against the father, with the odds now less favourably disposed towards the heavy-handed patriarch.

The second of the three sons in terms of age, but the first of them to appear on-stage, Lenny – a shady, nocturnal figure – impersonates the darker side of the Kafkan protagonist. By far the most resourceful and quick-witted of the fraternal trio, Lenny may not have tarried long in the groves of Academe, but what he lacks in the way of abstract knowledge, he more than makes up for in sharp practice. A formidable strategist in his deployment of language, Lenny evinces a high degree of verbal fluency together with an extensive and colourful vocabulary drawn from both ends of the cultural spectrum. His speeches, as well as being sprinkled with vulgar Anglo-Saxon expressions, are spiced with a variety of words and phrases that seem quite foreign to someone of his socio-economic background (for example, 'hypothesis' (III 36), 'criterion' (III 39), 'envisage' (III 41), 'ruminate' (III 44), 'equivocal' (III 72), 'je ne sais quoi' (III 73), and so on). Shrewdly observant and wilfully discursive, Lenny revels in his talent for impromptu story-telling, as demonstrated in several extremely lurid anecdotes – all of which incidentally betray a maleficent obsession with the female sex. The true nature of what Lenny euphemistically calls his 'occupation' (III 73) remains concealed until very near the end of the play, when it emerges that he is in fact a ponce, living off the immoral earnings of a stable of whores who operate in the vicinity of Greek Street.

The Homecoming opens with a kind of parodic inversion of the initial confrontation between Georg Bendemann and his father in 'The Judgement'. In Pinter's play, it is the rebellious son who occupies the position of paternal superiority, and the widowed father who pursues a decidedly puerile agenda. Like Bendemann Snr, Lenny is seated and studies a newspaper. Enter Max in search of a pair of scissors. It transpires that while the son reads the paper like an adult, the father wants only to cut something out of an earlier edition like a child. Enthroned *in loco parentis*, Lenny pays little attention to Max's babbling tantrums. Every so often, though, his patience begins to fray, whereupon he scolds the old man with gruff indignation: 'Why don't you shut up, you daft prat?' (III 15); 'Plug it, will you, you stupid sod, I'm trying to read the paper' (III 17). Dressed in a shabby cardigan and carrying a walking-stick, the patriarch, despite his pompous sound and fury, would seem to have abdicated all but nominal authority to his maverick son. Max brandishes his rugged sceptre to intimidate the lad – in a manner reminiscent of Mr Samsa in 'The Metamorphosis' – but fails to convey any real sense of majesty or menace. Instead, the father becomes an object of ridicule, as Lenny (in a speech which mimics the ending of James Joyce's story 'Counterparts'[34]) taunts him with the sardonic evocation of childhood fears:

> Oh, Daddy, you're not going to use your stick on me, are you? Eh? Don't use your stick on me Daddy. No, please. It wasn't my fault, it was one of the others. I haven't done anything wrong, Dad, honest. Don't clout me with that stick, Dad. (III 19)

Still, Lenny is very much his father's son; and even his genius for sarcasm has to some extent been inherited from the old man himself. (We only have to check out some of Max's scathing jibes at Sam to find proof of his paternity.) Having evidently been beaten with this *shtick* as a small boy, Lenny is now apt to turn it on the past master. The words 'Daddy' and 'Dad' are repeatedly enunciated by the son and glazed with venomous treacle in a calculated attempt to embarrass Max. Through this subversive use of the terminology of endearment, Lenny debunks the mawkish ideal of the patri–filial relationship and thereby highlights his contempt for the governor:

MAX: Stop calling me Dad. Just stop all that calling me Dad, do you understand?
LENNY: But I'm your son. You used to tuck me up in bed every night. He tucked you up, too, didn't he, Joey?

Pause.

He used to like tucking up his sons.

LENNY *turns and goes towards the front door.*

MAX: Lenny.
LENNY (*turning*): What?
MAX: I'll give you a proper tuck up one of these nights, son. You mark my word.

They look at each other.
LENNY *opens the front door and goes out.*
Silence. (III 25)

All this talk about Max tucking up his sons explicitly parallels the carphological exchange in 'The Judgement', when Georg had set about covering his father up with the bedclothes:

'Am I well covered up now?' asked his father, as if he were not able to see whether his feet were properly tucked in or not.
'So you find it snug in bed already,' said Georg, and tucked the blankets more closely round him.
'Am I well covered up?' asked his father once more, seeming to be strangely intent upon the answer.
'Don't worry, you're well covered up.'
'No!' cried his father, cutting short the answer, threw the blankets off with a strength that sent them all flying in a moment and sprang erect in bed. Only one hand lightly touched the ceiling to steady him.
'You wanted to cover me up, I know, my young sprig, but I'm far from being covered up yet. And even if this is the last strength I have, it's enough for you, too much for you. [. . .]' (CSS 84)

As Erich Heller has pointed out, Kafka plays rather ponderously here on the *double entendre* of the German word *zudecken* – 'to cover with a blanket', but also 'to squash' or 'to render powerless'.[35] The covering up is therefore clearly meant to symbolize the emasculation of the father and his apparent surrender to senility. Correlatively, in *The Homecoming*, Lenny insinuates that Max, teetering on the brink of his second childhood, has lost all his fatherly potency and is thus no longer able to tuck up his sons. As far as Lenny is concerned, the old man is now 'sexless' (III 80) and liable to need tucking up himself. Max, however, refuses to take this affront to his virility lying down, and threatens to put the hubristic son in his place, just as old Mr Bendemann had done in 'The Judgement'.

In a fiendishly black and vicious tirade – which exemplifies what Kafka had called 'the pruriency of a child over-fed with meat' (WPC 205) – Lenny interrogates his father about the circumstances and pleasures involved in the act that led to his conception:

> I'll tell you what, Dad, since you're in the mood for a bit of a . . . chat, I'll ask you a question. It's a question I've been meaning to ask you for some time. That night . . . you know . . . the night you got me . . . that night with Mum, what was it like? Eh? When I was just a glint in your eye. What was it like? What was the background to it? I mean, I want to know the real facts about my background. I mean, for instance, is it a fact that you had me in mind all the time, or is it a fact that I was the last thing you had in mind?
>
> *Pause.*
>
> I'm only asking this in a spirit of inquiry, you understand that, don't you? I'm curious. And there's lots of people of my age share that curiosity, you know that, Dad? They often ruminate, sometimes singly, sometimes in groups, about the true facts of that particular night – the night they were made in the image of those two people *at it*. It's a question long overdue, from my point of view, but as we happen to be passing the time of day here tonight I thought I'd pop it to you. (III 44)

Here, Lenny unleashes his rancour like a poisoned arrow aimed squarely at the basis of his parentage. It is significant that Kafka should also have declared 'this bond of blood' to be 'the target of [his] hatred' (DII 167):

> the sight of the double bed at home, the used sheets, the nightshirts carefully laid out, can exasperate me to the point of nausea, can turn me inside out; it is as if I had not been definitively born, were continually born anew into the world out of the stale life in that stale room, had constantly to seek confirmation of myself there, were indissolubly joined with all that loathsomeness, in part even if not entirely, at least it still clogs my feet which want to run, they are still stuck fast in the original shapeless pulp. (DII 167)

In response to Lenny's onslaught, Max delivers what is perhaps the most powerfully charged line in the entire play: 'You'll drown in your own blood' (III 44). Once again the obvious analogy is with 'The Judgement', wherein Mr Bendemann had likewise condemned his incorrigible son to 'death by drowning' (CSS 87). More specifically, though, the fate of being suffocated by haematic submersion is itself redolent of another Kafka story – namely, 'The Vulture', in which the moribund narrator euphorically consoles himself with the thought that he can feel the eponymous bird of prey 'drowning irretrievably in [his] blood, which was filling every depth, flooding every shore' (CSS 443). In addition, the sentence pronounced by Max effectively amplifies one of the precepts of Mosaic Law:

> For every one that curseth his father or his mother shall be surely put to death: he hath cursed his father or his mother; his blood shall be upon him. (Leviticus 20:9)

The patriarch thus portends that the son's animosity towards his own kin will ultimately rebound upon himself. (This danger is swiftly confirmed – first on a visual and then on a visceral level – by two encounters between Max and Joey in the early morning sequence which concludes Act 1.) Nevertheless, the impenitent Lenny ignores his father's censure and, determined to have the last word, snarlingly retorts that he would have no objection if Max preferred 'to answer the question in writing' (III 44). This riposte is doubly important: firstly, it anticipates the Kafkaesque mode of indirect communication at the heart of *Family Voices*; secondly, it suggests that the roles in 'Letter to his Father' should be reversed, with the old man having to put down on paper what he is afraid to relate to his son face to face.

Lenny's affiliation with Kafka is further accentuated by his claim that he is unable to sleep because of some insistent yet inscrutable auditory nuisance:

> TEDDY: Oh. Did I . . . wake you up?
> LENNY: No. I just had an early night tonight. You know how it is. Can't sleep. Keep waking up.
>
> *Pause.*
>
> TEDDY: How are you?
> LENNY: Well, just sleeping a bit restlessly, that's all. Tonight, anyway.
> TEDDY: Bad dreams?
> LENNY: No, I wouldn't say I was dreaming. It's not exactly a dream. It's just that something keeps waking me up. Some kind of tick.
> TEDDY: A tick?
> LENNY: Yes.

TEDDY: Well, what is it?
LENNY: I don't know. (III 33)

Himself a lifelong insomniac, Kafka was forever tormented by an acute sensitivity to all kinds of environmental noise. Indeed his personal writings are littered with fretful references to the incessant and insoluble din which seemed to rage all around him from morning till night. Time and again, he records how he was being 'kept from sleep, from work, from everything by the noise' (DII 119). Even when fatigue dragged him downwards into slumber, some discordant sound would always jolt him violently awake again (FEL 179). He described his room in the family domicile as 'the very headquarters of the uproar' (DI 133): 'When the breakfast clatter ceases on the left, the lunch clatter begins on the right. Doors are now being opened everywhere as if walls were being smashed' (FFE 70). In desperation, he tried blocking up his ears with Ohropax, a kind of wax wrapped in cotton wool, which he had to order from Berlin (FEL 449; FFE 329). This was a messy, stopgap nostrum, by which he could muffle the cacophony, but never shut it out completely. The impenetrable silence which he craved more than anything else continually eluded him, 'as water on the beach avoids stranded fish' (FEL 496). A similar yearning for peace and quiet is expressed in *Silence* by Bates, who recently complained to his neighbours about the 'unendurable racket', only to be told that he 'would have to bear it in order to pay for being alive' (III 193).

Back in *The Homecoming*, it is only fitting that Teddy, the logician on call, should put forward a rational explanation for Lenny's ticklish problem. Teddy conjectures that his brother's repose is probably being disrupted by the activity of some rogue time-piece:

TEDDY: Have you got a clock in your room?
LENNY: Yes.
TEDDY: Well, maybe it's the clock.
LENNY: Yes, could be, I suppose.

Pause.

Well, if it's the clock I'd better do something about it. Stifle it in some way, or something. (III 33)

After he has seen Teddy off to bed, Lenny returns holding a small clock, which he places in front of himself. Here it stands – accused – while he teases the matter out with Ruth:

> Eh listen, I wonder if you can advise me. I've been having a bit of a rough time with this clock. The tick's been keeping me up. The trouble is I'm not all that convinced it was the clock. I mean there are lots of things which tick in the night, don't you find that? All sorts of objects, which, in the day, you wouldn't call anything else but commonplace. They give you no trouble. But in the night any given one of a number of them is liable to start letting out a bit of a tick. Whereas you look at these objects in the day and they're just commonplace. They're as quiet as mice during the daytime. So . . . all things being equal . . . this question of me saying it was the clock that woke me up, well, that could very easily prove something of a false hypothesis. (III 36)

All clocks were anathema to Kafka. It seemed to him as if they had been designed primarily to create noise – a function which they discharged with steely efficiency. The fact that they also registered the passage of time was wholly incidental. Throughout his life, the author had waged a furious campaign against the chronometer, which he regarded as a baneful and intractable thorn in his side. When he lived with his parents, he was wont to hide the clock in his coat pocket in a vain attempt to eliminate its obstreperous ticking (FEL 134). Later, unable to tolerate the perpetual hullabaloo of the family home any longer, he found an apartment of his own. On moving in, the first thing he did was silence the clock (FEL 445). However, he was then harassed by its counterpart next door, which, as if in sympathy, began to strike all the louder: '[. . .] I try not to hear the minutes, but the half-hours are proclaimed with a deafening if melodious sound; but I cannot play the tyrant and demand that this clock be stopped as well' (FEL 445).[36]

Joey, '*a man in his middle twenties*' (III 14), is the youngest and least obviously Kafkaesque of the three sons in *The Homecoming*. The name 'Joey' is of course a pet form of Joseph, and thus recalls the praenomen of K. in *The Trial* and the pseudonym of K. in *The Castle* – both of whom are supposedly ciphered surrogates of Kafka himself. From an intellectual standpoint, Joey has been totally eclipsed by the antipodean brilliance of his elder brothers. Unable to match either the streetwise savvy of Lenny or the bookish erudition of Teddy, he epitomizes brawn at the expense of brain. This cerebral deficiency on the part of Joey is reflected in his awkward and inarticulate use of language. It is therefore symptomatic that he should have proportionately less to say than anyone else in the play. His sentences are short. Monosyllables predominate. More often than not, he is prompted or interrupted by others. When he does attempt to speak at any length, his efforts are hampered by a slow delivery and multiple fractures of syntax – all of which brings to mind Kafka's diagnosis of his own 'hesitant, stammering mode of speech' (WPC 170).

Suitably employed 'in demolition' (III 59) during the daytime, Joey spends most of his evenings down at the local gym, where he trains tirelessly in pursuit of his burning ambition 'to hit the top' (III 83) as a professional boxer. Surprisingly perhaps, it is this last detail which galvanizes his association with Kafka. Possessing neither the temperament nor the constitution of an athlete himself, Kafka had nevertheless related on more than one occasion how he was always having to 'make decisions from moment to moment, like a boxer, without doing any boxing' (FFE 33; 32). Even more significant is the fact that the author felt that the eternal struggle of the son against the father could best be described as 'shadow boxing' (CK 69). This notion is echoed with peculiar clarity towards the end of Act 1 of *The Homecoming*, when we are told in a stage direction that Joey '*shadowboxes, heavily, watching himself in the mirror*', while Max, standing to the side, looks on '*in silence*' (III 45). Through this brief dumb show, Pinter develops a stark correlation between the zealous sciamachy of youth and the cynical degeneracy of old age. Accordingly, the true antagonist of the filial boxer is not the father, but the mercurial enantiomorph of his own ego, which automatically matches his fancy footwork and trades blow for blow, until eventually it, like the son himself, grows to resemble that old man with the stick. As Kafka pointed out: 'Age is the future of youth, which sooner or later it must reach. So why struggle? To become old sooner? For a quicker departure?' (CK 69). The novelist made the above remarks during a discussion of J.M. Synge's tragicomedy *The Playboy of the Western World*;[37] and, by an intriguing coincidence, the symbol of the mirror also features prominently in that play's patri-filial shenanigans. It is reported that Christy Mahon, the eponymous anti-hero, was often to be found 'making mugs at his own self in the bit of a glass'[38] hung on the wall of his father's house. The trouble was that the misshapen countenance which gawked back at the son whenever he stared in this, 'the divil's own mirror',[39] seemed to be a reflection not of himself, but of the old man's characterization of him as 'An ugly young streeler with a murderous gob on him'.[40] Later, after he has 'destroyed his da'[41] and been granted asylum in Flaherty's shebeen, Christy catches sight of himself for the first time in an unbiased mirror and is so entranced by his handsome visage that he takes the glass from the wall in order to get a closer look. Startled by the arrival of a trio of female admirers, this Celtic Narcissus then tries unsuccessfully to hide the mirror behind him: 'Well, I never seen to this day a man with a looking-glass held to his back. Them that kills their fathers is a vain lot surely'.[42]

Instinctively, Joey seems to realize the sheer futility of engaging in single combat with his father. He prefers simply to go along with the situation on the home front, not so much out of resignation, as out of bullish insensibility. And even when he falls victim to paternal aggression – in the play's only moment of physical violence – it is noticeable that Joey chooses not to retaliate. The mêlée in question is precipitated when Max calls upon his muscular son to 'chuck out' the intrusive Teddy and Ruth (III 50). In his reluctance to assume the office of bouncer, Joey clumsily implies that his father's ill-humour is the result of senile decay, and thereby challenges the old man's title to supremacy. The stage is set for a championship bout, with the disgruntled patriarch seeking to demonstrate that he is 'still strong' (III 16) enough to see off the impudent young contender. Recalling the triumphant comebacks of Messrs Bendemann and Samsa, Max punches Joey in the solar plexus; but unlike his rejuvenated antecedents in 'The Judgement' and 'The Metamorphosis', the old man overreaches himself and collapses alongside the stricken son.

Despite this shemozzle, the father evidently finds it much easier to relate to the pugilistic aspirations of Joey than he does to the (respectively) anaemic and inglorious activities of Teddy and Lenny. In the vigorous demeanour of his youngest son, Max recognizes something of the fire and excitement that had distinguished his own heyday, when he and his sparring partner MacGregor were two of the toughest fighters in the West End of London. (Is it really just a coincidence that the names of the two men with whom Max is most closely associated – MacGregor and Sam – virtually replicate that of the protagonist of 'The Metamorphosis'?) Consequently, he feels well qualified to offer the lad some paternal, if rather jaundiced, advice on the noble science of fisticuffs:

> Boxing's a gentleman's game.
>
> *Pause.*

I'll tell you what you've got to do. What you've got to do is you've got to learn how to defend yourself, and you've got to learn how to attack. That's your only trouble as a boxer. You don't know how to defend yourself, and you don't know how to attack.

Pause.

Once you've mastered those arts you can go straight to the top. (III 25–6)

Oddly enough, the same sporting metaphor is deployed to similar effect in *Family Voices*, where the patriarchal Mr Withers addresses the son as 'boxer' (IV 297), and then delivers the decidedly oracular exhortation: 'Keep your weight on all the left feet you can lay your hands on. Keep dancing' (IV 297). Boxing clearly typifies on a literal level the kind of 'chivalrous fighting, in which', according to the paternal puppet in 'Letter to his Father', 'the forces of independent opponents are measured against each other, each one remaining alone, losing alone, winning alone' (WPC 216). The antithesis of such gallantry is to be found in the mercenary tactics favoured by 'vermin, which not only sting but, at the same, suck the blood, too, to sustain their own life' (WPC 216). Kafka himself, for all his Queensberry-style qualms, is ventriloquiously denounced in the 'Letter' as a prize specimen of the parasitic breed.

The third and eldest of Max's sons is Teddy, whose homecoming gives the play its name. Accompanied by Ruth, his sphinx-like wife, Teddy has returned from the United States, a futuristic land of milk and honey, to visit his past in England, now a foreign country where they do things differently.[43] It is interesting that Teddy should have chosen to settle in America, since that continent had also provided both the locale and the eventual title of Kafka's first novel. Furthermore, Karl Rossmann, the hero of the novel, had left his family for reasons quite similar to those which hastened Teddy's elopement. (A full exposition of this and other parallels with *America* will be given in the next chapter with respect to *Family Voices*.) Like many of his contemporaries, Kafka had been enchanted by 'dreams of a marvellous America, of a wonderland of unlimited possibilities' (CK 144). This brave New World on the other side of the Atlantic promised a rapturous vista of liberty and opportunity as an antidote to the incestuous and claustrophobic decadence of Europe – perhaps most quaintly epitomized by the city of Venice, from which, as it happens, Teddy and Ruth have just departed. (Venice, incidentally, is also the setting of Ian McEwan's novel *The Comfort of Strangers*, brilliantly adapted for the screen by Pinter and director Paul Schrader, in which a young English couple are menacingly wooed by a father-fixated magnifico. And let us not forget that the pivotal scene in *Betrayal*, wherein Emma admits to Robert that she has been cuckolding him with his best friend, takes place in a Venetian hotel room.)

It is particularly appropriate that the entrance of Teddy should be heralded by Max's exclamation, 'I remember my father' (III 27); since there is about the returning son an air of self-conscious nostalgia. Absence has evidently made the wanderer's heart grow fonder. (The same could also be said of the young man in *Family Voices*, who paradoxically feels closest to his parents when he is furthest away from them.) On crossing the threshold of his father's house, Teddy assures Ruth that his kinsfolk are 'very warm people' (III 31); and even though this is glaringly contradicted by the far from cordial reception accorded to the couple by Max, the son is only too ready to take up the old man's somewhat specious offer of 'a nice cuddle and kiss' (III 51). Teddy's responsiveness is instantly hailed by the laughing Max as proof that, despite everything, the eldest boy 'still loves his father!' (III 52). (Significantly, however, the spectacle of the proposed embrace is stymied by the descent of the curtain marking the end of Act 1.) Throughout his years in exile, Teddy would seem to have cultivated a ridiculously schmaltzy imago of his dear old papa, which, curiously enough, is not unlike the satirical portrait of Max so unlovingly painted by Lenny. Indeed the difference here between the pimp and the pedant is not nearly so clear-cut as it may at first appear. The true feelings of the sons towards their father can perhaps best be gauged from the way in which they use the word 'Dad': Lenny, as we have seen, takes a sly delight in the detonation of this term, which is probably the most effective weapon in his acerbic arsenal; Teddy, on the other hand, simply utilizes the expression as a kind of phatic emollient to palliate the arid formality of his attempts at conversation. Ultimately, though, it would seem that neither Lenny nor Teddy is capable of investing this pet name with even a scintilla of genuine affection. Joey, for his part, apparently cannot bring himself to use the word 'Dad' at all.

Academically the most distinguished of the brothers, Teddy, given free rein to learn whatever he wanted, has followed the example of Kafka and turned his back on his father's business to pursue his own 'loftier ideas' (WPC 183). Moreover, like Franz, he has studied for and been awarded a doctorship.[44] This qualification is 'a great source of pride' (III 73) to the family; yet it is also, in practical terms, a measure of the son's estrangement from them. Teddy's education has now become his career. He occupies a prestigious position in a 'highly successful' (III 58) philosophy department of an American university. Teddy enjoys his work and thrives in the 'very stimulating environment' (III 58) of college life. An accomplished man of letters, his tenure has been consolidated and his reputation enhanced with the publication of an impressive series of 'critical works' (III 69). Significantly, though, his father has never bothered to read any of them. Hermann Kafka had displayed a similar lack of enthusiasm for his son's literary exploits. As far as Kafka Snr was concerned, the novelist was not only wasting his time, but was also damaging his health by sitting up to all hours at his writing-desk.[45] And whenever Franz presented the old man with a copy of some freshly printed opuscule (a case in point being the slim volume *A Country Doctor*, which, as a conciliatory gesture, had been specially inscribed with the agonizing dedication – 'To My Father'), Hermann would always brusquely snort: 'Put it on my bedside table!' (WPC 197). But whereas Franz, whose estimation of his own worth depended on the judgement of his father more than anything else, was deeply hurt by this philistine response, Teddy nonchalantly maintains his 'intellectual equilibrium' (III 70), recognizing that the verdict of the barbarous Max is of absolutely no consequence, since the old man 'wouldn't have the faintest idea of what [the works] were about' (III 69).

If Teddy's connection with Kafka can be said to have a linchpin, then it is perhaps to be found in the vexed question of his marriage to Ruth. Kafka once described marriage as the 'greatest terror' of his life (WPC 202). Certainly, no other single issue had caused the author so much pain and anxiety. At times, the very thought of matrimony was enough to drive him to a state of almost zombie-like distraction:

> from the moment when I make up my mind to marry I can no longer sleep, my head burns day and night, life can no longer be called life, I stagger about in despair. (WPC 210)

He even attributed the onset of his tuberculosis to 'the strain of the superhuman effort of wanting to marry' (WPC 199). Kafka's gamomania was therefore not simply an occasional fancy or a sudden compulsion, but 'a permanent, decisive and indeed the most grimly bitter ordeal' (WPC 202). Every so often, he tried to balance the pros and cons of getting married by listing them side by side in his notebooks (for example, WPC 232–3; DI 292–3), and, in so doing, found a modicum of solace by comparing his own connubial conundrum with those of several of his literary heroes, such as Grillparzer, Flaubert and Kierkegaard. Chief among his worries was that, as a married man, he would have less time and energy to devote to his writing. Rather than let this happen, Kafka vowed that he would 'Live as ascetically as possible, more ascetically than a bachelor' (DI 296). Yet he knew very well that celibacy would bring him little comfort and no joy; and, despite his concerns about wedlock, he did not wish to suffer the same fate as the hollow men who dwelt in his house of fiction:

> It seems so dreadful to be a bachelor, to become an old man struggling to keep one's dignity while begging for an invitation whenever one wants to spend an evening in company, having to carry one's meal home in one's hand, unable to expect anyone with a lazy sense of calm confidence, able only with difficulty and vexation to give a gift to someone, having to say good night at the front door, never being able to run up a stairway beside one's wife, to lie ill and have only the solace of the view from one's window when one can sit up, to have only side doors in one's room leading into other people's living rooms, to feel estranged from one's family, with whom one can keep on close terms only by marriage, first by the marriage of one's parents, then, when the effect of that has worn off, by one's own, having to admire other people's children and not even being allowed to go on saying: 'I have none myself,' never to feel oneself grow older since there is no family growing up around one, modelling oneself in appearance and behavior on one or two bachelors remembered from one's youth. (DI 150–1)[46]

In addition to these social and psychological pressures, Kafka also had to reckon with the whole canon of Mosaic and rabbinical teachings, wherein the need to marry is stressed as both a religious obligation and a biological imperative. In the Torah, it is written that 'a man [shall] leave his father and mother, and shall cleave unto his wife: and they shall be one flesh' (Genesis 2:24); while the Talmud, as Kafka himself noted, is even more damnatory in its prescriptiveness: 'A man without a woman is no person' (DI 162).

The infallible logic of such holy ordinances persuaded the novelist that to have a wife who understood him in his entirety 'would mean to have support from every side, to have God' (DII 126).

Obviously a man of luminous intelligence and rare sensitivity, and by all accounts a sparkling conversationalist, Kafka, with his dark, rather fey good looks, seems to have held a strange attraction for the opposite sex. Yet, despite being intimately involved with a succession of nubile young women, all his attempts to marry were to result in disappointment. Twice he was betrothed to Felice Bauer, and twice he broke off the engagement. In the interim, he appears to have had a clandestine liaison with Grete Bloch (Felice's familiar), whereupon she is rumoured to have conceived his child.[47] There followed a somewhat precipitate infatuation with Julie Wohryzek, the daughter of a synagogue custodian. In this instance, the banns were even published; but accommodation difficulties prompted Kafka to call off the wedding just forty-eight hours before it was due to take place. He then began a passionate long-distance romance with his Czech translator, Milena Jesenská-Pollak, who was in fact already married and, what is more, a gentile. This affair lasted for more than two years, but ended in great unhappiness. Finally, as he lay on his deathbed, his hopes of marrying Dora Dymant, his devoted young mistress and sick-nurse, were cruelly dashed when her family's rabbi refused permission.

Nevertheless, for all his honourable intentions, the plain truth is that none of Kafka's attempts at marriage stood even the slightest chance of success. The reasons for failure were of course many and complex: however, the decisive factor resided not in any external impediment, but in the aspiring groom's conviction that he was 'intellectually incapable of marrying' (WPC 210). Try as he might, Kafka could no more rationalize his obsessive 'fear of marriage' (WPC 212) than he could obliterate the baleful influence of his father. This indeed is hardly surprising, since the former was in fact a symptom of the latter. Accordingly, it is no coincidence that the author's most concerted and comprehensive bid to resolve his connubial neurosis should come in the dramatic climax of 'Letter to his Father'. Yet if marriage was to be the last battle in the psychological war with the father, then the best the son could hope for was a Pyrrhic victory. Over the years, Kafka had developed an impossibly 'high idea of marriage' (WPC 212) from the example of his own parents – which in his view was a model union as regards constancy, mutual help, number of children, and stability in the face of adversity. Thus he had become unshakeably convinced that what was essential to sustaining a marriage was everything that his father epitomized, and therefore necessarily everything that he himself lacked. Moreover, if the father in all his power and glory still had to struggle to make married life a success, what chance had the wretched son?

Not only did Kafka consider himself mentally unsuited to marriage, but he also felt that he was morally unfit to enter into this most holy and 'shameless' (WPC 206) of institutions. This pathological sense of unworthiness was crystallized by a particularly disastrous teenage escapade which he recalls in 'Letter to his Father'. One evening, while out walking with his parents, the adolescent Kafka began to tease them about their negligence in having failed to warn him against the perils of sexual licence. Speaking 'in a stupidly boastful' yet 'stammering manner', he went on to hint that there was no longer any need for them to worry, since, thanks to his schoolmates, he now 'knew everything' (WPC 205). In recognition of his son's rakish progress, Hermann Kafka responded by offering to give the boy 'some advice about how [he] could go in for these things without danger' (WPC 205). Franz could not have been more horrified by this proposal; nor was he in any doubt as to the enormity of its implications:

> you were pushing me, just as though I were predestined to it, down into this filth, with a few frank words. And so if the world consisted only of me and you, a notion I was much inclined to have, then [the] purity of the world came to an end with you and, by virtue of your advice, the filth began with me. (WPC 206–7)

Despite advising his son to do 'the filthiest thing possible', the father remained outside his own advice, 'a married man, a pure man, exalted' far above such shameful things (WPC 206). He was after all merely seeking to ensure that none of this filth – which appeared to be his son's natural element – would be brought into the family home. The father in *The Homecoming* is similarly concerned about preserving the purity of his household. When confronted by the dressing-gowned figures of Teddy and Ruth, Max is scandalized that his son should have picked up 'a filthy scrubber off the street' (III 50) and spent the night with her under his roof. (Teddy had in fact anticipated just such a reaction, when, before retiring, he cautioned Ruth that they must get up early, since it 'Wouldn't be quite right' (III 31) if his father were to find them in bed.) Max's indignation is prompted not by any meretriciousness in the outward appearance or behaviour of Ruth, but rather by his own foreknowledge of Teddy's moral turpitude. Neither father is in the least surprised that his son should have a predilection for filth, but both insist that 'the slopbucket' (III 50) must be kept outside the front door.

Whenever either Teddy or Ruth mentions their marital status, the other characters are apt to: (a) completely ignore the remark and carry on talking, (b) abruptly change the subject, or (c) recite sugar-coated platitudes about domestic bliss. It is perfectly obvious that the rest of the family – with the exception of Sam (III 77–8) – do not recognize this as a *bona fide* union. In their view, the ostensible marriage is no more than a convenient façade which has been cobbled together to lend a spurious legitimacy to unbridled fornication. Hermann Kafka had indeed been equally sceptical about his son's proposed marriage to Julie Wohryzek. Moreover, he too was of the opinion that only 'the most abominable, crude, and ridiculous' (WPC 208) of instincts could be behind such an arrangement:

> 'She probably put on some specially chosen blouse, the thing these Prague Jewesses are good at, and straightaway, of course, you made up your mind to marry her. And, what's more, as fast as possible, in a week, tomorrow, today. I can't make you out, after all, you're a grown man, here you are in town, and you can't think of any way of managing but going straight off and marrying the next best girl. Isn't there anything else you can do? If you're frightened, I'll go along with you myself.' (WPC 207–8)

The devastation which Kafka *fils* felt at this rebuke was compounded by the fact that an uncanny premonition of the entire incident had emanated from his own pen some seven years earlier in 'The Judgement'. In that story, would-be bridegroom Georg Bendemann had received the following indictment from his father:

> 'Because she lifted up her skirts,' his father began to flute, 'because she lifted her skirts like this, the nasty creature,' and mimicking her he lifted his shirt so high that one could see the scar on his thigh from his war wound, 'because she lifted her skirts like this and this you made up to her, and in order to make free with her undisturbed

> you have disgraced your mother's memory, betrayed your friend and stuck your father into bed so that he can't move. But he can move, or can't he?' (CSS 85)

By the same token, in *The Homecoming*, Max's antipathy to Teddy's alliance with Ruth may have been inspired in part by Jack Pinter's misgivings about his son's decision to wed Vivien Merchant, who – like Ruth's namesake in the Old Testament – was a *shiksa*.[48] (The atmosphere in the Pinter household was certainly not helped by the fact that Harold had arranged to have the knot tied in a registry office on the Day of Atonement.[49]) Significantly, it was Ms Merchant, a talented and engaging actress, who gave the definitive interpretation of Ruth on both stage and screen. Furthermore, Pinter himself, while remaining understandably reticent about this possibly autobiographical dimension to the play, has implied that the role was tailor-made for his first wife: 'There's never quite been a Ruth like Vivien' (CP 128).

As we have seen, Max initially pours scorn on his son's nuptials by assailing the reputation of the sometime bride. In a barrage of brickbats and disparaging home-truths, he reviles the unblushing Ruth as:

> a 'dirty tart' (III 49);
> 'a smelly scrubber' (III 49);
> 'a stinking pox-ridden slut' (III 49);
> 'a filthy scrubber' (III 50);
> 'a whore' (III 50);
> 'the bedpan' (III 50);
> 'the slopbucket' (III 50);
> 'that disease' (III 50).

At the start of Act 2, however, the father, having apparently undergone a miraculous change of heart during the interval, not only gives his blessing to the match, but also commends Teddy for having made such 'a wonderful choice' (III 57). What is more, he even says that, had he been informed of the couple's plans, he would gladly have borne the expense of a white wedding with all the trimmings. Ruth is now characterized in the most flattering of terms:

> 'a lovely daughter-in-law' (III 53);
> 'a nice feminine girl with proper credentials' (III 57);
> 'a charming woman' (III 57);

> 'an intelligent and sympathetic woman' (III 59);
> 'a lovely girl' (III 67);
> 'A beautiful woman' (III 67);
> 'a woman of quality' (III 68);
> 'a woman of feeling' (III 68).

At the same time, though, the old fellow claims to understand why his son did not tell him before about his consort: Teddy probably thought that his father would have been 'annoyed' (III 67) at him for having married a woman beneath him. Max reassures the boy, however, that he is 'a broadminded man' (III 67); yet the loose connotation of the word 'wife' is once again insinuated when he adds:

> Look, next time you come over, don't forget to let us know beforehand whether you're married or not. I'll always be glad to meet the wife. Honest. I'm telling you. (III 67)

Notwithstanding the shady undercurrent of Ruth's faltering speech about her 'modelling' (III 65) career, or whether indeed she ever was, actually is or will eventually become a 'whore', these seemingly contradictory statements which Max makes about Teddy's partner may in fact be directly related to the son's own ambivalence about the marriage. A compelling parallel can be drawn here with the final section of 'Letter to his Father', where Kafka's deeply equivocal attitude to matrimony is exposed by the deposition of the prosopopoeic patriarch:

> when you recently wanted to marry, you wanted – and this you do after all admit in this letter – at the same time not to marry, but in order not to have to exert yourself you wanted me to help you with this not-marrying, through my forbidding you to make this marriage on account of the 'disgrace' that this union would bring upon my name. Now as it happened I did not dream of doing this. First of all, here as elsewhere, I never wanted 'to be an obstacle to your happiness', and secondly I never want to have to hear such a reproach from my own child. But was my having overcome my own feelings, and so leaving your way open to this marriage, any help to me? Not in the slightest. My dislike of the marriage would not have prevented it; on the contrary, it would in itself have been for you an added stimulus to marry the girl, for the 'attempt at escape', as you put it, would thus of course have become complete. And my consent to the marriage did not prevent your reproaching me, for you do prove that I am in any case to blame for your not marrying. (WPC 216–17)

Paternal hostility is also the *sine qua non* for the unorthodox marriage in *The Homecoming*. Once Ruth has been welcomed into 'the bosom of the family' (III 84) and made to feel at home, she is no longer desirable or useful to her husband. As far as Teddy is concerned, Ruth herself has now become part of the constrictive organism from which she had once helped him escape. Thus the phlegmatic philosopher relinquishes his conjugal rights with the minimum of fuss. For all his specious objections – and he is careful not to protest too much – Teddy seems quite happy to rubber-stamp the family's enterprising plans for his already estranged wife, and actually volunteers to put their proposals to her himself.

The very fact that Teddy got spliced the day before he took flight to America suggests that he may have shared Kafka's view of marriage as 'the pledge of the most acute form of self-liberation and independence' (WPC 210). The novelist had indeed supposed that by marrying, setting up home and founding a family, he would not only achieve 'the utmost a human being can succeed in doing at all' (WPC 204), but also – and even more importantly – he would match the supreme achievement of his own father. This would 'be like a fairy-tale' (WPC 211) come true. The anxiety, weakness, self-contempt and shame which had characterized his relations with the old man would be instantly dispelled and soon forgotten. For the first time, father and son would stand together on the same level, as *equals*. But there's the rub. By assuming the status of a *paterfamilias*, Kafka feared that he would virtually be holding a mirror up to the illustrious figure of his father, and that, as a result, he himself would be a mere simulacrum, with no real aseity and no separate identity. It seemed to him that, in order to become a truly autonomous individual, a young man needed to establish himself in a walk of life that had absolutely no connection with his father. (For both Kafka and Teddy, the declaration of independence would be drafted and defended in the republic of letters.) The bridal path, while appearing to represent the most auspicious escape route, might just as well be an elaborate treadmill of the father's design:

> It is as if a person were a prisoner and he had not only the intention of escaping, which would perhaps be attainable, but also, and indeed simultaneously, the intention of rebuilding the prison as a pleasure-seat for himself. But if he escapes, he cannot do any rebuilding, and if he rebuilds, he cannot escape. (WPC 211)

This dilemma is keenly reflected in the experience of Teddy. His marriage has in effect been slavishly modelled on that of his father – a second-rate copy of an old master. Like Max, Teddy espouses a woman of dubious virtue ('I've never had a whore under this roof before. Ever since your mother died' (III 50).), who bears him three male children ('All boys? Isn't that funny, eh? You've got three, I've got three' (III 58).).

Ultimately, Kafka felt that he himself had been barred from the estate of matrimony because this was his father's 'most intimate domain' (WPC 211):

> Sometimes I imagine the map of the world spread out flat and you stretched out diagonally across it. And what I feel then is that only those territories come into question for my life that either are not covered by you or are not within your reach. And, in keeping with the conception that I have of your magnitude, these are not many and not very comforting territories, and above all marriage is not among them. (WPC 211–12)

It is all the more ironic therefore that Hermann Kafka should have threatened to emigrate rather than be a party to his son's unholy alliance with Julie Wohryzek (WPC 212–13). Teddy, on the other hand, saves his old man the trouble by going into exile himself. Yet it is not altruism but expediency which impels Teddy's expatriation. Indeed his nuptial vows are tenable only so long as he abides in the New World – that is, outside the sphere of paternal influence. As soon as he returns to England, his fatherland, the contraband marriage is automatically dissolved.

* * *

Perhaps the most striking resonance from the work of Kafka is contained in the title itself of Pinter's play. For *The Homecoming*, in what may well be a conscious *hommage*, shares its name with a short prose piece written by Kafka in late 1920, which delineates the impressions of a son on his return to the home of his father after a long absence:

> I have returned, I have passed under the arch and am looking round. It's my father's old yard. The puddle in the middle. Old, useless tools, jumbled together, block the way to the attic stairs. The cat lurks on the banister. A torn piece of cloth, once wound round a stick in a

> game, flutters in the breeze. I have arrived. Who is going to receive me? Who is waiting behind the kitchen door? Smoke is rising from the chimney, coffee is being made for supper. Do you feel you belong, do you feel at home? I don't know, I feel most uncertain. My father's house it is, but each object stands cold beside the next, as though preoccupied with its own affairs, which I have partly forgotten, partly never known. What use can I be to them, what do I mean to them, even though I am the son of my father, the old farmer? And I don't dare knock at the kitchen door, I only listen from a distance, I only listen from a distance, standing up, in such a way that I cannot be taken by surprise as an eavesdropper. And since I am listening from a distance, I hear nothing but a faint striking of the clock passing over from childhood days, but perhaps I only think I hear it. Whatever else is going on in the kitchen is the secret of those sitting there, a secret they are keeping from me. The longer one hesitates before the door, the more estranged one becomes. What would happen if someone were to open the door now and ask me a question? Would not I myself then behave like one who wants to keep his secret? (CSS 445–6)

Quite apart from the similarities of the title and theme, we should also note how the taut psychological realism of Kafka's 'Home-Coming' clearly adumbrates Pinter's characterization of the homing son. As it stands, this *morceau* could easily have been written by Teddy, arguably the protagonist of Pinter's play, so accurately does it describe that character's state of mind. Indeed the rhetorical structure of 'Home-Coming' – wherein the quiet scrutiny of external phenomena gradually gives way to a quizzical spiral of reminiscence and apprehension – perfectly captures the hesitancy of the self-absorbed epistemologist as he comes into collision with his ruder origins. Equally remarkable is the fact that the verbal texture of the prose piece, its diction, iterancy and cadence, should bear such a close resemblance to the deliberate and scholastic timbre of Teddy's speech.

Nothing actually happens in 'Home-Coming'. Kafka dispenses with the need for action and instead presents us with an archetypal tableau of filial alienation. Everything has been stripped down to the bare minimum. We know nothing about the narrator's history, his appearance, his reasons for coming home, where he has been or what he intends to do. We are simply provided with a static situation. The arrival of this quasi-prodigal son, like that of Teddy, is as unexpected as it is unannounced. No welcome or salutation awaits him. Only the smell of coffee being prepared for supper greets his anxious nostrils – the fatted calf has evidently been spared for a more festive season. Surveying the old farmstead with new eyes, he is struck by the foreignness of the familiar and filled with a mistrust of the mundane. The puddle in the middle of the yard, the rag fluttering in the breeze, the cat lurking on the banister, the smoke escaping from the chimney are all observed with growing consternation, as if they portend some imminent danger. With his sensory faculties on full alert, he stands next to the house – silent, motionless, alone: afraid to knock or open the door; afraid that someone from within might open it and find him there. Perhaps he plans to wait until the occupants have retired for the night, and then enter the building – as Teddy and Ruth do – with the stealth of a burglar. For the moment, though, he does not move: he remains transfixed, unable to quit his poignant vigil. This is the place of his birth – the house in which he spent his childhood; but he does not belong here anymore. His home is somewhere else. The house and all it represents is rooted in his past; yet that is his only connection with it. No other link can ever be established. Like Teddy, he might still be thought of as 'an integral part' (III 73) of the family unit, but only to the extent that when they 'all sit round the backyard having a quiet gander at the night sky, there's always an empty chair standing in the circle, which is in fact' his (III 73). Despite his proximity to the house and his kinship with its inhabitants, the narrator is discomfited by an acute sense of his own psychological remoteness; and it is this, rather than any physical barrier, which ultimately excludes him from the hoped-for hospitality of the hearth. Furthermore, he is only too aware that the longer he dwells at the threshold, the more of a stranger he becomes. If anything, the position of the son is actually worse than that of a stranger: because his relationship with those who live in the house is fixed, stale and problematical; whereas a stranger would always be at liberty to form an acquaintance unprejudiced by the past. The question of estrangement is also posed at the end of *The Homecoming*, when Ruth says to Teddy, as he is just about to leave for the airport, 'Don't become a stranger' (III 88). Significantly, this pregnant cliché elicits no reply from her deserting husband, who promptly turns on his heels and exits with his luggage, shutting the front door behind him.

In what is manifestly a symptom of severe alienation, the narrator of 'Home-Coming' raises the issue of people being regarded in terms of, what a Marxist commentator might call, their 'use-value'.

'What use can I be to them [. . .]?' he asks himself with respect to those inside the farmhouse. By the same token, he might just as well ask, 'What use can they be to me?' The plain truth is that these folks can be of no more service to him than the 'Old, useless tools' which obstruct the passage to the attic stairs. With neither unction nor utility to commend them, the other members of the family are effectively deprived of their personalities and envisioned with an air of almost clinical detachment:

> My father's house it is, but each object stands cold beside the next, as though preoccupied with its own affairs, which I have partly forgotten, partly never known.

This pattern of reification is virtually duplicated by the returned *émigré* in Pinter's play. In an ironic variation on the parable of the lost son, Teddy declares that it is not himself but the various members of his father's household who have been wandering around in a state of mindless perdition:

> You're just objects. You just . . . move about. I can observe it. I can see what you do. It's the same as I do. But you're lost in it. You won't get me being . . . I won't be lost in it. (III 70)

Such an uncommon feeling of aloofness makes any real communication with the others impossible. In the case of 'Home-Coming', the son cautiously resolves to assume the posture of 'an eavesdropper'. He listens intently, but his perception is clouded by vague recollections and distant echoes. Consequently, he hears nothing. Nothing, that is to say, except the chimerical chiming of a half-remembered clock. (One wonders if this could be the same chronometer as that which Teddy suspects has been keeping Lenny awake at night with its infernal ticking?) At the same time, he dare not make a sound himself for fear that his presence might be discovered. No longer privy to the affairs of the household of which he was once a member, he feels certain that the others are concealing something from him. Yet he himself is apt to behave as though he has a secret of his own to keep. This pervasive concern about being kept in the dark also surfaces in *The Homecoming*, when Max, disturbed by the midnight skirmish between Lenny and Ruth, comes downstairs to investigate and finds his son tight-lipped and alone:

> He was talking to someone. Who could he have been talking to? They're all asleep. He was having a conversation with someone. He won't tell me who it was. He pretends he was thinking aloud. What are you doing, hiding someone here? (III 43–4)

As a matter of fact, every character in the play would appear to have something to hide – a deep-seated anxiety, a past indiscretion, an unfulfilled desire, a chink in their emotional armour which dare not be exposed.

Some two years after he wrote 'Home-Coming', Kafka, in what might well have been meant as a postscript to the prose piece, registered the following *pensée* in his diary:

> How long the road is from my inner anguish to a scene like that in the yard – and how short the road back. And since one has now reached one's home, there is no leaving it again. (DII 226)

Once again, therefore, it would seem that, for Kafka's filial protagonist, the return home is as final as death itself. As far as Teddy is concerned, however, the homecoming is no more than a brief stopover. For all his theoretical nostalgia, the visiting professor, having already tasted freedom, is determined not to stay long enough to get trapped again in this Daedalean labyrinth. Within twenty-four hours of his arrival, he has left his father's house and is on his way back to America. (Like Lot, on his precipitate departure from Sodom (Genesis 19), he abandons his inconstant wife to her own fate.) Teddy evidently believes, as Kafka himself did, that he can best preserve his feeling for the family – even if only in a negative sense – by breaking away from it (WPC 189–90). There comes a time when, said the novelist, 'One has to go abroad in order to find the home one has lost' (CK 188). And indeed it is this paradox which will be explored by Pinter in *Family Voices*.

3

More Strange Than a Stranger: *Family Voices*

> How would it be if you were merely to observe the life of your family? The family would think that you were sharing their life and were content. And in fact this would be partly true. You would be living with your family, but on different terms from them. That would be all. You would be outside the circle, with your face turned inwards towards the family, and that would be enough. Perhaps now and then you might even see your own image reflected in your family's eyes – quite small and as if drawn on a glass ball in the garden. (CK 183)

Although the most fundamental and insistent of the various elements in *The Homecoming*, the troubled relationship between father and son did not figure again in Pinter's writings for many years. By contrast, several of the more peripheral motifs in that play quickly came to prominence and remained at the forefront of his work from the mid-1960s right up to the end of the next decade. Between *The Basement* (1967) and *Betrayal* (1978), the dramatist published a total of eight plays, in the course of which he continued to explore and amplify such themes as the battle for indoor ascendency, the interchangeability of men – or perhaps the fickleness of women – as sexual partners, and the encroachment of the past into the present. These same concerns were to some extent simultaneously reflected in Pinter's periodic excursions into the realm of screen-writing.

At the start of 1981, however, the issue which had been at the very heart of *The Homecoming* was wonderfully refurbished and given fresh significance with the first radio and stage productions of *Family Voices*. (A few weeks after receiving its première on BBC Radio 3, the play opened as a 'platform performance' at the National Theatre in London.) Those who tend to estimate the value of a dramatic work in terms of time and motion would no doubt be inclined to regard *Family Voices* – which lasts for just over half an hour and involves no physical activity whatsoever – as a very slight piece indeed. Nevertheless, this beguilingly *bijou* composition deserves to be recognized as one of the most extraordinary and accomplished of all Pinter's works. For despite its brevity and apparent lack of kinetic energy, the play is literally 'packed with incident' (CP 151), and is equally rich in both humour and pathos. The result is an oddly affecting, almost Chekhovian study of the passions, conceits and memories that are stirred in the wake of domestic disintegration.

What makes *Family Voices* so unusual is the fact that it takes the form of a series of dead letters which revolve elliptically around the three *dramatis personae* – a young man, his mother and his recently deceased father. Just as early exponents of the novel (such as Richardson, Rousseau and Laclos) had used an epistolary method to bring the kind of psychological insight to contemporary prose fiction that the soliloquy had introduced to drama, so Pinter, in an audacious piece of eclecticism, employs a similar technique in *Family Voices* to objectify the interior monologue and thus facilitate its triplication. The external business of letter-writing, moreover, provides the playwright with a key to the inner lives of his characters, allowing him to unlock the torrent of words – unspoken and unspeakable – that swells up under silence. Pinter is thereby able to sustain a level of intimacy which would not be possible in direct speech, especially since the latter is no more than 'a constant stratagem to cover nakedness' (I xiii).

Prior to *Family Voices*, Pinter's most telling use of an epistolary device had been in *Betrayal*. In Scene 6 of that play, Jerry explains to Emma how he had misplaced her latest *billet-doux* and then panicked at the thought that it might be found by his wife. But what Jerry does not know, and Emma does not tell him, is that a week or so earlier, Robert – her husband and his best friend – had discovered the truth about their infidelity, after chancing upon of one of Jerry's letters to her. In addition, the motif of letter-writing is featured very conspicuously in two of the screenplays which Pinter penned during the 1970s. The first of these is *The Go-Between* (adapted from the novel by L.P. Hartley), where Ted and Marian, the socially mismatched lovers, conduct their furtive romance with the help of Leo, the innocent little 'postman', who smuggles dispatches back and forth between them. The second is *Langrishe, Go Down* (based on the novel by Aidan Higgins), which ends with Imogen Langrishe – in a re-enactment of an earlier episode – reading through a whole bundle of letters that she wrote but never sent to her former *inamorato,* Otto Beck; the missives having been discreetly appropriated by her elder sister, Helen, who kept them hidden in a drawer in her own bedroom.

There is in fact something curiously Kafkaesque about the psycho-dynamics of letter-writing – a mode of communication which both presupposes and accentuates the element of distance between the parties concerned, while encouraging them to express their inmost thoughts and deepest feelings. Kafka himself, although a compulsive and prolific letter-writer (indeed his collected epistles represent a substantial portion of his literary remains), had always been painfully aware of the limitations of this sort of far-flung intercourse. He often chose to register his frustration at writing letters by writing about it in his letters: a signal example of the double-think that held sway over both his life and work. 'How little use meetings in letters are', he wrote in 1908 to Hedwig Weiler, the first of his postal muses; 'they're like splashings near the shore by two people who are separated by an ocean' (FFE 28). He later found it necessary to add the qualification: 'but I did not say the splashing could be heard' (FFE 28). By 1922, having written what would amount to whole volumes of correspondence to Felice Bauer, Milena Jesenská-Pollak, his sister Ottla, and countless others, Kafka was convinced that he had fallen under the spell of the 'evil sorcerer of letter-writing' (MIL 234), and in consequence had been liable to endure a Job-like succession of unnatural afflictions. 'All the misfortune of my life', he claimed, 'derives, one could say, from letters or from the possibility of writing letters' (MIL 229). Over the years, the obsessive mechanics of drafting a letter had grown to resemble the operation of the punitive apparatus of 'In the Penal Colony', wherein the pen becomes a pantographic 'harrow', the paper becomes human flesh, and the scribing motion becomes an act of mutilation. And since his letters were '*born of torture, incurable torture*', the author believed that they in turn could '*create only torture*' (MIL 224).

Hoping perhaps for some brief respite from this endless cycle of epistolary torment, Kafka would every now and then call upon one of his fictional *alter egos* to take his place on the (letter-)rack. Try as he might, though, the perversely subjective narrator found it impossible to detach himself from these whipping-boys, who were after all mere extensions of his own troubled personality.

Instead of securing his relief at their expense, Kafka tended rather to preside over the sufferings of his characters with an ambivalent blend of *Schadenfreude* and sympathy: in short, he was availing himself of the supposed time-out not to lick his wounds, but to rub salt into them. The malignant influence of the letter, which had gradually poisoned almost every area of the author's private life, thus began to infect the main body of his literature. In Kafka's fiction, the letter is never simply a vehicle for imparting information, but characteristically insinuates itself into the narrative with an air of surreptitious formality; like a Trojan Horse ready to spill forth its secret cargo of destruction.

The most obvious case in point is undoubtedly that of 'The Judgement'. Indeed this is hardly surprising in view of the fact that the story was written only two nights after the momentous occasion of Kafka's first correspondence with Felice Bauer. For the opening third of its length, 'The Judgement' concentrates almost exclusively on the implications of a letter which the hero, Georg Bendemann, has just finished writing to his friend in St Petersburg. The (alleged) *raison d'être* of this epistle is to notify the distant comrade about the arrangements that have been made in respect of Georg's forthcoming wedding celebrations. Nevertheless, the prospective bridegroom conveys these tidings with a singular reluctance, not least because he has deliberately, even systematically, misrepresented the issue of his engagement in several previous dispatches to the Russianized expatriate. Visibly uneasy as to the effect this disclosure might have on the friend, Georg ponders over the latest missive for some considerable time, hanging on its every word. Eventually, he rises from his desk and, crossing the small lobby to his father's room, slips the letter into his pocket, as if it were a piece of evidence which might incriminate him in the eyes of the old man. This precaution notwithstanding, the subsequent trial of strength between father and son is sparked off when Georg, in his eagerness to usurp a paternal blessing, inadvertently allows the aged parent to catch sight of the epistle. From the old man's point of view, this letter is proof positive of Georg's treachery, and therefore, to all intents and purposes, a warrant for the boy's execution. It only remains for the father – who himself professes to have entered into secret correspondence with the 'learned' friend – to designate the manner of that execution: whereupon Georg is unhappily dispatched to a watery grave.

A more subtle though no less arbitrary brand of (in)justice is brought to bear on the adolescent protagonist of Kafka's first novel, *America* (described by the author as 'a sheer imitation of Dickens' (DII 188)), who finds himself endowed with great expectations after the passage of one epistle, only to be thrown back on hard times with the advent of another. When his ship docks in New York harbour, Karl Rossmann, much to his surprise, is met by his Uncle Jacob, a successful politician and business tycoon, who has received a letter from Europe alerting him to the young man's predicament. While he has always regarded the Rossmanns with a mixture of contempt and suspicion, Senator Jacob feels obliged to take the friendless Karl under his wing. Commendably zealous in his patronage, he makes provision for the boy's education and cultural adjustment, yielding freely to his every whim. Before long, however, this *entente cordiale* begins to turn sour. Matters come to a head when Karl, despite the wishes of his uncle, accepts an invitation to stay overnight at the country residence of Mr Pollunder. Seething with self-righteous indignation that his 'principles' (A 103) should have been so compromised by Karl's recalcitrance, the Senator determines to disown his nephew post-haste. In accordance with the dictates of protocol, their alliance, having been cemented by one letter, is formally dissolved with the drawing-up of a counter-missive, which Uncle Jacob contrives to have served on the boy, like a writ, at the stroke of midnight.

This kind of red-tape is of course the very lifeblood of the body politic in *The Castle*. At the centre of that novel stands K., the 'ostensible Land Surveyor',[1] whose every attempt to take up the post to which he has been appointed leaves him floundering against a tide of bureaucratic blankness. Twice, when he has all but given up hope of official recognition, his benighted campaign is briefly illuminated with the arrival of a somewhat glibly worded communiqué, which purports to have been written by the mysterious Klamm. However, since these memoranda are both obscure and inconsistent, they present the hero with more questions than answers, and thus conspire to heighten rather than alleviate his sense of existential uncertainty. (K.'s namesake in *The Trial* finds himself on the horns of a similar dilemma, when the letters of solicitation which he addresses to Fräulein Bürstner are neither answered nor returned.) Yet during his visit to the parental home of Barnabas – the naïve young fellow who brings him the letters – the Land Surveyor learns that every missive from the Castle, regardless of its contents, is in fact a sign of grace, and as such must be received in a spirit of deference and humility. The wretched plight of those who have come to be known as 'Barnabas's people' (C 258) can it seems be traced back to an incident which occurred three years earlier, when their youngest daughter, Amalia, was delivered a summons in the shape of an obscene *billet-doux* from a high-ranking Castle minister called Sortini. Overcome with anger and disgust, the maiden automatically tore up this 'abominable' (C 241) subpoena-*cum*-valentine and threw the fragments into the face of the official messenger. The provocative character of the letter notwithstanding, Amalia's reaction was interpreted by many as a hubristic snub to the Castle hierarchy and an unprecedented challenge to its sovereign authority. Fearing the worst, Barnabas's clan – then held 'in high esteem' (C 231) as paragons of diligence and propriety – pleaded for mitigation on the grounds that the girl had acted out of modesty rather than malice: but such was the enormity of Amalia's crime that nothing short of immediate and exemplary retribution would suffice. Thus, without further ado, the entire family were thrown out of their home and into a state of purgatorial disgrace. Here, reviled and ostracized by everyone else in the community, they struggle to eke out a miserable existence in the forlorn hope that some day their trespass might be forgiven them.

Casting his mind back over a lifetime of epistolary exertions which had brought him neither consolation nor communion, Kafka sank into a funereal despondency:

> The easy possibility of letter-writing must – seen merely theoretically – have brought into the world a terrible disintegration of souls. It is, in fact, an intercourse with ghosts, and not only with the ghost of the recipient but also with one's own ghost which develops between the lines of the letter one is writing and even more so in a series of letters where one letter corroborates the other and can refer to it as a witness. How on earth did anyone get the idea that people can communicate with one another by letter! Of a distant person one can think, and of a person who is near one can catch hold – all else goes beyond human strength. Writing letters, however, means to denude oneself before the ghosts, something for which they greedily wait. Written kisses don't reach their destination, rather they are drunk on the way by the ghosts. (MIL 229)[2]

These lines from a letter to Milena, besides being a terrifying summation of Kafka's scribal defeatism, could almost be said to encapsulate the very essence of *Family Voices*. From this haunting passage, Pinter might easily have drawn not just a blueprint for the thematic structure of his epistolary drama, but also the inspiration for its most daring use of metaphor: since *Family Voices* actually features a ghost who writes 'A last kiss' (IV 301) to his son in the form of a letter. Furthermore, like the 'written kisses' mourned by Kafka, all of those which comprise *Family Voices* remain undelivered, and thus fall short of their purpose. (One wonders if the busses mailed between mother and son have been imbibed *en route* by the vampiric father? The old spook himself hints that he has been assimilating the contents of his wife's dispatches.) Accordingly, and as the title would suggest, it is perhaps more apt to regard such 'letters' as the cathartic objectification of inner voices. By the same token, the fact that these utterances are never acknowledged clearly has no effect upon their production; because, like late-night radio hams, the family trio continue to transmit their messages, not knowing if they are being received. All the while, however, Pinter allows the audience to 'listen in' to this three-part disharmony, like the insatiable spectres before whom the correspondents must denude themselves.

* * *

In the context of *Family Voices*, the term 'letter-writing' is inevitably something of a misnomer; since, paradoxically, it does not denote a literary activity *per se*, but rather alludes to the meditative processes involved therein. Pinter disencumbers the letter of all formal trappings, while preserving both the spirit and the integrity of its psychological evolution. Moreover, even though the epistolary motif is carried throughout the play, neither the name nor, for that matter, the address of any of the correspondents is ever disclosed. Instead the three speaking parts are identified numerically, in order of appearance: an arrangement which coincides with the graduated diminution in the relative amounts that each of the roles has to say. Through this digital anonymity, the dramatist contrives to present his characters as archetypal figures in a universal saga of familial estrangement.

The first voice is that of a young man, 'still under twenty-one' (IV 302), who is writing to his mother. He represents the nucleus of the play, insofar as the other voices exist only in relation to him. It would seem that the young man has – for reasons which are implied but never stated – absconded some time ago from the parental home. He now lives as a lodger in a very comfortable and exclusive tenement, somewhere in an 'enormous city' (IV 288). Here, cocooned from the bustle of external affairs, the insularity of the boy's position is all but total: he hardly ever leaves the house; he has no regular employment; nor has he any contact or association with anyone outside. His entire world is bound up within the walls of the tenement – a circumstance which is reflected in the letters that he writes to his mother. Indeed, collectively, these missives read like an intimate chronicle of domesticity, wherein Voice 1 records his changing impressions of and occasional encounters with the other members of the household. There are in fact five other people living in the building – three women and two men – all of whom are apparently related, though the nature of their affinity remains shrouded in secrecy. The young man does not so much mention these characters in his dispatches, as bring each of them to life through a series of teasingly evocative vignettes.

The eldest of the three women is the landlady, Mrs Withers. She is seventy years old and, according to Voice 1, 'an utterly charming person, of impeccable credentials' (IV 288). Nevertheless, on reading between the lines, it emerges that this grand old dame has a fairly prodigious thirst for alcoholic beverages – gin, *vin rosé* and Campari are those mentioned by name. The young fellow – who starts off by saying that he is 'dead drunk' (IV 287) and then moments later claims to be a strict teetotaller – confesses that he himself regularly joins her for a couple of drinks, not just in the house but also at The Fishmongers Arms.[3] During these all-consuming bouts of liquorishness, Mrs Withers is apt to recall the days of her youth and, in particular, her experiences as a member of the Women's Air Force in the Second World War. Her fond memories, though, are blighted by the fact that the man she loved was killed at sea: she feels certain that, if they had married, she would have 'had tons of sons' (IV 298). As a result, the permanently maudlin dowager is inclined to look upon Voice 1 as 'her solace' (IV 289), and 'Sometimes she gives [him] a cuddle, as if she were [his] mother' (IV 292). This portrait of the overly maternal landlady clearly harks back to Pinter's characterization of Meg in *The Birthday Party*.

The second woman is initially distinguished by her penchant for wearing red dresses. (Mindful perhaps of the meretricious connotation of this colour, our young correspondent subsequently 'decides' that her attire 'wasn't red but pink' (IV 292).) Her name is Lady Withers; however, once she becomes better acquainted with the boy, she asks him to call her 'Lally' (IV 292). Although apparently middle-aged, the woman still possesses an 'amazingly young' 'alabaster neck' (IV 296). She lives in an improbably spacious room, which is extravagantly decorated 'with sofas and curtains and veils and shrouds and rugs and soft materials all over the walls, dark blue' (IV 292). Here, she entertains visitors, especially at night. Several aspects of Lady Withers' character suggest an affinity with the figure of Brunelda in *America*, who likewise favours a red gown and dwells in an apartment cluttered with a wide assortment of fabrics and furnishings. Both women, moreover, display a talent for classical music: Lady Withers, we are told, plays Schumann on the piano; while Brunelda has led a highly successful career as an opera singer.

The third female denizen is a fifteen-year-old schoolgirl called Jane. At first, Voice 1 believes that she is the daughter of Mrs Withers, but later concludes that she must be the old woman's grand-daughter. The boy recounts to his mother how he had recently sat next to Jane on a sofa, while partaking of tea and buns in Lady Withers' room. Jane was dressed entirely in green – apart from her black-clad toes, which she perched on his lap:

> Jane [. . .] chewed almost dreamily at her bun and when a currant was left stranded on her upper lip she licked it off, without haste. I could not reconcile this with the fact that her toes were quite restless, even agitated. Her mouth, eating, was measured, serene; her toes, not eating, were agitated, highly strung, some would say hysterical. My bun turned out to be rock solid. I bit into it, it jumped out of my mouth and bounced into my lap. Jane's feet caught it. It calmed her toes down. She juggled the bun, with some expertise, along them. I recalled that, in an early exchange between us, she had told me she wanted to be an acrobat. (IV 293)

This episode is strangely reminiscent of: (a) the incident in Chapter 3 of *America*, where Karl finds himself pinned to a sofa after a similar *tour de force* by an equally agile nymphet; and (b), with its concentration on the freakish nature of Jane's toes, the scene in Chapter 6 of *The Trial*, where Leni shows her 'pretty little paw' (T 124) to Joseph K.. Voice 1 is somewhat puzzled that Jane, while she continues to do a great deal of homework, never appears to attend any school. (Perhaps she receives her lessons through a correspondence course.) All the same, he is extremely impressed by the fact that she 'keeps her nose to the grindstone' (IV 290), and recognizes 'within her eyes, raw, untutored, unexercised but willing, a deep love of learning' (IV 294). Inspired by her enthusiasm, he considers offering himself out as a private academic coach. Jane, he fancies, would be an ideal pupil. His offer to help Jane with her homework, though, is coolly rejected by the tutelary Lady Withers, who seems determined to supervise the girl's education herself.

None of the three women is on speaking terms with either of the senior male occupants of the house, who are themselves alienated from one another. The elder of the two men is an eccentric old hermit-like figure called Mr Withers, about whom very little is known. The other man, Riley, who claims to be a police-officer, tries hard to square his pederastic impulses with his devotion to the Almighty. Both these characters will be analysed in detail later.

The idea of running away from home – as epitomized by the young hero of *Family Voices* – had often suggested itself to Kafka, who was inclined to regard his parents as 'persecutors' (FEL 55), holding him captive in, what he described as, 'a prison specially constructed for myself, which is all the harsher because it looks like a perfectly ordinary bourgeois home' (CK 53). The semi-incarcerated writer was in fact thirty-two years old before he eventually managed to cut loose of his leading-strings and break out of his room in the parental apartment. He knew in advance, however, that even if, as a result of such a move, he were to effectuate a more liberal domestic environment, he would still have to grapple with the bars which he carried within him (CK 22–3). In one of his 'He' aphorisms (which exemplifies his predilection for writing self-analysis in the third person), the author touched upon the true nature of his inherent compulsion:

> He does not live for the sake of his personal life, he does not think for the sake of his personal thoughts. It seems to him that he lives and thinks under the compulsion of a family, which certainly has more than enough vitality and intellectual power of its own, but for which he constitutes, in obedience to some law unknown to him, a formal necessity. Because of this unknown family and these unknown laws he cannot be released. (GWC 110)

Kafka was indeed constrained by a cell – yet it was not an architectural compartment such as one might expect to find in a penitentiary or monastic institution: rather it was the ultimate element of his own organic structure. Try as he might, the author realized that he could no more breach the wall of this cell, than crack his own genetic code. As he lamented to Gustav Janouch: 'every attempt at escape is useless. One cannot break one's chains when there are no chains to be seen' (CK 53).

By contrast, the young man in Pinter's play would appear to have shaken off these invisible ties, when he flees 'the oppressive, poison-laden, child-consuming air of the nicely furnished family room' (FFE 297) for a new life in the world at large. Yet the fugitive boy, accustomed to the sheltered security of custodial existence, soon finds himself ill-prepared for the pressures and responsibilities brought on by his freshly discovered independence. Alone in a city of faceless strangers, his first act as a 'free' individual is to deliver himself into the clutches of a surrogate brood, where he is 'content' (IV 300) to reside once again under virtually permanent house arrest. For all his delusions of emancipation, Voice 1 has, in reality, neither the will nor the resource to be anything else but a prisoner. No sooner has he entered into his new abode than he automatically begins to resume the position that he had formerly occupied *en famille*: 'Oh mother, I have found my home, my family. Little did I ever dream I could know such happiness' (IV 297). Rather than escape, therefore, the young man merely 'begs to be moved out of the old cell, which [he] hates, into a new one which [he] must first learn to hate' (GWC 81).

Consanguinity notwithstanding, the sophisticated veneer of cosy domesticity which prevails in the Withers household scarcely conceals the quiet despair and strained civility of living amongst a group of people with whom one has little or nothing in common. Indeed it is particularly ironic that the two women who came to the front door claiming to be the boy's mother and sister should have been told that 'This was a family house, no strangers admitted' (IV 295), since so many of the residents themselves behave as if they are in fact complete strangers to each other. This sense of familial estrangement corresponds almost exactly to that felt by Kafka himself while living in the domicile of his parents. In November 1912, the author confided to Felice Bauer:

> I have never found in any family, whether of friends or relations, as much coldness and false friendliness as I have always felt obliged to show towards my parents (through my fault as well as theirs). (FEL 56)

The following year, in a draft of a letter to Fräulein Bauer's father, Kafka went on to elaborate:

> [. . .] I live in my family, among the best and most lovable people, more strange than a stranger. I have not spoken an average of twenty words a day to my mother these last years, hardly ever said more than hello to my father. I do not speak at all to my married sisters and my brothers-in-law, and not because I have anything against them. The reason for it is simply this, that I have not the slightest thing to talk to them about. (DI 299–300)

By the same token, the young man in *Family Voices*, despite his continual assertions to the contrary, would ultimately appear to have no genuine rapport with either of his respective meinies, anymore than he has with the people he passes on his fanciful perambulations through the city. And as he says of these anonymous pedestrians:

> they look at me, they try to catch my eye, they expect me to speak. But as I do not know them I do not speak. Nor do I ever feel the slightest temptation to do so. (IV 288)

If indeed mutual knowledge is the *sine qua non* for all interpersonal relations, then Voice 1 – who knows so little about his kith, and about whom his kin know so little – must himself be regarded as a virtual stranger in both house and home.

In terms of Kafka's fiction, the most specific and pronounced parallels with *Family Voices* are to be found in *America*, which like Pinter's play focuses on a young man living in emotional and geographical isolation from his parents. It was in fact Max Brod – Kafka's literary executor – who decided that the novel should be called *America*. The author himself, while working on the manuscript, had indicated in a diary entry that his intention had been to use the title *Der Verschollene* (DII 107) (variously translated as 'The Man Who Disappeared', 'The Missing Person' or 'The Boy Who was Lost'). Needless to say, this original designation – with its emphasis on the fate of the central character rather than the New World into which he merges – makes the point of comparison with *Family Voices* much more explicit. Still, Brod's editorial oversight/presumption notwithstanding, the special affinity with Pinter's play is evident from the very start of the novel. In the opening sentence, Karl Rossmann (the hero) is introduced as 'a poor boy of sixteen who had been packed off to America by his parents because a servant girl had seduced him and got herself with child by him' (A 13); similarly, the young scamp in *Family Voices*, if we are to believe his mother, had also – and on more than one occasion – been caught with his pants down in the company of a female employee of his parents' household:

> Women were your downfall, even as a nipper. I haven't forgotten Françoise the French maid or the woman who masqueraded under the title of governess, the infamous Miss Carmichael. (IV 302)

(There are two very striking connections here with the person of Kafka himself. Firstly, the novelist was only too aware of the danger of falling into 'the female trap' (CK 178). As he admonished the callow Gustav Janouch: 'Women are snares, which lie in wait for men on all sides in order to drag them into the merely finite' (CK 178).[4] Secondly – and almost incredibly – Kafka's earliest memories of erotic awakening also involved a 'governess or some French woman'.[5]) Furthermore, not only does Voice 1 commit the same offence as the debauched Rossmann, but he also suffers the same consequence: displacement from hearth and home. Because of his below-stairs liaison, Kafka's juvenile delinquent is banished to the United States, and, although the protagonist of *Family Voices* never divulges his place of exile, we should remember that it was to the land of the Stars and Stripes that Teddy had fled in *The Homecoming*, after entering into a clandestine *mésalliance* with a girl whom his family would have considered beneath him.

Unlike his opposite numbers in *Family Voices* and *The Homecoming*,[6] Karl Rossmann adheres to 'a fixed resolution' (A 113), made on the evening of his departure, never to enter into any correspondence with his folks; and this despite the fact that both of his parents '(and his father very strictly on leaving him at Hamburg) had enjoined him' (A 113) to keep in contact. Only once does he consider breaking his vow of silence. This moment of hesitation occurs at the beginning of Chapter 4, when Karl, having received his marching orders from Uncle Jacob, spends the night in a dingy flop-house on the outskirts of New York City. There, while taking inventory of his box of belongings, he comes across an old, half-forgotten photograph of his mother and father. (At the end of *The Homecoming*, Teddy is given a small photograph of his father to take with him on his journey back to the USA (III 87).) Karl 'wondered if it might not be better to write to his parents' (A 113) after all, and, gazing at the portrait, began to scrutinize their faces, 'as if to read in them whether they still wanted to hear news of their son' (A 114). We have already touched upon the significance of the letter-writing motif in *America*. At this juncture, however, Kafka, who in his earlier use of epistles had been concerned primarily with the advancement of the plot, actually anticipates the central thesis of *Family Voices*, by relating the wistful ruminations of the *dépaysé* protagonist to the possibility of writing letters. In essence, the photograph, like the letter, is no more than an embellished scrap of paper, which, while affording only indirect communion, would nevertheless claim to 'convey with such complete certainty the secret feelings of the person [represented] in it' (A 113). (Kafka himself was highly sceptical of the camera and its fabrications: 'Nothing can be so deceiving as a photograph' (CK 152), he once declared.) Despite the frozen expressions and treacherous gloss, Karl comes to cherish the picture as a precious relic, since it constitutes his sole remaining link with his *Heimat*. When (in circumstances which defy explanation) the photograph later vanishes, the boy is finally – if fleetingly – brought to the realization of himself as a virtual orphan, cut adrift from his roots and dispossessed of his past. More important, though, is the fact that Kafka, in delineating the young man's interpretation of and response to the photograph, accurately prefigures the disposition of the three correspondents in *Family Voices*:

> [. . . Karl] tried to catch his father's eye from various angles. But his father refused to come to life, no matter how much his expression was modified by shifting the candle into different positions; nor did his thick, horizontal moustache look in the least real; it was not a good photograph. His mother, however, had come out better; her mouth was twisted as if she had been hurt and were forcing herself to smile. (A 113)

What we have here is, to all intents and purposes, a prototype of Pinter's play, with the abortive exchange of letters taking place inside the head of the central character.

* * *

The second voice belongs to a woman in the autumn years of her life. She is evidently the mother to whom the boy is writing. From her home near the coast, the woman complains that she never hears from her son. Although he is always in the forefront of her thoughts, she sometimes wonders if the boy even remembers that he still has a mother. Voice 2 claims to have written several months ago to the young man, informing him that his father had passed away. This letter – like all her others – was never acknowledged. As far as she can ascertain, no one knows where her son might be or even if he himself is alive or dead.

What distinguishes the mother from the other correspondents is that she alone is constantly yearning for a response: the son is too wrapped up in the affairs of the Withers household; the father has long since given up the ghost. This solicitude on the part of the woman is reflected most noticeably in the interrogative character of her dispatches. Her first letter, in particular, contains no less than fourteen question marks – ten of which occur within the opening fifty-eight words:

> Darling. Where are you? The flowers are wonderful here. The blooms. You so loved them. Why do you never write?
>
> I think of you and wonder how you are. Do you ever think of me? Your mother? Ever? At all?
>
> Have you changed your address?
>
> Have you made friends with anyone? A nice boy? Or a nice girl? (IV 289)

Inevitably, though, such questions, falling as they do on deaf ears, can never be answered, and merely serve to perpetuate a dizzy spiral of bafflement and anxiety.

Voice 2 is clearly something of a throw-back to the gallery of maternal portraits which had dominated much of Pinter's early work: Rose in *The Room*, Meg in *The Birthday Party*, Flora in *A Slight Ache* and Mrs Stokes in *A Night Out*. Common to all such figures is the innate desire to (re)kindle the spirit of symbiosis which imbues a mother's relations with her infant child. This aspiration is thrown into sharp relief in *Family Voices*, where the woman becomes intoxicated with a lush nostalgia for the halcyon days when no one or nothing could come between herself and the little boy:

> [. . .] I was washing your hair, with the most delicate shampoo, and rinsing, and then drying your hair so gently with my soft towel, so that no murmur came from you, of discomfort or unease, and then looked into your eyes, and saw you look into mine, knowing that you wanted no-one else, no-one at all, knowing that you were entirely happy in my arms [. . . .] (IV 296)

For Kafka, this kind of devotion was fundamentally narcissistic – a dervish-like whirling of the ego about an immaterial object: 'The love that parents have for their children is animal, mindless, and always prone to confuse the child with their own selves' (FFE 296). Discussing this phenomenon at some length in a quartet of weighty epistles, written in the autumn of 1921 to his eldest sister (Elli), the novelist was reminded of an old school-book poem[7] which

> tells of the wanderer who, after many years, returns to his native village and whom no one recognizes but his mother. 'The mother's eye her son did know.' That is the true miracle of mother love and a great truth is expressed here. But only half a truth, for the corollary is missing, that if the son had stayed at home, she would never have known him, for her daily association with the son would have made him completely unrecognizable to her and so the very opposite of the poem would have happened and anyone else would have known him better than she. (Granted that she would not have had to recognize him, since he would never have come back to her.) (FFE 296)

Several years earlier, Kafka – speaking specifically about his own mother – had confided to Felice:

> All parents want to do is drag one down to them, back to the old days from which one longs to free oneself and escape; they do it out of love, of course, and that's what makes it so horrible. (FEL 55)

Similarly, in *Family Voices*, the woman engages in wishful fantasies which anticipate a time when, reunited with her son, she will again clasp him to her maternal bosom:

> perhaps you will arrive here in a handsome new car, one day, in the not too distant future, in a nice new suit, quite out of the blue, and hold me in your arms. (IV 294)

In a desperate bid to engineer such a homecoming, Voice 2 resorts to emotional blackmail. She paints a bleak picture of herself, bereft of her husband and forsaken by her son, sitting 'alone by an indifferent fire, curtains closed', in a winter of 'eternal night' (IV 296). Later, she claims that she is ill and implores the boy to come to her sick-bed. Still she receives neither comfort nor sympathy. Embittered by the young man's apparent lack of concern, the mother allows her frustration to spill over into indignation: 'I wait for your letter begging me to come to you. I'll spit on it' (IV 297). At one point, the woman even declares the boy to be 'a monster' (IV 293), momentarily forgetting that, like Mrs Samsa in 'The Metamorphosis', it was she herself who 'gave birth to' (IV 290) this *bête noire*. In a frantic flourish of threats and accusations, the mother announces that she has supplied the police with a full description of the young man and informed them of her suspicion that he is 'in the hands of underworld figures who are using [him] as a male prostitute' (IV 302). Having eventually given her son up 'as a very bad job' (IV 302), Voice 2 concludes her correspondence on a note of wounded resignation. She signs off with a final reproach to the boy, delivered characteristically in the form of a forlorn question: 'Tell me one last thing. Do you think the word love means anything?' (IV 302).

At no stage during the play does the young man attempt to correspond directly with his father, despite the fact that he still believes 'the old boy' (IV 302) to be very much alive. All communication is relayed, in theory at least, via the mutual connection with the mother – an arrangement which brings to mind the intercom system which operated in the Kafka household:

> [. . .] I did not dare to ask, and later from habit did not even really much think of asking, you [the father] anything directly when Mother was there. It was much less dangerous for the child to put questions to Mother, sitting there beside you, and to ask Mother: 'How is Father?' so guarding oneself against surprises. (WPC 173)

Relations in *Family Voices* are of course terminally complicated by the circumstance that the mother and son are not even on the same wavelength and thus remain totally oblivious to each other's repeated attempts at communication.[8]

Although cast in the role of mediatrix, the maternal figure is not exactly a free agent, and indeed can only ever be expected to pay lip-service to the principles of neutrality. Like Frau Kafka before her, Voice 2 is compelled, on an emotional if not intellectual level, to both echo and endorse the judgements and condemnations which the patriarch has pronounced on their wanton son

(WPC 183): 'Perhaps I should curse you as your father cursed you. Oh I pray, I pray your life is a torment to you' (IV 297). Ultimately, therefore, the mother, while appearing to occupy the middle ground, is 'too devoted and loyal' to her husband 'to constitute an independent spiritual force [. . .] in the child's struggle' against the father (WPC 183). Moreover, such is the sanctity of this allegiance that it can never be impeached, even in widowhood – as Albert Stokes discovers in *A Night Out*:

> MOTHER: You promise?
> ALBERT: Promise what?
> MOTHER: That . . . that you won't upset your father.
> ALBERT: My father? How can I upset my father? You're always talking about upsetting people who are dead!
> MOTHER: Oh, Albert, you don't know how you hurt me, you don't know the hurtful way you've got, speaking of your poor father like that.
> ALBERT: But he is dead.
> MOTHER: He's not! He's living! (*Touching her breast*) In here! And this is his house! (I 335)

Also conceived and originally performed as a radio play, *A Night Out* clearly foreshadows – albeit on a less ethereal level – the tripartite domestic tension of *Family Voices*; since it too focuses on a restless young man, his anxiously possessive mother and her dead husband. At one point, Mrs Stokes even chides her son: 'Your father would turn in his grave if he heard you raise your voice to me' (I 334).

* * *

The third and last of the familial voices is that of an elderly man, who quickly identifies himself as the father of the young fellow and the husband of the woman. Making his vocal entrance relatively late in the proceedings, the *paterfamilias* – in the first of his two messages to the lad – immediately sets out to scotch the rumour that he is no longer alive:

> I know your mother has written to you to tell you that I am dead. I am not dead. I am very far from being dead, although lots of people have wished me dead, from time immemorial, you especially. (IV 300)

Like his counterpart in 'The Judgement' (with whom he appears to share a quasi-divine omniscience), the father has felt threatened by what he reckons are the malignant aspirations of his son:

> It is you who have prayed for my death, from time immemorial. I have heard your prayers. They ring in my ears. Prayers yearning for my death. But I am not dead. (IV 300)

The old man then breaks off this solemn preamble and, in a surprise *volte-face*, wryly announces that he has 'been leading [his son] up the garden path' (IV 300). He now confirms that he is in fact 'As dead as a doornail', and addressing the boy from the periscopic station of his 'glassy grave' (IV 301). All his erstwhile assertions to the contrary were, he explains, intended simply as a 'bit of fun' (IV 300). The narrator of Kafka's story 'Unhappiness' had indeed warned us about the shifty comings and goings of such phantasmal communicants:

> One never gets straight information from them. It's just a hither and thither. These ghosts seem to be more dubious about their existence than we are [. . . .] (CSS 394)

Although continuing in an ironic vein, the tone of the father's epistle veers increasingly towards sarcasm; and nowhere more so than when he directs his jibes at the schmaltzy ideal of the patri–filial relationship. (This line of attack had of course been deployed with much greater virulence by Lenny, during his war of words with Max in *The Homecoming*.) Voice 3 describes his letter as 'A last kiss from Dad', which, he says, he has taken the trouble to write because he has always had 'such a loving son' (IV 301). Yet, for all its gallows humour and barbed sentimentality, this missive betrays a serious and heartfelt desire on the part of the old man to break through the wall of silence that has long existed between himself and his son.

This ambivalence of the father towards his son is conveniently epitomized in the two apparently conflicting versions that the mother gives of her husband's final moments. According to the first of these reports, the old man spoke of the youngster frequently, and 'with tenderness', as his life ebbed away; and, in 'One of his last sentences', requested his wife to give the lad 'a slap on the back' from his father (IV 291). Later, however, Voice 2 declares that the patriarch had actually cursed the name of his son as he lay on his deathbed, and thus expired 'in lamentation and oath' (IV 293). Although there is insufficient evidence to substantiate either of these statements, a case can be made for each by simply calling into question the veracity of its obverse. If, for example, we assume that the first representation is accurate, then the second may be seen as a perjurious symptom of the woman's growing vexation at her wayward son. Alternatively, if we suppose that the second account is true, then the first could be viewed as a white lie, which the mother tells in order to spare the feelings of the boy, but which, in her exasperation, she subsequently retracts. Nevertheless, it should be pointed out that the two propositions are not necessarily at variance with one another. A useful parallel can be drawn here with the story about the door-keeper and the man from the country, as told in Chapter 9 of *The Trial*.[9] During their discussion of the parable, the priest instructs Joseph K. that 'it is not necessary to accept everything as true, one must only accept it as necessary' (T 246):

> The story contains two important statements made by the door-keeper about admission to the Law, one at the beginning, the other at the end. The first statement is: that he cannot admit the man at the moment, and the other is: that this door was intended only for the man. If there were a contradiction between the two, you would be right and the door-keeper would have deceived the man. But there is no contradiction. The first statement, on the contrary, even implies the second. (T 241)

Correlatively, in *Family Voices*, there need not be any discrepancy between the two statements that the woman makes about the mood of her husband at the time of his death. Indeed, if read in tandem, both are entirely consistent with Kafka's assertion that paternal love 'often wears the face of violence' (CK 24). In addition, it is worth noting that the situation variously described by Voice 2 is inversely comparable to the circumstances of Kafka's own demise: since the dying father's paradoxical attitude to his obmutescent son effectively mirrors Hermann Kafka's mixed feelings about the correspondence of the moribund Franz. The last few months of the novelist's life were spent in a sanatorium near Vienna, from which he wrote to his parents, expressing his desire to see them.[10] As he lay on his deathbed, with his larynx so ravaged by tuberculosis that he was scarcely able to speak, Kafka registered on a slip of paper how his father had been 'glad to receive the special-delivery letters, but also annoyed by them' (FFE 420).

Behind all the frustrations and disappointments, the pain and resentment, the fear and suspicion, there is undoubtedly a deep-seated and enduring affection between Voice 3 and his son. The mother recalls happier times, when father and son would walk along the cliff path and sit together at the top, 'munching' away at the cheese sandwiches she had prepared for them (IV 290). And, in his urban isolation, the young man manages to sustain a kind of fellowship by meditating upon the wholesome heritage of his formative years:

> [. . .] I am not lonely, because all that has ever happened to me is with me, keeps me company; my childhood, for example, through which you, my mother, and he, my father, guided me. (IV 288)

(Interestingly, Kafka – despite his feelings of estrangement and persecution – was also obliged to acknowledge the nurturing influence of his folks: 'they are my parents after all, indispensible elements of my own being from whom I constantly draw strength, essential parts of me, not only obstacles' (DII 167).) Furthermore, when the boy learns from Riley about the visit of the two 'imposters' (IV 295) who claimed to be his mother and sister, he wonders, with the same blend of raillery and regret which is so characteristic of Voice 3, why his father 'wasn't bothered to make the trip' (IV 295). The tragedy is that when the lost son finally expresses his 'longing' to return home 'to clasp [his] father's shoulder' and 'to have a word with him' (IV 302), the old man has already been dead for several months. The dream of such a joyful homecoming – always a source of comfort, if only a remote possibility – has disappeared forever, taking with it all hope of reconciliation.

The story, however, does not end here. There can, it seems, be neither escape nor repose – even in death. As a consequence perhaps of their failure to resolve their differences, father and son are both haunted by cryptic murmurs and rueful reverberations. Just before we hear that the young man has been christened 'Bobo' (IV 301) by the other denizens of the tenement, who talk to him as if he were the family pet,[11] the father, wrapped in the glacial stillness of his tomb, relates how he is harassed by the intermittent cry of a Cerberian hound:

> While there is, generally, absolute silence everywhere, absolute silence throughout all the hours, I still hear, occasionally, a dog barking. I hear this dog. Oh, it frightens me. (IV 301)

Kafka himself had used almost exactly the same image on a number of occasions. For example, on 13 December 1911, the author described in his diary how he had had a particularly 'disgusting' nightmare: 'A dog lay on my body, one paw near my face. I woke up because of it but was still afraid for a little while to open my eyes and look at it' (DI 175). Moreover, in the fragment 'Temptation in the Village', the hero is likewise startled from deepest slumber when he apprehends that a 'repulsive little lap dog' (DII 55) is lurking beside his ear. This tyke is later taken away by a group of children, who – curiously enough – stand it on a sheet of letter paper upon which a woman has just been writing. A third and even more arresting instance of this canine motif occurs in an epistle which Kafka wrote to his friend Oskar Baum in 1919:

> This house still harbours a memory of you, or rather of your boy. A small Pomeranian belonging to the letter-carrier at whose house you boarded could not endure Leo's pesterings and was bought by Fräulein Stüdl, that is, rescued. The dog has long been dead, but you, as father of your son, will not be forgotten. The dogs are just now barking gloriously outside the house; they take their revenge against me for the Pomeranian every night. But that is no great matter; the inner dogs are more dangerous to sleep. (FFE 211–12)

From his room, Bobo – the pup in *Family Voices* – can hear nocturnal whispering and footsteps on the stairs, which, being too timid to investigate, he attributes to the unseen 'guests' (IV 300) who visit Lady Withers' chamber. Back home, his mother is disturbed by similar noises, though she is convinced that they are made by the unquiet spirit of her dead husband. As the play ends, the father, in his eerie, plangent voice (broadcast through only one stereo channel), delivers an elegiac quatrain (typographically disguised as prose): 'I have so much to say to you. But I am quite dead. What I have to say to you will never be said' (IV 303).

* * *

According to Kafka, we should regard 'our neighbour, whom God puts in our path and to whose actions we are directly exposed', as 'a messenger from the outer world' (CK 94). Two such emissaries are assigned to the young man in *Family Voices*. Even though Voice 1 may never actually come face to face with his father, the latter is given a kind of vicarious presence in his son's world through the agency of the two senior male occupants of the tenement. In the course of their separate encounters with the boy, Mr Withers and Riley both intimate a passionate and queerly paternal interest in him. Despite the many differences between them, these characters are clearly meant to adumbrate complementary versions of fatherly authority. And it is surely no coincidence that we first learn about the existence of the two gentlemen immediately after the mother mentions the death of her husband.

The concept of the paternal proxy is one of the key elements of Kafka's work. The author may well have claimed that his writing 'was all about' (WPC 197) the conflict with the father, nevertheless, after the devastating battles of 'The Judgement' and 'The Metamorphosis', he evidently found it too painful to go on confronting the old adversary head on. Both those stories end with the death of the son – an outcome which is hardly surprising given the filial tendency to view the father as divine. The Bible, after all, warns that anyone who even sets eyes on God – let alone dares to challenge His sovereignty – will not live to tell the tale (Exodus 33:20). Resplendent in His power and glory, God is too holy to look upon – or to be looked upon by – sinful man. And yet, because of His grace, He does not abandon mankind altogether. Instead He contrives to reveal Himself to the sons of men in sundry indirect and temporary ways. Occasionally, He may make Himself manifest in the form of a theophany; an example of this phenomenon is the burning bush from which He spoke to Moses (Exodus 3). More often, though, He chooses to communicate His will through a range of heavenly and human intermediaries – primarily, the angels and prophets. These divinely appointed envoys therefore have a crucial part to play in promoting understanding and reconciliation. In deference perhaps to this biblical protocol, Kafka became convinced that it was more beneficial, and certainly 'much less dangerous' (WPC 173), to rely upon the good offices of some such intermediary in his relations with his own numinous father. We have already seen how both Kafkas, *père et fils*, were inclined to use the mother as a go-between, rather than address each other directly: the difference being that the father elected to do so from a position of superiority, while the son was motivated solely by the need to 'guard' himself (WPC 173). At one point in 'Letter to his Father', the author speculates about how much better things might have been if he had grown up away from his father's overpowering influence:

> I should probably have [. . . become] quite different from what I really am, and we might have got on with each other excellently. I should have been happy to have you as a friend, as a chief, an uncle, a grandfather, even indeed (though this rather more hesitantly) as a father-in-law. Only as what you are, a father, you have been too strong for me [. . . .] (WPC 159)

This extract contains the rationale for virtually all of Kafka's literary attempts to attenuate the *force majeure* of the paternal personality. In the bulk of his fictions, the omnipotent patriarch does not actually appear *in propria persona,* but is instead represented *per procurationem.* The paternal proxy, although always a man of some prestige, can come in a variety of guises. For example, he might be an uncle, a boss, a bureaucrat, a clergyman, an officer of the law or a member of the armed forces. Through his dealings with such ambassadors, the Kafkan hero is given to believe that he can petition and eventually propitiate the forbidding father – or rather some metaphorical evocation of the old man's 'ultimate authority' (WPC 162), such as the Court in *The Trial* or the secretariat in *The Castle.*

Interestingly, a similar reluctance to confront the father can also be detected in the work of Pinter. Only in *The Homecoming* do we see the familial antagonists engaged in a physical showdown. Elsewhere the struggle against the father is pursued indirectly and from a distance. Nevertheless, even *in absentia,* the old man can still be a force to be reckoned with. In quite a few of Pinter's plays, a father, while not involved in the thick of the action, manages to make his formidable presence felt in the affairs of his progeny. This ubiquity of the pater is manifest not just in the consanguineous contexts of *Family Voices* and *Moonlight,* but also in the more diverse circumstances of *The Room, The Birthday Party* and *One for the Road.*[12] In each of these instances, moreover, the father's shoes are once again filled by an authoritative deputy – or perhaps one should say 'attorney', because the Pinterian *demi-père* nearly always has some connection with the law.

In the case of *Family Voices,* the problem of communication between father and son is mirrored in the boy's (non-)relationship with Mr Withers – the inscrutable old recluse 'to whom no-one talks, to whom no-one refers, with evidently good reason' (IV 300). We know only what the son himself knows – or rather what he imparts to his mother – about this character, which is to say, tantalizingly little. Indeed the information we have on the old man is so meagre that even the most prosaic detail seems to assume mysterious significance. The full extent of our knowledge in this respect is as follows: the old fellow is called Benjamin Withers; he is bald, anchoretic by nature, and retires early to his room, where there are three quite conspicuous objects – a jug, a basin and a bicycle. Although he shares the same name as the women who rule the roost, we remain uncertain as to whether or not the old man is in fact affiliated to this particular branch of the Withers family tree. 'And which Withers is he anyway?' ponders the bemused Voice 1: 'I mean what relation is he to the rest of the Witherses?' (IV 300).

Seldom has Pinter devised a more truly Kafkaesque episode than that which unfolds when Voice 1 tells his mother how he has just 'had the most unpleasant, the most mystifying encounter, with the man who calls himself Mr Withers' (IV 297). Here, as with other such meetings with members of the household, the boy reconstructs the whole experience in eidetic flashback. Accosting our anonymous hero as 'son', the old fogy bids him to enter his chamber, which he describes as 'a true oasis' (IV 297). Ordinarily, this usage of the word 'son' – a hackneyed form of address to any junior male, regardless of parentage – would be unremarkable; however, in the context of *Family Voices*, it is tantamount to an assertion of Mr Withers' patriarchal legitimacy. Having enticed the unsuspecting youth into his sanctum sanctorum, the old man then launches into a breathless and dithyrambic tirade – an exotic mishmash of polyglottal gibberish which quite literally mesmerizes the listener:

> This is the only room in this house where you can pick up a caravanserai to all points West. Compris? Comprende? Get me? Are you prepared to follow me down the mountain? Look at me. My name's Withers. I'm there or thereabouts. Follow? Embargo on all duff terminology. With me? Embargo on all things redundant. All areas in that connection verboten. You're in a diseaseridden land, boxer. Keep your weight on all the left feet you can lay your hands on. Keep dancing. The old foxtrot is the classical response but that's not the response I'm talking about. Nor am I talking about the other response. Up the slaves. Get me? This is a place of creatures, up and down stairs. Creatures of the rhythmic splits, the rhythmic sideswipes, the rums and roulettes, the macaroni tatters, the dumplings in jam mayonnaise, a catapulting ordure of gross and ramshackle shenanigans, openended paraphernalia. Follow me? It all adds up. It's before you and behind you. I'm the only saviour of the grace you find yourself

> wanting in. Mind how you go. Look sharp. Get my drift? Don't let it get too mouldy. Watch the mould. Get the feel of it, sonny, get the density. Look at me. (IV 297–8)

For the purpose of this logorrhoea, Michael Kitchen, who played the part of the son in the original radio production, virtually became Mr Withers, drivelling out the old timer's words in a bravura display of demoniacal ventriloquism. The impression was not unlike that created by Jonathan Pryce's powerful and controversial interpretation of Hamlet at London's Royal Court Theatre in 1980. Under the direction of Richard Eyre, Pryce effectively internalized the famous ghost scene by reading both parts in the exchange between Hamlet and his dead father, as if the Prince were possessed or suffering from schizophrenia. By an intriguing coincidence, this episode from Shakespeare's Danish tragedy is echoed not just in *Family Voices* – which likewise features a sire who addresses his scion from beyond the grave – but also in *One for the Road,* where Nicolas refers to Gila's late father as a 'perturbed spirit' (IV 389),[13] and in *Moonlight,* where several of the Bard's lines are mischievously quoted by Jake and Fred (M 59–60).[14]

It comes as no surprise when, soon after this *tête-à-tête,* the young man confesses to feeling 'bewildered, anxious, confused, uncertain and afraid' (IV 300). Yet the primary cause of such consternation appears to lie not in what Mr Withers says, or even in the manner in which he says it, but in the fact that the lad does not understand him. To convey the boy's sense of incomprehension to the audience, Pinter exaggerates the weirdness of the old codger's speech by seasoning it with words from various foreign languages. This idea of a linguistic barrier between father(-figure) and son was something which had been instilled into Kafka at an early age. The everyday influence of sundry nursemaids, cooks and servants meant that the infant Franz spoke mostly Czech until he started school. However, his parents found it difficult to confabulate in Czech and so usually spoke German to their son. Kafka would later explore this confusion of tongues in his fiction, most notably in 'The Metamorphosis' and the sequence with the Italian visitor in *The Trial*. Now, in *Family Voices,* it may be that the son cannot understand the old man because he speaks nonsense: then again, bearing in mind that the entire episode is related from the boy's point of view, the old man might only appear to speak nonsense because the son cannot understand him. In any event, Mr Withers, like the father, is unable to get through to the lad, and, frustrated by the vehemence of his own endeavour, only succeeds in alienating him still further. Throughout this, his one and only interview with Mr Withers, the son remains utterly dumbfounded; and although he later claims to 'talk freely' (IV 300) to all the other inmates, he emphasizes that he has no further contact with the glabrous dotard. One is reminded here of the passage in 'Letter to his Father' in which Kafka describes how, traumatized by paternal harangues, he 'lost the capacity to talk' (WPC 170):

> at a very early stage you forbade me to talk. Your threat: 'Not a word of contradiction!' and the raised hand that accompanied it have gone with me ever since. What I got from you [. . .] was a hesitant, stammering mode of speech, and even that was still too much for you, and finally I kept silence, at first perhaps from defiance, and then because I couldn't either think or speak in your presence. [. . .] I was too docile, I became completely dumb, cringed away from you, hid from you, and only dared to stir when I was so far away from you that your power could no longer reach me, at any rate directly. (WPC 170–1)

Similarly, in *Family Voices,* the boy's inability and/or reluctance to speak to the old man accords completely with the attitude that he adopts towards his own father. Moreover, given the father's posthumous aversion to things canine, it is only natural that his *locum tenens*, Mr Withers, should refrain from the jocular practice of calling the youngster by his doggish pet name:

> The only person who does not call me Bobo is the old man. He calls me nothing. I call him nothing. I don't see him. He keeps to his room. I don't go near it. He is old and will die soon. (IV 301)

Indeed Voice 1 would appear to be waiting for the demise of the old man just as earnestly as he is alleged to have prayed for the death of Voice 3. The religious dimension to the character of Mr Withers is elusive yet unmistakable. The old man's praenomen even has a biblical pedigree. Benjamin was the name of the youngest son of Jacob, and as such has the meaning 'son of the right hand' or 'son of my old age'. While this is not without interest, Mr Withers would seem to have a much more pronounced affinity with another figure from the Old Testament. Certain parts of the old man's speech suggest that he is actually a kind of deranged

Moses. There are indeed a number of details which could be interpreted as manic references to the Pentateuch. Consider the following, for example:

(1) 'Up the slaves' – the captive Israelites?
(2) 'in a diseaseridden land' – the various plagues visited upon Egypt?
(3) 'follow me down the mountain' – Mount Sinai?
(4) 'Embargo' and 'verboten' – matters prohibited under the Law?
(5) 'oasis' and 'caravanserai' (coupled with Riley's allusion to the 'desert') – the years of wandering in the wilderness?

Mr Withers and Moses are both prophets. Each has, *mutatis mutandis,* been commissioned to act as an intermediary for a dreaded and unapproachable being. Just as Moses had imparted the various ordinances of the Lord to the Children of Israel, so Mr Withers attempts to proclaim a message from the father to the young man in *Family Voices.* The outlandish diction which characterizes the old man's oration is in fact one of the hallmarks of prophetic discourse:

> In the Law it is written: 'Through men of strange tongues and through the lips of foreigners I will speak to this people, but even then they will not listen to me,' says the Lord. (1 Corinthians 14:21; cf. Isaiah 28:11–12)[15]

(If Mr Withers' role as a divinely appointed spokesman is implied rather than stated, there is nothing tacit about the afflatus of Nicolas in *One for the Road,* who indeed repeatedly trumpets the fact that he is the mouthpiece of Jehovah: 'God speaks through me. I'm referring to the Old Testament God, by the way, although I'm a long way from being Jewish' (IV 374). Nicolas clearly sees himself as following in the venerable tradition of the *nabî'* – the Hebrew term for one who communicates God's message through human lips.) As well as being a prophet, Moses could be described as the saviour of his people, since it was he, after all, who led the Hebrew slaves out of Egypt and brought them to the Promised Land. Correspondingly, in *Family Voices,* when Mr Withers declares, 'I'm the only saviour of the grace you find yourself wanting in' (IV 298), he would appear to be claiming to have the ability to deliver the boy from his place of exile.

It seems fairly obvious that Voice 1 left home not to make his father proud of him, as the mother initially suggests (IV 291), but because he wanted to escape from the crucible of paternal jurisdiction. The young man's predicament is in fact closely analogous to the sense of biblical displacement which Kafka had outlined in his diary on 28 January 1922:

> why did I want to quit the world? Because 'he' would not let me live in it, in his world. Though indeed I should not judge the matter so precisely, because I am now a citizen of this other world, whose relationship to the ordinary one is the relationship of the wilderness to cultivated land (I have been forty years wandering from Canaan); I look back at it like a foreigner, though in this other world as well – it is the paternal heritage I carry with me – I am the most insignificant and timid of all creatures and am able to keep alive thanks only to the special nature of its arrangements [. . . .] Should I not be thankful despite everything? Was it certain that I should find my way to this world? Could not 'banishment' from one side, coming together with rejection from this, have crushed me at the border? Is not Father's power such that nothing (not I, certainly) could have resisted his decree? It is indeed a kind of Wandering in the Wilderness in reverse that I am undergoing: I think that I am continually skirting the wilderness and am full of childish hopes (particularly as regards women) that 'perhaps I shall keep in Canaan after all' – when all the while I have been decades in the wilderness and these hopes are merely mirages born of despair, especially at those times when I am the wretchedest of creatures in the desert too, and Canaan is perforce my only Promised Land, for no third place exists for mankind. (DII 213–14)

Here, Kafka expounds his own personal variation on the paradox of the restless expatriate – from the prodigal son in St Luke's Gospel to Dorothy in *The Wizard of Oz*[16] – who comes to identify the Promised Land with the home he (or she) left behind. In *Family Voices*, Mr Withers effectively offers to show his charge the way to Canaan, though evidently, like Moses, he will not live long enough to enter it himself. The old man insinuates that, since the law of the father is both ineluctable and sacrosanct, the boy must be prepared to follow the path of obedience. In the course of his testimony, he publishes a number of apparently irrefragable edicts and admonishes the listener to walk with probity and circumspection. Moreover, given that one of the commandments promulgated by Moses – and cited incidentally by Goldberg in *The Birthday Party* (I 71) – stresses the need to 'Honour thy father and thy mother' (Exodus 20:12), it seems reasonable to suppose that Mr Withers is exhorting young Bobo to go back to the parental home with his tail between his legs. The consequence of not being reconciled with the father is vividly conveyed to the whelp when (at the behest of Mr Withers) he turns his eyes upon the face of his cabbalistic guru: thereupon he is confronted with a truly horrifying vision of Gehenna. 'It was', as he later tells his mother, 'like looking into a pit of molten lava' (IV 298). Then again, the blazing countenance of the old man also brings to mind the intense radiance of Moses' visage immediately after he had received the tablets of stone from Jehovah (Exodus 34:29–35).

If Mr Withers could be said to represent the mystical and ancient aspects of the patriarchal personality, then Riley, the other senior male occupant of the house, might be described as the embodiment of fatherly strength and ascendancy. Our young correspondent begins his characterization of Riley with a terse yet extremely telling sentence: 'He is big' (IV 291). Stature, as we have seen, is perhaps the single most important measure of paternal authority. Thus it would appear that Voice 1 is inclined to view Riley in much the same light as that in which Franz, Georg, Gregor and Max had regarded their respective big daddies. This perception is accentuated during the description of the episode in which Riley comes into the bathroom while the young man is lying, presumably 'quite naked' (IV 287), in the tub: a sequence that is strangely reminiscent of Kafka's account of how vulnerable he used to feel as a boy when undressing in the same bathing-hut as his father. (On such occasions, Franz was always completely overawed by what he saw as the sheer majesty of his father's physique. Hermann Kafka – a veritable mountain of a man, 'strong, tall, broad' (WPC 163) – would characteristically stride out of the hut displaying his virility with aplomb rather than embarrassment; by contrast, his son – an awkward little skeleton, 'skinny, weakly, slight' (WPC 163) – would feel painfully exposed and deeply ashamed.) Sitting bullishly on the edge of the bath, Riley is a supremely impressive combination of muscularity and magnitude. His masculine vigour is underscored by the fact that he is strikingly hirsute, boasting not just a fine head of black hair, but also 'black eyebrows and black hair on the back of his hands' (IV 291). Only too aware of the destructive potential of his tremendous might, he subsequently sounds a note of warning: 'I'm a big man, as you see, I could crush a slip of a lad such as you to death [. . .]' (IV 299). Nevertheless, Riley does not despise the youngster's smooth and delicate body. On the contrary, he actually congratulates the boy on having such a surprisingly 'wellknit yet slender frame' (IV 295). (Later, while declaring that he is not a practising pederast, Riley confesses to having taken a 'fancy' (IV 299) to the lad and evidently believes that, should he ever succumb to temptation, his little 'chum' (IV 299) would make an ideal catamite.) When Voice 1 bashfully acknowledges this compliment, the lusty hulk replies: 'Don't thank me [. . .] It's God you have to thank. Or your mother' (IV 295). A clear vindication of Riley's role as a paternal proxy, this statement both highlights and articulates the young man's barely suppressed apprehension of his father's divinity. Moreover, if the boy's father is in fact God, then it must surely follow that the boy himself is the Son of God. And indeed this would seem to be confirmed when Voice 3 applies the phrase 'from time immemorial' (IV 300) to both himself and Voice 1 – the implication being that the two persons have existed together *ab initio*, like God the Father and His Son. (Incontrovertibly the *idée fixe* of each of Kafka's filial protagonists, this pseudo-Christological concept of sonship will be developed much more fully by Pinter through the amateur dramatics of Jake and Fred in *Moonlight*.)

The name 'Riley' occurs in two of Pinter's other plays. Firstly, there is the figure of the blind Negro in *The Room*, who indeed is himself something of a paternal proxy: appearing briefly at the end of that play, he tells Rose (or Sal, as he calls her) that her father wants her to come home, and then – in an idiomatic transposition which is very typical of the Old Testament prophets – switches to the first person to proclaim: 'I want you to come home' (I 108). Secondly, there is the mysterious individual mentioned in *Moonlight*: in an ironic allusion to the ascetic regimen of the homonymous homosexual in *Family Voices*, Fred testifies that he himself had once 'lived the life of Riley' (M 50); whereupon Jake points out that the celebrated *bon viveur* who inspired this proverbial phrase was directly descended from a Nephilim-like race of theanthropic heroes (M 50–2).[17]

The inspiration for Pinter's portrait of the big man in *Family Voices* may well have come from *The Trial*. Riley could easily be a composite of two of the more memorable and distinctive characters from Kafka's most famous legal fiction. Firstly, on a physical level, he bears a remarkable resemblance to Hasterer, the prosecuting counsel who appears in one of the novel's unfinished chapters. Like Riley, Hasterer is described as a 'giant of a man' (T 266) with 'great hairy hand[s]' (T 264). Moreover, with respect to Riley's predilection for male company, it is worth noting that Hasterer has an exceptionally intimate friendship with Joseph K.. On their nights out, the pair often link arms and walk each other home (T 265–6). Hasterer even gets rid of the lascivious woman who has been living with him, when she begins to disrupt the time he spends with K.. Secondly, on a philosophical level, Riley has a good deal in common with the prison chaplain who accosts K. during his visit to the cathedral. Like this unnamed priest, Riley personifies the corporate power of the law and the Church; because although he is 'a policeman by trade', his 'deepest disposition is towards religion' (IV 299). While claiming to be 'highly respected' (IV 299) in both legal and ecclesiastical circles, Riley concedes that he is ostracized by the other people in the tenement, who apparently view him with the utmost contempt:

> They don't give a shit for me here. Although I've always been a close relation. Of a sort. I'm a fine tenor but they never invite me to sing. I might as well be living in the middle of the Sahara desert. (IV 299)[18]

The ladies of the house in particular shun him because his refusal to comply with the ordinary conditions of bourgeois domesticity insinuates a slight to their gender. 'There are too many women here, that's the trouble' (IV 299), he complains to the young man. These women, he says, treat him 'like a leper' (IV 299). (In Pinter's work, the word 'leper' would appear to be used specifically to convey the idea of sexual repugnance. The most striking example of this occurs in *The Birthday Party*, when Goldberg enunciates the word twice in quick succession to highlight, respectively, Stanley's alleged aversion to Lulu and his venereal corruption: 'Why do you treat that young lady like a leper? She's not the leper, Webber!' (I 41–2).) Not surprisingly, therefore, Riley shares – and exaggerates – the priest's mistrust of the daughters of Eve. In *The Trial*, the cleric reproaches K. for believing that the Circean troop of female solicitors that he has enlisted will help to advance his cause:

> 'You cast about too much for outside help,' said the priest disapprovingly, 'especially from women. Don't you see that it isn't the right kind of help?' (T 236)

Riley, for his part, has a much more overtly misogynistic temper, as exemplified in his unceremonious dismissal of the two ladies who come to the front door claiming to be the boy's mother and sister. (Ironically, Voice 2 herself acknowledges that women in general are to be blamed for the 'downfall' (IV 302) of her son.)

The chaplain stands apart from the rest of the minions of the Court insofar as he is not a 'petticoat-hunter' (T 236). By taking holy orders, he has deliberately chosen to resign himself to a life of steadfast and unremitting celibacy. Similarly – though in quite a different way – Riley also exempts himself from the Sisyphean struggle for female favours: his pederastic tendencies afford him (un)natural immunity from the allure of the opposite sex. The ultimate goal of both these men is evidently not sexual liberation, but rather liberation from sex. Each seeks to elude the yoke of sexual orthodoxy by yielding instead to the rigour of an authoritarian order. As Kafka himself once observed:

> Man voluntarily limits his own self, surrenders his highest and most real property, his own person, in order to find salvation. By outward restraint he tries to achieve inner freedom. That is the meaning of self-submission to the Law. (CK 169)

The road to freedom, though, is rarely a circuitous route, and this particular method of escape is potentially a merry-go-round of masochistic wish-fulfilment. Certainly, it is a curious kind of freedom which demands that the individual should impose such punishing constraints upon himself. The mortification of the flesh is of course an intrinsic part of sacerdotal existence, and therefore necessarily embodied in the character of the priest. In the case of Riley, however, this idea of chastening the senses is expressed in a bold and frankly perverse diction which dove-tails nicely with his image as a bent copper. Riley's fetishistic obsession with the trappings of bondage is not – as he himself believes – a safeguard against carnal activity: on the contrary, it reeks of pornographic indulgence. Recalling Max's equation of sexual excitement and equestrian prowess in *The Homecoming* (III 18) (which incidentally anticipates the *leitmotiv* of Peter Shaffer's play *Equus*), Riley declares that he must 'keep a tight rein on [his] inclinations' (IV 299). 'My lust', he says, 'is unimaginably violent but it goes against my best interests, which are to keep on the right side of God' (IV 299). For that reason, he has to keep his 'desires shackled in handcuffs and leg-irons' (IV 299). In theory, he should be 'good at that sort of thing' (IV 299), since such devices are, after all, standard equipment for one in his profession. Yet Riley's status as a limb of the law is itself something of a moot point. Admittedly, his cautionary remarks to the two 'imposters' at the front door do mimic the supposed idiom of the typical British bobby: but why does he threaten to 'call a copper' (IV 295) if he is in the force himself? This, coupled with the fact that he hardly ever leaves the house, would seem to suggest that Riley has merely assumed the persona of constable to lend a tawdry glamour to the otherwise drab rites of self-discipline. Voice 1 is perhaps not so far off the mark when he surmises that his sturdy neighbour 'must be a secret policeman' (IV 300).

There are a number of interesting parallels here with the motion picture *Cruising*, which went on general release one year before the first performance of *Family Voices*. The film – which was written and directed by William Friedkin, with whom Pinter had collaborated on the screen version of *The Birthday Party* – focuses on a young police-officer (Al Pacino) who, after a series of sadistic murders in the homosexual *demi-monde* of New York City, agrees, on the promise of swift promotion, to pose as a decoy on the streets and in gay bars. Very soon, however, the protagonist finds himself caught up in a priapic circus, bristling with forbidden pleasures, identity crises and Oedipal terrors. Moustachioed musclemen, clad in black leather and heavy chains, ape the cop, who gradually betrays a lurid fascination for the role which he in turn plays with increasingly ominous conviction, as he begins to lose himself in the mass of squirming bodies. In the course of the investigation, two details emerge about the killer which have a particular relevance to *Family Voices*: firstly, he has been writing letters for ten years to his dead father; secondly, his *modus operandi* involves binding the hands and feet of his victims.

Riley's attempts to hold his libido in check amount to an erotic inversion of the angst by which Kafka was seized during the reception given to celebrate his first engagement to Felice Bauer. A few days after that occasion, the author recorded in his diary how he

> Was tied hand and foot like a criminal. Had they sat me down in a corner bound in real chains, placed policemen in front of me and let me look on simply like that, it could not have been worse. (DII 42)

Kafka and Riley concur in that each relates his feelings of sexual paranoia through symbols of captivity. The difference between the two men is that, in this dungeon of the senses, Riley is the gaoler, whereas Kafka is the prisoner: the former keeps his 'desires shackled in handcuffs and leg-irons', while the latter is himself 'tied hand and foot' because of his desires. However, the fact remains that both men are locked in a prison mentality – albeit on opposite sides of the bars.

What makes the above diary entry so significant is that it contains the seed from which *The Trial* itself would subsequently spring. Indeed, as Elias Canetti has shown, Kafka's account of the arrest of Joseph K. in the opening chapter of the novel is replete with sublimated references to his own infelicitous engagement party.[19] It is of course impossible to say with any degree of certainty whether or not Pinter is deliberately alluding to this seminal text through the *soi-disant* policeman in *Family Voices*. Nevertheless, when the dramatist returned to the subject of the father–son relationship some twelve years later, there can be little doubt that it was *The Trial* which had prompted him to do so.

4

The Final Blasphemy: *Moonlight*

> Be careful how you talk about God. He's the only God we have. If you let him go he won't come back. He won't even look back over his shoulder. And then what will you do? You know what it'll be like, such a vacuum? It'll be like England playing Brazil at Wembley and not a soul in the stadium. Can you imagine? Playing both halves to a totally empty house. The game of the century. Absolute silence. Not a soul watching. Absolute silence. Apart from the referee's whistle and a fair bit of fucking and blinding. If you turn away from God it means that the great and noble game of soccer will fall into permanent oblivion. No score for extra time after extra time after extra time, no score for time everlasting, for time without end. Absence. Stalemate. Paralysis. A world without a winner. (AA 39–41)

In the year which followed the first production of *Family Voices*, Pinter wrote another two short plays – *A Kind of Alaska* and *Victoria Station*. All three of these pieces were subsequently published and performed under the collective title *Other Places* (1982). In retrospect, this title can now be viewed as an ironic signpost; an indication of the fact that the playwright was about to turn his attention elsewhere. In later years, Pinter had become increasingly alarmed at what was happening in other places – places like Chile, South Africa, Turkey, Nicaragua, East Timor, Israel and Nigeria. The dramatist who had long specialized in the representation of domestic intrigues and interior uncertainties was now forced to acknowledge that for most of his professional life he had been 'sleepwalking'[1] – impervious to the systematic cruelty that was being inflicted daily on his fellow human beings around the world. The time had come for him to answer the clarion call and to try to do something about this state of affairs. Frustrated and incensed at the antics of the British political establishment, he became actively involved in a number of liberal and humanitarian pressure groups, including Amnesty International, PEN,

CND and the 20th of June Society.[2] He began to use his position as a public figure to highlight the plight of prisoners of conscience, persecuted writers and their families. He made it his business to speak out against injustice, whether at home or abroad, and set about exposing the hypocrisy of Western governments, championing the spirit of emerging democracies, and opposing censorship, discrimination and intolerance.

Throughout the 1980s and early 1990s, it was clear that Pinter had decided to devote more of his energies to espousing political causes than to writing for the stage. Many were convinced that England's 'best living playwright'[3] had finally abandoned the craft through which he had made his reputation. When he did make the occasional foray into the theatre, it was generally to practise his directorial skills – he took the helm for revivals of classic plays by Jean Giraudoux and Tennessee Williams and for productions of more recent works by Robert East, Simon Gray, Donald Freed and Jane Stanton Hitchcock – yet this only served to highlight his own lack of new material. During an interview in 1990, Pinter rejected as 'absolute nonsense' the suggestion that the curtain might already have descended on his playwrighting career, and, in a self-qualifying assertion worthy of Kafka, added: 'I've got plenty left in me, I think'.[4] However, there was no escaping the fact that the creative fountain of this once extraordinarily prolific dramatist (who at the start of his career had penned seven plays – including *The Birthday Party, The Hothouse* and *The Caretaker* – and ten revue sketches within the space of two years) had latterly been reduced to a spasmodic trickle. Indeed, in the decade which followed *Other Places*, Pinter's gross theatrical product amounted to just three short plays – *One for the Road* (1984), *Mountain Language* (1988) and *Party Time* (1991) – and a couple of dramaticules – *Precisely* (1983) and *The New World Order* (1991). Not surprisingly, the author's more overt political concerns came top of the agenda in every one of them. Written with a combination of moral ferocity and surgical precision, each of these playlets is set in some undisclosed country peopled by mandarins and martinets, torturers and tyrants, and their prisoners and pathics. They describe in stark and sometimes chilling detail the sordid brutalities of everyday life under a totalitarian regime. Nevertheless, if all five of these pieces were to be performed consecutively on the same evening, the entire programme would last for less than two hours.

There was one area of literary activity where Pinter not only maintained but actually managed to increase his output in the 1980s – that of preparing screen adaptations of the work of other writers. It was no coincidence, however, that most of the novels which he agreed to transcribe for the cinema and television during this period should also have been set against some kind of political backdrop. Among these were Margaret Atwood's *The Handmaid's Tale*, which portrays a futuristic police state where fertile women are enslaved and exploited by a fundamentalist elite; Fred Uhlman's *Reunion*, which evokes painful memories of a boyhood friendship marred by the anti-Semitism of the Third Reich; and Elizabeth Bowen's *The Heat of the Day*, which focuses on a conflict of loyalties in wartime Britain, where national security is pitted against an *affaire de coeur*. This pattern was all the more remarkable when we consider that only one of Pinter's previous eleven screen adaptations – namely, *The Quiller Memorandum*, based on a novel by Adam Hall,[5] in which an American secret agent is sent to Berlin to infiltrate a group of neo-Nazis – had involved any obvious political dimension.[6]

When the BBC announced in the summer of 1989 that Pinter had been commissioned to write a screenplay of Kafka's *The Trial*, it seemed that the dramatist had chosen yet again to embark on a project which would reflect his concomitant passions for film and politics. One of the great landmarks of modern fiction, *The Trial* has often been construed as a grim premonition of the totalitarian terrors which would blight the map of Europe for much of the twentieth century. Ironically, however, this view – which has always been more popular among those who have never bothered to read the book or whose memory of it has been distorted by time – was not shared by Pinter, who stressed that he himself did not regard *The Trial* as a particularly political work (CP 88; 136). Part of what attracted him to the idea of doing the adaptation appears to have been a conviction that Kafka's narrative, for all its peculiarities, describes a potentially universal human predicament, and does so moreover with a perpetual sense of urgency. As if to emphasize this, he declared that he simply would not be interested in scripting a film of something like *Darkness at Noon* – Arthur Koestler's famous anti-Stalinist novel, which, on the surface, has some affinities with *The Trial*, yet is, by comparison, far less relevant to us today, because, according to Pinter, 'it's so specifically of its time and place' (CP 88).

Certainly, it is interesting that Pinter's fascination with *The Trial* should have been highlighted at a time when his own work had shown a marked politicization; but what made the proposed adaptation especially significant was that it would bring the playwright back to his literary roots. Pinter had initially discussed the project with the producer Louis Marks in 1982, yet had actually dreamt of making a film of Kafka's novel ever since he read it some thirty-five years earlier.[7] He was seventeen when he first became acquainted with the strange case of Joseph K.. The impact it had upon him could scarcely have been more profound. After scouring the shelves of his local public library, he shut himself away for several weeks and read everything that he could find by Kafka. He reportedly told Marks that it was this experience which had fired his ambition to be a writer.[8] Although technically hearsay, this acknowledgement is manifestly of enormous importance. Pinter had of course previously alluded to the fact that Kafka had made a lasting impression on his work; never before, though, had the nature, source and extent of this influence been so clearly spelt out. By working on a screenplay of *The Trial*, he would have an opportunity to explore again and celebrate the mysteries of this inspirational text. It also meant that he could give proper and permanent testimony to his unique affiliation with the novelist.

The Trial had in fact been filmed before. In 1962, Orson Welles, the vagabond genius of American cinema, had fashioned a tremendously atmospheric but deeply problematic interpretation of the book, starring Kafka-lookalike Anthony Perkins as the hapless Joseph K..[9] Welles, characteristically, had felt no obligation to remain faithful to his source material – any more than he had done in his equally idiosyncratic treatments of works by Shakespeare and Cervantes – and freely tampered not only with the plot, but also with the personality of the protagonist. The contemporary critical response to the film was largely negative. Many commentators thought that it was misconceived, overblown and cluttered with a surfeit of phantasmagoric gimmickry. Pinter evidently shared this opinion. While busy working on his own screenplay, the dramatist indicated, in a public conversation with Mel Gussow at New York's 92nd Street YMCA, that his cinematic vision of the novel bore little resemblance to Welles' 'incoherent' effort (CP 88). He insisted that the new adaptation would be set not in some Expressionistic shadowland of 'spasmodic, half-adjusted lines, images, [and] effects' (CP 89), but rather in the normal everyday world. The main priority for Pinter was 'to tell the story straight'.[10] His intention was to represent the action as 'a hard, taut, objective series of events'.[11] As he explained to Gussow and his audience: 'The nightmare of [Kafka's] world is precisely in its ordinariness. That is what is so frightening and strong' (CP 88).

Having resolved to disregard all extraneous factors, Pinter cut through the jungle of critical theories that over years have twisted themselves like noxious weeds around Kafka's text. He chose instead to concentrate on capturing the essence of the novel – its narrative thrust, ironical timbre, dramatic tension and philosophic truth. The scrupulousness of his methodology is indeed reflected in the finished screenplay, which is, by any standards, a masterpiece of clarity, economy and fidelity. The dramatist had originally intended to direct the movie himself,[12] but, in the event, agreed to hand over the reins to the capable David Jones,[13] who had previously found favour in the eyes of many with his sympathetic renderings of Pinter's screenplays of *Langrishe, Go Down* and *Betrayal*. The production itself was distinguished by an impeccable cast which featured many of Britain's most outstanding thespians, together with the award-winning American actor Jason Robards, who played the part of Dr Huld, the Advocate. The leading role was taken by another American – Kyle MacLachlan, best known for his appearances in two typically bizarre films by David Lynch, *Dune* and *Blue Velvet,* and for his role as FBI agent Dale Cooper in Lynch's cult TV series *Twin Peaks. The Trial* was shot on location in Czechoslovakia, and at Prague's Barrandov Film Studios, during the spring of 1992. The entire script was committed to celluloid, though, with Pinter's acquiescence, a number of scenes were consigned to the cutting-room floor. The film opened in UK cinemas in June 1993. It was subsequently transmitted on BBC television at Christmas of that year. (There are several important issues which could be discussed here: the extraordinary and ubiquitous influence of *The Trial* on Pinter's *oeuvre*; the subtlety and selectiveness of Pinter's adaptation of the novel; the merits and deficiencies of the motion picture itself. Each of these matters clearly warrants detailed and systematic investigation. They are, however, too vast and complex to be accommodated within the fairly strict confines of the present volume.)

Within a few months of the release of the film and the publication of the screenplay, *Moonlight,* Pinter's first full-length play since *Betrayal* (1978), received its world première at the Almeida Theatre in London. What could be more appropriate than for the dramatist to follow up his adaptation of *The Trial* with a play in which he focused yet again on the quintessentially Kafkan theme of the struggle between father and son? Furthermore, given that this play marked the end of something of a fifteen-year hiatus, we are tempted to conclude that the experience of being absorbed once more in 'the book that had inspired him to become a writer'[14] had helped to rekindle Pinter's enthusiasm for writing for the theatre itself. Indeed, only months before he was commissioned to script *The Trial*, the dramatist had in fact confessed that he did not think he could ever write another full-length play for the stage (CP 76).

Moonlight is arguably the most self-referential of all its author's plays. A veritable compilation of Pinter-related preoccupations, this symphonic *multum in parvo* reverberates with a seemingly infinite number of verbal, visual and thematic echoes of many of his other works. Although technically a one-act play (and intended to be performed without an interval), *Moonlight* has a highly complex, even episodic structure. By turns poignant and puzzling, hilarious and haunting, it consists of no less than seventeen unnumbered segments – sharp, irregular and iridescent – which are joined together like the pieces of some elaborate mosaic. As in both *Silence* and *Family Voices*, the action takes place in three quite distinct areas – a spatial configuration which eloquently reflects the strained emotional relations between the various *dramatis personae*:

(1) The first area is a 'well-furnished' bedroom, where Andy, a cantankerous ex-civil servant, lies in the final throes of an unspecified terminal illness. By his side, and ministering to him throughout, sits Bel, his placid and dutiful wife.
(2) The second area is a 'shabby' bedroom (in a different location) which belongs to Fred, the younger of the couple's two sons. Fred – who for much of the play is also confined to bed – is invariably attended by his elder brother, Jake. Both young men are in their late twenties.
(3) The third area is a twilight zone of spirits, dreams and memories which is inhabited by Bridget, the teenage daughter of Andy and Bel. At one point, the parents themselves briefly appear here with her in an eerie and elegiac nocturne. This

area is also the forum for a bewilderingly mundane flashback sequence involving all three children at an earlier stage of their development.[15]

In addition to this disbanded quintet of nuclear family members, there are two other characters – Ralph and Maria. Once very good friends of Andy and Bel, Ralph and Maria each pay a visit to the two boys, and later come together to see the married couple.

Just as in *The Homecoming* Pinter had apparently paid homage to a homonymous prose-piece by Kafka, so in *Moonlight* he sounds a subtle titular tribute to another of the Czech maestro's works. Fittingly, on this occasion, the dramatist's point of reference is *The Trial*, and in particular the harrowing dénouement of the novel, wherein Joseph K. is escorted by two gentlemen across the deserted moonlit streets of the city to the place of his execution. Indeed we find that the word 'moonlight' is repeatedly echoed throughout this famous sequence:

> In complete harmony all three now made their way across a bridge in the moonlight [. . .] (T 252);
>
> The water, glittering and trembling in the moonlight [. . .] (T 252);
>
> The moon shone down on everything with that simplicity and serenity which no other light possesses (T 253);
>
> Then one of them [. . .] drew a long, thin, double-edged butcher's knife, held it up, and tested the cutting edges in the moonlight (T 254).

Incidentally, in the original German text, the author employs two slightly different substantives – *das Mondlicht* and *der Mondschein*; however, English translators (in this case, Willa and Edmund Muir, who were responsible for the definitive English versions of so many of Kafka's works) have been constrained to use 'moonlight' in all instances. Despite its Teutonic etymology, the parallel English noun 'moonshine' is no longer a literal expression, but a colloquial figure of speech (cf. 'sunshine'); and while *The Concise Oxford Dictionary* lists two quite distinct meanings for that word – (1) visionary talk or ideas, (2) illicitly distilled or smuggled alcoholic liquor – neither of them has any relevance to the situation in the final chapter of *The Trial*.

Among the myriad of symbolic connotations that have been

ascribed to the moon since ancient times is one which suggests that the lunar sphere represents a kind of celestial repository for wasted opportunities, broken vows, unanswered prayers and unfulfilled desires. It is singularly appropriate therefore that Pinter, like Kafka, should have chosen the image of the moon to illuminate the wistful thoughts of the protagonist in the face of his impending death.

With his memory fading and his reason failing, the quinquagenarian Andy sits propped up on his bed, like a latter-day Canute trying to turn back the inexorable tide of his own mortality. As he stares out at the bleak and ever-shrinking horizon, his thoughts are awash with the flotsam of a wrecked existence. Temperamental and at times delirious, he rambles on dogmatically about family, friends, work, sex and death. In one of his more philosophical moments, he tries to imagine what eternity might hold for him. He wonders if there will be 'unceasing moonlight with no cloud', or if it will be 'pitch black for ever and ever' (M 46). He himself tends towards the former scenario, not least because the idea of perpetual darkness would seem to suggest that all human life is utterly pointless. In any event, Andy – having apparently taken to heart the advice which Dylan Thomas gave to his moribund father – does not intend to 'go gentle into that good night', but will 'rage against the dying of the light'.[16]

At the start of the play, Andy is preoccupied by the fact that he has heard nothing from his two sons. The estranged and unsettled nature of his relationship with the young men is immediately established by his opening words: 'Where are the boys?' (M 2). Like the bedridden father in *Family Voices*, Andy himself is apparently incapable of – and evidently unpractised at – communicating directly with his sons, and must depend instead upon his wife's continual attempts at interposition. Initially bewildered by the boys' apparent refusal to come to him in his hour of need, he laments abstractedly to himself: 'Two sons. Absent. Indifferent. Their father dying' (M 35). Nevertheless, his attitude quickly changes to one of bitter exasperation as he begins to recall how Jake and Fred had both defied and disappointed him in the past. At the height of his wrath, the old man even goes so far as to repudiate the legitimacy of his sons (just as Max had done in *The Homecoming*): 'They were bastards. Both of them. Always' (M 35). He finally banishes the filial duo from his mind with the fiery conviction that they are nothing but 'A sponging pair of parasitical ponces. Sucking the tit of the state!' (M 36): and this the same State that Andy himself has served so assiduously, by sweating 'over a hot desk all [his] working life' (M 17).

After a long and distinguished career as a government official, Andy would appear to have been forced to take early retirement because of his infirmity. Work has clearly been the corner-stone of his existence. He declares that his aptitude and application were both exemplary; that his working procedures were above reproach; and that, in all his years of service, there was never the slightest suggestion of malfeasance, incompetence or dereliction of duty on his part. As far as Andy is concerned his was not so much a job as a vocation. It is no coincidence therefore that he should employ religious terminology when speaking about his erstwhile occupation. He claims to have been an inspiration to all the young men and women who worked under him, and to have encouraged them to remain diligent and 'keep faith at all costs' (M 17) in the administrative apparatus of the State. Like Max in *The Homecoming*, Andy not only extols the righteousness of work, but also alludes to the sacerdotal aspect of his own particular office. A 'first class civil servant' (M 17) he may well have been, but more than that he was 'an envied and feared force in the temples of the just' (M 17–18). Andy's quasi-ministerial calling is later echoed by Jake and Fred, who claim that the father was known to his colleagues under the 'celebrated' (M 61) – and indeed ecclesiastical – nickname of 'The Incumbent' (M 62).

While he enjoyed the admiration and respect of all those who worked under him, Andy is at pains to emphasize that he was not loved by these fellow workers; nor indeed did he ever want to be loved by them. 'Love', he says, 'is an attribute no civil servant worth his salt would give house room to. It's redundant. An excrescence' (M 17). Within any organized working environment, demonstrations of affection between management and junior staff are actively discouraged, if not explicitly prohibited, on the grounds that such undue sentimentality threatens to undermine discipline, efficiency and productivity. In one of his diary entries, Kafka suggests that the optimum regime for harmonious industrial relations is not an atmosphere of love, but the exact opposite:

> every director is dissatisfied with his employees; the difference between employees and directors is too vast to be bridged by means of mere commands on the part of the director and mere obedience on the

> part of the employees. Only mutual hatred can bridge the gap and give the whole enterprise its perfection. (DII 73)

Notwithstanding his own experience of working within different bureaucratic organizations, Kafka may well have developed this theory after observing the operation of his father's wholesale business. A man of formidable commercial talents, Hermann Kafka was so greatly superior to everyone else who came to work in the business that they could never even begin to satisfy him (WPC 182). Yet, while he despised these employees and frequently referred to them as 'paid enemies' (WPC 181), he was determined to get both the better of them and the best out of them. As a result, he would persistently harass, hector and revile them, to the point that they lived in constant dread of his approach.

Kafka Snr was so completely tied to the business that he scarcely saw his son once a day: when their paths did cross, the impression on the child was all the more profound (WPC 161). Hardened perhaps by the daily cut and thrust of his mercantile concerns, the old man seemed to be virtually incapable of showing tenderness to the boy. What is more, he was deeply cynical about any expression of paternal affection on the part of other men. In a rare moment of intimacy with the lad, he touched upon their signal lack of hearty emotional contact:

> 'I have always been fond of you, even though outwardly I didn't act towards you as other fathers do, and this precisely because I can't pretend as other people can.' (WPC 158)

Clearly, Hermann had found it very difficult to exchange the harsh persona which he wore all day on the shop-floor for a more benign countenance in the evenings at home. By the same token, Andy's asseveration that he wouldn't have given 'house room to' love strongly implies that his much-vaunted air of professional sternness also carried over into his domestic affairs. This confusion of the roles of parent and employer meant that both governors, Hermann and Andy, were wont to regard their sons not as beloved heirlings, but as misbegotten hirelings. Growing up in his father's chancery, the young Franz had been made to feel like 'a defaulting bank-clerk', who, while 'still holding his job', was forever 'trembling at the thought of discovery' (WPC 201). (Incidentally, the flip-side of this metaphorical coin can be glimpsed in 'Prosecuting Counsel', one of the unfinished chapters of *The Trial*, where

Joseph K. – himself a bank-clerk labouring under a judicial Sword of Damocles – who 'had never known a father's care, his own having died very young' (T 270),[17] is subject to the paternal patronage of the Bank Manager.) Similarly, the two sons in *Moonlight* are characterized by Andy as 'Lazy idle layabouts' (M 35) – a triple denunciation of their incorrigible indolence.

In 'Letter to his Father', we are told that Hermann Kafka took great delight in using rude and indecent expressions. He would often trumpet these forth 'in the loudest possible voice' (WPC 176) and then double up with unrestrained laughter, thus ensuring that even a trite little obscenity was savoured as if it were a truly inspired stroke of wit. By the same token, the father in *Moonlight* also has a prodigious and zestful predilection for ribaldry. Andy's Fescennine tendency, which he blithely demonstrates throughout the play, is epitomized by his long-suffering wife:

> all your life in all your personal and social attachments the language you employed was mainly coarse, crude, vacuous, puerile, obscene and brutal to a degree. Most people were ready to vomit after no more than ten minutes in your company. (M 19–20)

Kafka *fils* was himself nauseated at any kind of scurrilous talk. In 1908, he resigned from his position at the Assicurazioni Generali,[18] because, as he explained to the director, he could not stomach the incessant cursing and swearing of those around him (WPC 180–1). Such language seemed to him to have a particularly horrible and corrosive effect on all man's sensibilities: it was, he declared, almost as if one were being exposed to 'some smoking fire which burns one's lungs and eyes' (CK 39).

Oddly enough, Kafka could never recall being lambasted directly by his father in downright offensive terms: yet it was not really necessary for the son to be singled out in such a way; because, whether at home or at the family business, he still had to breathe in the air that had been sulphurated by the old man's maledictory broadsides:

> the words of abuse went flying around me in such swarms, as they were flung at other people's heads, that as a little boy I was sometimes almost stunned and had no reason not to apply them to myself too, for the people you were abusing were certainly no worse than I was and you were certainly not more displeased with them than with me. (WPC 171)

But whereas Hermann Kafka had been apt to throw vitriol with indiscriminate abandon, Andy prides himself on having been more circumspect in his use of unparliamentary language: 'I would never use obscene language in the office. Certainly not. I kept my obscene language for the home, where it belongs' (M 18). The link here between an off-duty civil servant and Limehousing has its origin in *The Castle*, where many of the bureaucrats are reputed to employ foul language outside office hours. This phenomenon would appear to be a peculiar consequence of the tremendous dedication that such men show towards their work: since it is reported that whenever the officials rise from their desks, they find it so difficult to adjust to the circumstances of the ordinary world that, in their derangement, they are liable to 'say the most beastly things' (C 239). (The antithesis of this protocol is perhaps to be found in the conversation of the real estate agents in David Mamet's *Glengarry Glen Ross* – a play which is incidentally dedicated to Pinter.) The high and mighty Klamm, for example, is 'notorious for his rudeness' (C 239); indeed people have been known to shiver at the sheer brutality of his outbursts: and then there is Sortini, an even more elusive official, who once propositioned the virginal Amalia in a letter which 'was couched in the vilest language' (C 235).

Paradoxically, even though Hermann Kafka himself 'cursed and swore without the slightest scruple', he would not tolerate and indeed roundly condemned anyone else who used such language (WPC 171). Here, as in all such matters, it seemed to Franz as if his father had about him an aura of 'enigmatic innocence and inviolability' (WPC 171). Similarly, in *Moonlight*, Bel marvels at the fact that Andy, for all his lewd and lunatic invective, has somehow still managed to retain 'a delicate even poetic sensibility' (M 20).

The paternal characters in both *Family Voices* and *The Homecoming* are also distinguished by a propensity for using profane language. According to the mother in *Family Voices*, her husband 'cursed everyone in sight' (IV 293) as he lay on his deathbed. Correspondingly, when *The Homecoming* opened in 1965, the salty vernacular of the *paterfamilias* had pushed at the very boundaries of what was permissible on the contemporary English stage. Times change, however; and when the play was revived a quarter of a century later, it was deemed necessary to modify the line in which Max tells his brother to 'flake off' (III 27), by replacing that expedient but euphemistic phrase with the uncompromising *mot juste* – 'fuck off'.[19] (Incidentally, it was particularly appropriate that the part of this more foul-mouthed Max should have been played by Warren Mitchell, who, as Alf Garnett (another cockney patriarch) in the hugely successful BBC TV comedy series *Till Death Us Do Part*,[20] had enjoyed a popular, if somewhat exaggerated, notoriety for turning the airwaves blue throughout the late 1960s and early 1970s.)

Back in 1966, Pinter had voiced his misgivings about what he saw as the 'scheme afoot on the part of many 'liberal-minded' persons to open up obscene language to general commerce'.[21] Four-letter words, in his opinion, were the basis of 'the dark secret language of the underworld', and therefore had to be 'used very sparingly' if they were to retain their power.[22] Nevertheless, in the later, more polemical phase of his career, the dramatist has generally ignored his own maxim and permitted his characters to rattle off these 'great, wonderful words'[23] in fusillades of ordure. It is worth noting that the half-dozen or so plays which immediately precede *Moonlight* in the Pinter canon are also those which feature his most extensive and egregious use of bad language. The fact that each of these pieces – *Victoria Station*, *Precisely*, *One for the Road*, *Mountain Language*, *The New World Order* and *Party Time*[24] – is essentially a nightmarish evocation of paternalistic domination can surely be no coincidence. What is more, of Pinter's earlier plays (and we are of course talking mainly about those written after 1968, when the Lord Chamberlain – that long-standing moral watchdog of the British theatre – finally hung up his censorial scissors[25]), only *No Man's Land* contains a comparable amount of verbal shock tactics, and it too is concerned with the peculiarly masculine politics of power. Thus, no taboo is left unbroken, as a bastard brotherhood of aggressive and overbearing male characters (Foster, Briggs, the Controller, Nicolas, the Sergeant, Lionel, Des, Terry) spit out every conceivable obscenity in their efforts to threaten, torment and humiliate. Indeed swearing is almost exclusively the preserve of the menfolk in Pinter's *oeuvre*. While it is true that Emma in *Betrayal* and the young woman who gives her name as Sara Johnson in *Mountain Language* both utter that most unladylike F-word (albeit in its proper sense) (IV 201; 411), and Charlotte in *Party Time* admits that her language has always been 'Appalling' (PT 27), these are very much the exceptions that prove the rule.[26] And the rule is that in the grammar of Pinter's dramatic language, the gender of all swear-words is invariably masculine.

During one of his conversations with Gustav Janouch, Kafka remarked: 'Swearing destroys man's greatest invention – language. It is an insult to the soul and a murderous offence against grace' (CK 39). In a later exchange, he warned that 'language destroyers' were liable to usher in 'a darkening of the world, a breath of the ice age' (CK 56). The destruction of language is of course the central theme of *Mountain Language*,[27] and indeed Pinter's portrayal of the linguistic vandals in that play may perhaps owe something to these comments by Kafka. The use of foul and abusive language on the part of those who seek to suppress the mountain dialect is certainly a very powerful and effective metaphor for the barbarity of their activities: the idiom of the military authorities is crude, harsh, full of sarcasm and peppered with obscenities; while that of the mountain people – as suggested through several deeply poignant voice-overs – is tender, compassionate and lyrical. If the same figurative logic is applied to the situation in *Moonlight*, then Andy's inveterate fondness for billingsgate could be said to have had a demonstrably deleterious impact on the conversation of his sons; since so much of what Jake and Fred say to one another is devoid of any received meaning. On the other hand, it should be noted that the young men are by no means averse to using the odd swear-word themselves. There are two possible reasons for this apparently un-Kafkaesque circumstance: firstly, like Sara Johnson, Jake and Fred may have decided that in order to survive they must speak in the tongue of the tyrant; secondly, like Lenny in *The Homecoming*, they may be deliberately parodying the (not-so-)niceties of their father's speech.

* * *

Bel is several years younger than her ailing husband. She remains by Andy's side throughout, tending to his every need. She does her best to ensure that he is physically comfortable, oversees his dietary requirements, tries to provide him with a degree of psychological reassurance, and even seeks to engender in him some hope of spiritual consolation. Impeccable in her bedside manner, she also attempts to humour Andy by sparring with him in feisty bouts of mordant banter. Bel appears not to mind being the butt of her husband's often vicious jokes, but strongly disapproves of his penchant for obscene language. Still, she manages to maintain an attitude of gracious tolerance even at the height of his Rabelaisian ravings. We are reminded here of Beth's solipsistic tranquillity in the face of Duff's provocative outpourings in *Landscape*.

In terms of temperament, Bel is as much a contrast to Andy as Kafka's mother had been to his father. Like Hermann Kafka, Andy is loud, brash, domineering, sardonic and volatile; while Bel, like Julie Kafka, is quiet, modest, sensible, scrupulous and stoical. The wife in *Moonlight*, moreover, has followed the example of Frau Kafka, who, despite being unequally yoked, 'always kept her independence, within the narrowest limits, delicately and beautifully, and without ever essentially hurting' her husband (WPC 183).

Bel's patient and genteel disposition is perfectly exemplified by the fact that she spends most of her time doing embroidery; an exercise which, like Penelope's web, seems to be always in hand but never ending. According to Homeric legend, Penelope, the wife of Odysseus and herself a paragon of domestic virtues, was pestered by various suitors while her husband was away at the seige of Troy. She contrived to keep these admirers at bay by declaring that she would only choose between them after she had finished weaving a shroud for her father-in-law. Every night, though, she would unravel the work she had done during the day, thus ensuring that her task would never be completed, and that the moment of decision would be postponed *ad infinitum*. Twenty years passed before Odysseus returned home, whereupon the importunate suitors were swiftly and sanguinarily dispatched. The parallel between *Moonlight* and this episode from Greek mythology is effectively confirmed when Andy, fascinated by Bel's interminable needlework, inquires:

> Oh, I've been meaning to ask you, what are you making there? A winding sheet? Are you going to wrap me up in it when I conk out? You'd better get a move on. I'm going fast. (M 34)

Yet there is also a common thread here with 'The Metamorphosis'. Because of the financial difficulties brought on by Gregor's transformation, Mrs Samsa is obliged to work from home as a seamstress for an underwear firm. In the evenings, Mr Samsa, like Andy, is intrigued as he watches his wife's incessant and assiduous stitching; and though wont to fall asleep in his armchair, he wakes up every so often and exclaims, 'What a lot of sewing you're doing today!' (CSS 123), before nodding off again.

In 'Letter to his Father', Kafka records that while Hermann had sometimes accused his wife of spoiling their children, this 'spoiling' was really no more than 'a quiet, unconscious counter-demonstration' against her husband's implacable disciplinarianism (WPC 184). Nevertheless, the novelist was prepared to acknowledge that even if it had been possible for his father's method of upbringing to produce in him some vestige of rebellious indignation, which in time might actually have prompted him to stand on his own feet, this would almost certainly have been cancelled out by his mother, who was always ready to make kind-hearted intercessions and underhanded concessions:

> [. . .] Mother merely shielded me from you in secret, secretly gave me something, or allowed me to do something, and then where you were concerned I was again the furtive creature, the cheat, the guilty one, who in his worthlessness could only pursue backstairs methods even to get things he regarded as his right. (WPC 177)

Correspondingly, in *Moonlight*, Andy suspects that Bel has been encouraging Jake and Fred in their waywardness and sloth by feeding them 'a few weekly rupees from [her] little money-box' (M 36). (The choice of currency here has a haughty significance; because the father not only addresses his consort with the imperious air of a governor during the British raj, but also implicitly brands the young men as untouchables.) Like the late lamented Jessie in *The Homecoming*, who ostensibly taught her sons 'Every single bit of the moral code they live by' (III 54), Bel is deemed solely responsible for the ethical outlook of the two boys. There is an interesting parallel here with Ibsen's *A Doll's House*, in which Torvald Helmer worries Nora, his furtively self-sacrificing wife, with the assertion that in nearly all cases of juvenile deliquency it is the mother who is to blame.[28] This idea appears with a vengeance in Pinter's political plays. In *One for the Road*, for example, Nicolas tells the tortured Gila that it is her fault that her son is 'a little prick' (IV 392); and in *Party Time*, it is even suggested that the chemical composition of a mother's milk is such that it can actually nurture perversion in her offspring (PT 25). By the same token, Andy's contempt for maternalistic indulgences is bitingly expressed in a Thatcherite caricature of the social security system as a monstrous mamma on which the likes of Jake and Fred greedily suck (M 36).

In what amounts to a kind of prequel to the extant correspondence of the mother in *Family Voices*, the maternal figure in *Moonlight* is actively seeking to mediate between her moribund husband and his errant sons. It appears that Bel has 'been trying for weeks' (M 2) to get in touch with the young men to let them know about their father's condition. She wryly acknowledges her lack of success, and attributes this to her own 'ineptitude' (M 3). Notwithstanding Andy's aspersions about her surreptitious supply of sops to the boys, Bel seems to be less fondly remembered by her sons than Voice 2 had been by the lad in *Family Voices.* We may recall that Voice 1, despite being lavished with the affections of Mrs Withers, was keen to emphasize that he had not forgotten that he still had a mother, and even went so far as to declare that she was 'the best mother in the world' (IV 292). What is more, whereas Voice 1 had spent the entire play intent on communicating with his mother, Jake and Fred, for all Bel's tireless efforts to contact them, are not inclined to reciprocate. (It is worth noting, however, that Fred – who implies that he is not descended from the same parents as his brother – does ask rather pointedly about Jake's mother on two separate occasions: in the first instance, Jake completely ignores the question (M 9); in the second, he angrily tells Fred not to 'talk dirty' (M 62) to him – a response which, by its startling inappropriateness, would appear to indicate a deep-seated sense of Oedipal anxiety.)

In the previous chapter, we saw how Kafka had described letter-writing – the mode of communication favoured by the characters in *Family Voices* – as 'an intercourse with ghosts' (MIL 229). Still, the fact that Bel prefers to use the telephone in her attempts to contact her sons would at least seem to hold out the prospect of greater immediacy. (After all, the very sound of the telephone ringing represents an insistent appeal to the young men in their mother's name.[29]) However, according to Kafka, the telephone – an obvious successor to the postal service – was itself invented by the same ever-hungry ghosts to ensure that they would not starve in an age when humanity, as it approached 'the moment of crashing', was desperately struggling to eliminate 'the ghostly element between people and to create a natural communication, the peace of souls', through such inventions as the railway, the motor car and the aeroplane (MIL 229). It is therefore not surprising that virtually all of the telephones in Kafka's fiction should appear to have been designed not to facilitate communication, but to frustrate it. A quick survey of the three novels will serve to illustrate this point.

When Karl Rossmann visits the nerve-centre of his Uncle Jacob's business empire in *America*, he learns that while telephonic communication is absolutely essential for such a mammoth commercial enterprise, it is also inherently unreliable. By way of precaution, the company has had to implement an elaborate screening procedure, whereby every telephone conversation is written down simultaneously by three separate operators: the different versions of the transcript are then compared to eliminate any mistakes (A 58). Later, in the porter's office of the Hotel Occidental, Karl discovers a bank of ultra-modern telephones which are so preposterously powerful that a person only has to whisper softly into the mouthpiece and the sound, transmitted like lightning to its destination, is amplified to such an extent that it becomes a deafening roar (A 211).

The telephone is featured sporadically throughout *The Trial*: during his arrest, Joseph K. is discouraged from making a 'senseless' phone call to Hasterer (T 20); he is later informed by telephone about the place and day (but unfortunately not the time) of his first interrogation; he also receives a phone call from Leni; however, having decided to dispense with the services of the Advocate, he feels that it would be more expedient to deliver this news in person, rather than risk the uncertainty of doing so over the telephone. Curiously, though, the motif of telephony is given much greater prominence in both the action and the dialogue of Pinter's screenplay of the novel. Indeed the dramatist actually goes so far as to devise several new scenes in which the telephone is the centre-piece. Moreover, the Joseph K. of the film version seems to be obsessed with the fact that there are never any telephone messages for him. It may well be that Pinter has decided to incorporate an allusion here to Kafka's other K. – the Land Surveyor in *The Castle*, who for a time feels as if he is 'at the mercy of the telephone' (C 33). (Incidentally, in the course of an abortive telephone conversation with someone up at the Castle, K. actually claims that his name is Joseph (C 34).) The Land Surveyor is initially convinced that the telephone at the Bridge Inn represents his best hope of securing some kind of official recognition from the Castle authorities. Before long, however, he begins to have serious doubts about the value of the telephone conversations concerning him and these doubts are confirmed during his visit to the Village Superintendent. The Superintendent is quick to point out that he himself would not give a telephone house-room: as far as he is concerned, the device is about as much use 'as a penny-in-the-slot musical instrument' (C 95). Although the telephones in the village are continually humming and singing, these sounds belie the fact that there is no fixed connection with the Castle, no central exchange to transmit the calls any further than the various subordinate departments. What is more, whenever someone from the village calls up the Castle, even the phones in the subordinate departments hardly ever ring, since the receivers are almost always left off the hook. On those very rare occasions when a telephone not only rings but is in fact answered, the reply is sure to be no more than a practical joke. Certainly, it would be foolish to assume that the person to whom one is speaking is actually who they claim to be. Even if the respondent were to claim to be a high-ranking official, it is much more likely that he is just some little copying clerk who has replaced the receiver out of sheer boredom and decided to amuse himself at the expense of the caller. At the same time, though, one can never entirely rule out the possibility – albeit a very remote one – that the speaker might indeed be the said high-ranking official.

Few telephones are to be found in Pinter's work for the theatre. The two most conspicuous examples occur in *The Collection* and *Tea Party*: both are striking because of their very perversity. In *The Collection*, a dimly-lit figure in a telephone kiosk makes a number of anonymous calls to Bill and Harry. This unidentified caller would seem to be James, who has presumably been trying to locate and disconcert Bill, the alleged violator of his wife, before confronting him in person. Later, Harry employs the same tactic on Stella, Bill's ostensible victim. An even more wanton use of the telephone occurs in *Tea Party*, where the apparatus in Disson's office becomes a fetishistic aid to erotic displacement. As a prelude to intimacy, Disson asks Wendy, his alluring secretary, first to bind his eyes with her chiffon scarf, and then to make a phone call to Newcastle. Now that she is unseen and otherwise engaged, he can bring himself to touch her – but only so long as she is actually speaking on the phone to a third party (III 117–18). Elsewhere in Pinter's *oeuvre*, a whole range of other quasi-telephonic gadgets bear witness to the treachery of communication technology. Into this category fall such gremlin-ridden devices as the speaking-tube in *The Dumb Waiter*, the various microphones, earphones and loudspeakers in *The Hothouse*, the intercom systems in *Tea Party* and *The Hothouse*, and the radio transceivers in *Victoria Station*. (Mention should also be made of 'Problem', a short story written in 1976, which concerns a telephone that suddenly begins to malfunction, causing the first-person narrator to fear that his life is in imminent danger.[30]) A notable exception to this pattern is the internal telephone used by the guard in *Mountain Language*. This instrument would appear to work quite normally. Still, there is presumably no need for ghosts in the machine, when other, more substantial forces are hell-bent on destroying human communication.

The problems that Bel comes up against in *Moonlight* are remarkably similar to those which had so bedevilled telephone communication with the Castle. On two occasions, we hear a telephone ringing in Fred's room. In the first instance, the telephone rings six times before the sounding of a mysterious click (M 48). In the second instance, we see Bel dialing a number on her telephone, after which its tintinnabulary counterpart is answered by Jake; though he and Fred wilfully ignore their mother's message about their father's illness, and pretend to be employees in a Chinese laundry (M 72–4).

Notwithstanding the fact that Kafka himself had once claimed to be Chinese (FEL 468), there is a rather intriguing connection here with the title of Josef von Sternberg's autobiography – *Fun in a Chinese Laundry*. A cinematic magician of light and shadow, von Sternberg was perhaps the greatest pictorial stylist ever to work within the Hollywood system. He is now chiefly remembered as the man who was responsible for creating and shaping the screen persona of Marlene Dietrich. She appeared for him as the archetypal *femme fatale* in a dazzling septet of exotic celluloid adventures, including *The Blue Angel*, *Shanghai Express*, *The Scarlet Empress* and *The Devil is a Woman*. The last of these was released in 1935, after which the *auteur* and his star parted company on rather less than amicable terms. But while Dietrich's career remained buoyant, von Sternberg's quickly took a nosedive and never recovered. Thirty years later, when he came to write his memoirs, the legendary Svengali, disgruntled that his own achievement had been eclipsed by the enduring popularity of his former protégée, could scarcely even bring himself to mention the 'incidental by-product'[31] by name. Von Sternberg's disavowal of the woman he once idolized is mirrored in the behaviour of the two sons in *Moonlight*, whose idea of fun in a Chinese laundry involves pretending that their own mother is a complete stranger.

In *The Castle*, the Village Superintendent, despite his lack of confidence in the telephone system, warns K. that even the most dubious reply to a telephone call can still be of very great significance (C 96). This would certainly seem to be the case with the 'Chinese laundry' charade in *Moonlight*. If we examine the two elements of this phrase, we find that the adjective 'Chinese' effectively underlines the sons' remoteness and estrangement from their parents, while the noun 'laundry' appears to represent an ironic attempt by the sons to persuade their mother of the cleanliness of their lifestyle.

Pinter first mooted the idea of a son needing to convince his mother of his cleanliness in *A Night Out*, where Mrs Stokes had admonished Albert not to dishonour the memory of his father by 'leading an unclean life' (I 335). Mindful of this injunction, Albert's opposite number in *Family Voices* is at pains to emphasize to his mother that the tenement-house in which he resides has a superb and extremely pleasant bathroom, where he and the other denizens enjoy the most 'lovely' ablutions – 'more or less unparalleled, to put it, bluntly' (IV 287). (She in turn tries to stave off fears of the boy's corruption by immersing herself in ecstatic memories of how she used to wash his hair (IV 296).) The theory seems to be that if the son can convince the mother of his cleanliness, then she, in her role as mediatrix, will communicate this fact to the reproachful father. Thereafter, it is hoped that whenever the patriarch begins to focus on the dirtiness of the son, he will be appeased somewhat by the assurances of his spouse. In time, as a corollary, it may even transpire that whenever the father's thoughts turn fondly to the mother, he will remember only the cleanliness of their son. This apparently is what happens in *The Homecoming*, where Max, during an unctuous panegyric about his dead wife, is prompted to recall how much he enjoyed giving each of his youngsters a bath: 'What fun we used to have in the bath, eh, boys?' (III 54). In *Moonlight*, however, the soft-soap approach succeeds only in working the old man up into a lather: thus when Bel mentions how the two lads had regularly helped her with the washing-up, Andy foamingly retorts that they were parasitical little bastards, and reminds her how Jake had once reacted with 'defiance' (M 36) when told to clean out the 'bloody filthy' (M 35) broom cupboard.

* * *

Before we come to look at the roles of Jake and Fred in detail, let us pause briefly to consider the three remaining characters in *Moonlight*: namely, Bridget, Maria and Ralph.

In addition to their two sons, Andy and Bel have (or rather had) a daughter called Bridget. She appears five times in the play. Each of her appearances is distinguished by an air of otherworldliness. In the list of *dramatis personae*, Bridget is described as 'a girl of sixteen'. However, in the flashback sequence, which – going by the relative ages of Jake and Fred – takes place ten years prior to the main action, we are told that she is already fourteen. The most logical explanation is that Bridget must have passed away some two years after this episode; that is to say, she has been dead for eight years before the start of the play. Yet since the fact of her death is too painful for the other characters to acknowledge, its circumstances – which were undoubtedly tragic – remain a complete mystery. While confirming that the wench is dead, Pinter has insisted that he himself does not know what happened to her (CP 106). Still, like Deborah in *A Kind of Alaska*, whose development was similarly (if not quite so finally) arrested, Bridget has been frozen in a limbo of perpetual adolescence.

Pinter has said that he regards Bridget as 'the crux of the play, because she informs everything' (CP 99). The pivotal position of the daughter would seem to be reflected in her unique association with the title. Not only does the play open and close with Bridget soliloquizing about the moon, but in the interim she also appears to her parents as a sylph-like creature bathed in lunar light. It is all the more appropriate therefore that her name – which is of Gaelic derivation – should mean 'shining bright'.[32]

Bridget claims that her father and mother, having devoted all their life, love and energies to their children, are now utterly exhausted. She sees herself as a kind of guardian angel, who has been specially commissioned to ensure that her parents sleep peacefully and wake up refreshed and reinvigorated: 'I must see that this happens. It is my task. Because I know that when they look at me they see that I am all they have left of their life' (M 1). This last remark is strangely reminiscent of the closing section of 'The Metamorphosis'. In the aftermath of Gregor's demise, the surviving members of the Samsa family, having taken the day off work, decide to travel by tram into the open countryside. In the course of this trip, Mr and Mrs Samsa are struck almost simultaneously by the fact that Grete, 'in spite of all the sorrow of recent times', has now 'bloomed into a pretty girl with a good figure' (CSS 139) and thus become the very personification of all their hopes for the future:

> And it was like a confirmation of their new dreams and excellent intentions that at the end of their journey their daughter sprang to her feet and stretched her young body. (CSS 139)

The fact that Bridget is dead and Grete very much alive eloquently accounts for the stark contrast in the prospects of their respective parents. Nonetheless, the two girls are, in Kipling's famous phrase, 'sisters under their skins'.[33] Although the youngest members of their separate families, Bridget and Grete feel similarly obliged to keep a watchful eye on their parents after their brothers demonstrate a total lack of filial responsibility. (Incidentally, there is evidence to suggest that Millie, the silent daughter in *Family Voices,* had been equally anxious about the welfare of her folks in the wake of her brother deserting his post (IV 293–4).) At the same time, both girls also appear to have an extraordinary emotional affinity with these self-centred male siblings. Just as Gregor had found Grete to be the person who was most sympathetic to him in his torpid condition, so Fred is convinced that Bridget would likewise understand his desire to stay in bed better than anyone else (M 53). Given her kind and helpful nature, it is only appropriate that Bridget should once have had an ambition to become a physiotherapist. As far as Fred was concerned, his sister would have made a 'wonderful' physiotherapist (M 32); even if he did joke that she would have had 'to play very soothing music so that her patients [wouldn't] notice their suffering' (M 31). We may recall that Grete's violin-playing had had a similarly soothing effect on the entomic invalid in 'The Metamorphosis'.

Pinter has indicated that the character of Bridget was inspired in part by Hirst's speech about the photograph album in *No Man's Land* (CP 98–9). As he meditates on the cryogenic faces of the forgotten and the departed, Hirst recommends that a person should always be willing to receive 'the love of a good ghost' (IV 141):

> They possess all that emotion . . . trapped. Bow to it. It will assuredly never release them, but who knows . . . what relief . . . it may give to them . . . who knows how they may quicken . . . in their chains, in

> their glass jars. You think it cruel . . . to quicken them, when they are fixed, imprisoned? No . . no. Deeply, deeply, they wish to respond to your touch, to your look, and when you smile, their joy . . . is unbounded. And so I say to you, tender the dead, as you would yourself be tendered, now, in what you would describe as your life. (IV 141)

In *Moonlight*, Bridget, who is 'much missed by all her family' (CP 99), exemplifies this perception of the dead as solicitous spirits who wait upon and watch over their loved ones in the land of the living. Andy in particular – no doubt because he himself is encamped in the valley of the shadow of death – has a very real sense of his daughter's presence in his life. 'But', as Pinter says, 'he can't define her. He can't hold her' (CP 124).

Whenever the father speaks of Bridget, he does so with a nostalgic tenderness which contrasts sharply with his attitude to his two sons. Andy remembers how he used to sing to the little girl and cuddle her, and how she would fall asleep in his arms (M 45). In his delirium, the old man seems to have blotted out the loss of his daughter – we are reminded here of Lear's anguished attempts to wish the dead Cordelia back to life[34] – and even imagines that she has borne him 'three beautiful grandchildren' (M 71). He continually yearns for her to bring these 'poor little tiny totlets' to his bedside, so that they might 'catch their last look of' their grandad and receive his blessing (M 45). (It is interesting that Max in *The Homecoming* should also have had three never-to-be-seen grandchildren.)

We first encounter Maria and her husband Ralph during their separate visits to Fred's bedroom, whereupon each of them delivers a long and splendidly baroque monologue about bygone days. Towards the end of the play, these secondary spouses accompany each other on a visit to the abode of Andy and Bel. On each of these occasions, Maria and Ralph (whether alone or together) appear suddenly, as if out of thin air, and start talking to the other characters. This would seem to suggest that the couple are actually spirits from the past – or, to borrow a phrase from Kafka, 'a memory come alive' (DII 193) – summoned both to witness the passing of Andy, in whose life they evidently played an important part, and to remind the errant sons of the parents on whom they have turned their backs.

Ralph and Maria are like euphoric *doppelgängers* of Andy and Bel. The two couples – who are identical in terms of age – have not seen each other for more than a decade. They were obviously very good friends at one time, but have completely lost touch in the intervening years. (If we are to believe Andy's Milesian tales of lust, lesbianism and adultery, these boon companions were all involved in a kind of eternal quadrangle. This is corroborated to some extent by Bel, who claims that Maria had been Andy's mistress (M 20) and declares that she herself had loved Ralph and should have married him instead (M 66).) In the course of their visit to Andy's bedroom, Ralph and Maria describe how they have been leading an idyllic life in the country, where they have taken possession of quite a large cottage – 'Not exactly a chateau' (M 69) – beside a small lake. Theirs is a world of cosy complacency and catalogue kitsch – a Laura Ashley evocation of domestic bliss, from which all reminders of suffering and death have been fastidiously eliminated. It is perhaps not surprising therefore that the couple should be so conspicuously disinclined to recognize the harsh reality of Andy's terminal illness. They spout Panglossian platitudes with an air of whimsical alacrity, yet display precious little empathy for either the patient or his nurse. Theirs is just a courtesy call. They are not directly involved in this private tragedy.

It just so happens that the marriage of Maria and Ralph has also resulted in the procreation of three children; the gender ratio (a boy and two girls) being the reverse of that which applies to Andy and Bel's progeny. Furthermore, the praenomens of Ralph and Maria's offspring – Lucien, Sarah and Susannah – effectively mirror those of the youngsters featured in the play. The boy's name (like Bridget) is associated with the idea of light, while those of the two girls (like Jake and Fred) have a connection with characters from the Old Testament. According to Maria, all three of her lot are 'in terribly good form' (M 16) and enjoying tremendous success in their chosen careers. They are, it seems, a real credit to their parents, and take after them both in a perfectly balanced way (M 68–9). The fact that there is so much here for Maria and Ralph to boast about reflects badly upon the fractured state of the play's nuclear family. Moreover, on the basis of their remarks to Jake and Fred, the couple would seem to have been called upon to act as the boys' airy godparents. It is rather fitting therefore that Maria should share her name with the Blessed Virgin, because, despite her record-breaking feats of fornication (M 38–9), she too is something of a maternal mediatrix. Correlatively, Ralph, by virtue of his experience as a football referee, serves as a vicegerent of divine – which is to say, fatherly –

authority: since, as Andy himself explains, the referee not only represents 'the law in action', but is also responsible for 'the articulation of God's justice' (M 68).

* * *

Like the young man in *Family Voices*, Jake and Fred are living in self-imposed exile from their parents. Moreover, despite the persistent efforts of their mother to get in touch with them, the two boys are evidently determined to remain incommunicado and perdu. Both in their late twenties, the brothers would appear to have failed to emulate the professional and personal achievements of their father. Neither of the sons seems to be gainfully employed, let alone in a prestigious position; nor it seems has either of them managed to get married or to become a father himself.

Curiously complementary and apparently inseparable, Jake and Fred follow in the wake of a whole procession of other male double-acts who have trod the boards of Pinter's theatre: the classic examples being Goldberg and McCann in *The Birthday Party*, Ben and Gus in *The Dumb Waiter*, Briggs and Foster in *No Man's Land*, and Des and Lionel in *The New World Order*. This binary pattern may remind us of the Beckettian motif of the 'pseudocouple',[35] as exemplified by such dubious duos as Vladmir and Estragon in *Waiting for Godot*, Pozzo and Lucky in the same play, Hamm and Clov in *Endgame*, and the eponymous anti-heros of *Mercier and Camier*. Nevertheless, it is worth nothing that there are perhaps just as many examples of male pairs in the work of Kafka. If we cast a cursory eye over Kafka's novels, for instance, we cannot fail to be struck by the semi-detached duality of such characters as Franz and Willem in *The Trial*, the nameless executioners in the same novel, Arthur and Jeremiah in *The Castle*, and Robinson and Delmarche in *America*.

Given the fact that all of the scenes involving Jake and Fred – with the exception of the flashback sequence – take place in the latter's 'shabby' bedroom, a parallel can also be drawn between *Moonlight* and *The Caretaker*, which likewise features two brothers and is set entirely in a dingy bedroom – albeit a makeshift one. In both these plays, moreover, one half of the fraternal dyad is suffering from a somewhat questionable health problem. Aston, the elder brother in *The Caretaker*, describes how as a teenager he had experienced symptoms which were apparently diagnosed as being consistent with delusional insanity: thanks to the tender mercies of quack psychiatry, he has long since been cured of his gentle 'hallucinations' (II 52), but is now severely traumatized by his memories of receiving electroconvulsive therapy. Aston's 'complaint' (II 53) is mirrored to some extent by the uncertified medical condition of the intermittently bedridden Fred in *Moonlight*.[36] Another issue which is common, if not central, to both *The Caretaker* and *Moonlight* is that of fraternal communication. Aston – who allegedly 'talked too much' (II 52) until he was subjected to ECT – and Mick, his spivish and rather sinister cognate, tend to relate to each other through an unusual, though not unsympathetic, code of silence. By total contrast, Jake and Fred give the impression of being engaged in a fast and furious game of verbal ping-pong. Their exchanges crackle with the sporty rhythm of stichomythia, and consist largely of riddles, puns and *non sequiturs*.

Jake and Fred appear seven times in the play. Two of these appearances – the flashback and the 'Chinese laundry' sequence – revolve around a conversation between the fraternal pair and a third party. In their five remaining scenes, the brothers appear alone together on the stage. (Although two of these duologues are curtailed by the apostrophic interventions of Maria and Ralph, respectively.) It is in this pentad of episodes that we see Jake and Fred trying to free themselves from the all-pervasive influence of their father. The two boys, having grown up under the shadow of a man who persisted in portraying himself as the infallible embodiment of temporal and spiritual authority, conspire to bring about a separation of these paternal powers, and thereby explode the mythical basis of Andy's supremacy. This iconoclastic revolt is prosecuted through a highly elaborate game of charades, in which the young men alternately assume the personae of biblical and bureaucratic protagonists. The brothers' contribution to the action of *Moonlight* may be summarized thus:

(1) First biblical charade (interrupted by Maria) (M 6–15);
(2) First bureaucratic charade (interrupted by Ralph) (M 23–7);
(3) Conversation with Bridget (flashback) (M 29–33);
(4) Second bureaucratic charade (M 41–4);
(5) Second biblical charade (M 49–62);
(6) Telephone conversation with Bel ('Chinese laundry') (M 73–5);
(7) Third bureaucratic charade (M 77–9).

In the sections which follow, I shall offer a detailed exposition of both the meaning and the mechanics of the different charades played by Jake and Fred. For the sake of simplicity, I shall begin with the bureaucratic cycle.

* * *

By way of response to Andy's insistent remarks about their inveterate laziness, Jake and Fred not only pretend to be in regular employment, but also purport to be following in their father's footsteps – something that none of the sons in *The Homecoming* had managed to do – and working for the Civil Service. The result is a crazy triptych of bogusly bureaucratic routines, wherein the two brothers roguishly burlesque the job to which the old man had devoted the best years of his life.

Jake and Fred may well be taking a leaf here out of one of Kafka's books. The novelist himself knew a great deal about bureaucracy. After all, he too had 'sweated over a hot desk' (M 17) for most of his working life. Having previously been employed in the legal business and then in the Prague offices of an Italian insurance company (Assicurazioni Generali), Kafka was recruited to a senior clerical position in the semi-governmental Workers' Accident Insurance Institute in July 1908. He continued to work there until 1922, when poor health forced him to retire. The day-to-day experience of being 'a solitary display-Jew' in this 'dark nest of bureaucrats' (CK 174) both informs and underpins so much of his literary work. Moreover, in the most famous of his fictions, Kafka, like the brothers in *Moonlight*, offers a dryly satirical perspective on the nature of administrative officialdom. What emerges from the pages of *The Trial* and *The Castle* is above all the sense of a world 'more fantastic than stupid' (MIL 127), with its polity of bumbling officials, tortuous procedures and inaccessible departments. (In *The Trial*, we even get two bureaucracies for the price of one, since the ill-fated Joseph K. is caught up in the nets of both the Bank and the Court.) Furthermore, it is interesting that the bureaucratic systems in both these novels should also have a patrilineal dimension. In *The Trial*, Titorelli, the Court portrait-painter, claims that he has inherited his position from his father: 'It's the only post that is always hereditary',[37] he tells K. – the clear implication being that other posts are sometimes hereditary too. Correspondingly, in *The Castle*, Schwarzer, who interrogates the newly arrived Land Surveyor with a bumptious blend of prudence and malice, and who is obviously grooming himself for future service at the Castle, informs K. that he is 'the son of the Castellan' (C 11). And while it later emerges that Schwarzer's father is actually one of the lowest-ranking officers, he is still reputed to have considerable influence (C 18).

Rampant red-tapism had been lampooned before in Pinter's theatre, notably in *The Hothouse* and *Precisely*. The exceptional thing about the bureaucratic buffoonery in *Moonlight*, however, is that it takes place in Fred's dilapidated bedroom. This idea of official business being conducted in a bedchamber is indeed a quintessential feature of the work of Kafka.[38] Moreover, the fact that the bedroom bureaucrats of *Moonlight* face each other across a table brings to mind the arrest of Joseph K. in *The Trial*, where a bedside table had been moved to the middle of Fräulein Bürstner's room to serve as a desk for the Inspector. There is in fact only one other quasi-administrative prop in *Moonlight* – a handful of papers which are shuffled and scrutinized by Jake. The illusion of officialdom is therefore created and sustained almost entirely through the verbal ingenuity of the protagonists. Indeed the bureaucratic fantasia is as much a testimony to the power of language as it is to the language of power. The two brothers persuasively evoke the enclosed world of Whitehall civil servants by deftly mimicking the salient features of its idiom. The talk here is of permanent secretaries and placements, off-the-record briefings and confidential meetings, with speeches being delivered, motions being tabled and votes being taken. As befits those involved in ministerial manoeuvres and occupational oneupmanship, Jake and Fred affect an attitude of chilly *politesse* and wily opportunism. Their interlocution is at times highly reminiscent of the casuistic chatter of Sir Humphrey Appleby and his magpie-like colleagues in BBC television's popular comedy series *Yes, Minister* (and its sequel, *Yes, Prime Minister*).[39] Furthermore, it is interesting that, while they are in their administrative roles, the two sons take care to observe Andy's ban on the use of obscene language in the office. (On other occasions, the conversation of the brothers is noticeably less decorous.) Admittedly, Fred does ejaculate two rather brusque words – 'bloody' and 'prat' (M 43) – towards the end of the second bureaucratic skit, but these particular expressions seem almost *de rigueur* given the Blimpish circumstances.

In the Civil Service – as in other male-dominated bastions of the British Establishment, such as public schools and the armed forces – surnames are the traditional and preferred mode of address. Having spent his entire working life in this rigidly impersonal environment, Andy would seem to have long since lost the ability to retain or recall the given names of other men. (However, as his frequent invocations to Bridget and Maria demonstrate, he does not appear to have the same problem with the Christian names of females.[40]) Try as he might, he cannot bring to mind the name of his 'old chum' (M 36), the amateur football referee; and even when Bel tells him that he is talking about Ralph, Andy is far from convinced that this is the right name. Moreover, while it is true that the father does mention Jake by name in the story about the broom cupboard, it is noticeable that he never utters the name of his younger son. Instead, Andy simply refers to Fred as 'the other one' (M 35). This *ad hoc* nomenclature bears a strong resemblance to K.'s pragmatic method of giving orders to Arthur and Jeremiah, the Tweedledum-and-Tweedledee-like assistants in *The Castle*:

> 'You're a difficult problem,' said K., comparing them, as he had already done several times. 'How am I to know one of you from the other? The only difference between you is your names, otherwise you're as like as . . .' He stopped, and then went on involuntarily, 'You're as like as two snakes.' They smiled. 'People usually manage to distinguish us quite well,' they said in self-justification. 'I am sure they do,' said K., 'I was a witness of that myself, but I can only see with my own eyes, and with them I can't distinguish you. So I shall treat you as if you were one man and call you both Arthur, that's one of your names, yours, isn't it?' he asked one of them. 'No,' said the man, 'I'm Jeremiah.' 'It doesn't matter,' said K. 'I'll call you both Arthur. If I tell Arthur to go anywhere you must both go. If I give Arthur something to do you must both do it, that has the great disadvantage for me of preventing me from employing you on separate jobs, but the advantage that you will both be equally responsible for anything I tell you to do. How you divide the work between you doesn't matter to me, only you're not to excuse yourselves by blaming each other, for me you're only one man.' (C 31)

Correlatively, in *Moonlight*, Andy's alternate use of 'Jake' and 'the other one' may also be born of the fact that he has found it impossible to distinguish between the two brothers. At any rate, as we shall see later, this phenomenon takes on a more peculiar symbolic significance within the context of the biblical extravaganza.

Each of the bureaucratic episodes in *Moonlight* resounds with a seemingly interminable roll-call of omnifarious surnames, ranging from the commonplace (Black, White, Kelly, Small) to the more recherché (Alabaster, De Groot, Bugatti, Ottuna). It is perhaps not surprising that many of these names – and especially the ones beginning with B – are constantly being mixed up: they are after all the names of corporate men in grey suits; faceless functionaries not discrete personalities. To make matters worse, some of those involved are known under different names to different people. One official, for example, is known to some of his acquaintances as Rawlings and to others as Manning. (Aliases have been used before in Pinter's work – most notably in *The Caretaker*, where the vagabond Davies explains how he has been living under the sobriquet of Jenkins, since finding an insurance card made out in that name (II 18).) A similar type of onomastic uncertainty also surrounds the brothers themselves, who incidentally never address each other by their forenames. In the first of the bureaucratic charades, Fred plays the part of a district commissioner who has come down to administrative headquarters expecting to be consulted on a matter of some urgency. Fred calls himself Macpherson, although Jake, playing the part of the jack-in-office who receives him, assumes that Fred's name is Gonzalez – an assumption which Fred does not contradict. When Jake suggests that it is Kellaway that Fred has come to see, Fred replies rather equivocally, 'Yours was the name they gave me' (M 24), and then indicates his belief that Jake is called Saunders; Jake appears to acknowledge that this is his name, but later reveals that Saunders is also known as Kellaway. All of this patronymic confusion is in fact symptomatic of the sons' deep-seated ambivalence about the personality of their own father. Custom dictates that a person's surname should correspond to that of his or her progenitor. For Jake and Fred, however, things are not quite so straightforward; since their paternity is disputed on two separate counts. Not only is Andy adamant that both boys are illegitimate, but the brothers themselves also imply in the course of the biblical tomfoolery that they do not share the same father.

Although the sole inspiration for this fantastical pantomime of strangers and brothers, Andy himself is never mentioned directly by either of the two principals. Just as Kafka, in both *The Trial* and *The Castle*, had contrived to represent the absent father as an elusive legislative authority, so Jake and Fred, in their bureaucratic fictions, conjure up the paternal spirit and cause it to dwell in the imposing but unseen shape of a martinettish administrator. Furthermore, in a mischievous combination of deference and disdain, the young men ascribe to this personage a grandiose, almost Ruritanian title – Lieutenant-Colonel Silvio d'Orangerie. An examination of the various elements of this appellation yields the following insights into its significance:

(1) 'Lieutenant-' hints that this figure may be a kind of deputy or substitute.
(2) 'Colonel' is indicative of a man whose true colours are obscured by his professional position. As *Brewer's Dictionary of Phrase and Fable* explains: 'When an officer in the British Army is promoted to the rank of colonel he loses his regimental identity and becomes a member of the Staff Corps'.[41]
(3) 'Silvio' has a definite association with the displaced parent of a pair of rival sons; since it is actually derived from the feminine '(Rhea) Silvia', who, according to Roman legend, was the mother of abandoned twins Romulus and Remus. (The name 'Ralph', incidentally, is an amalgamation of 'counsel' and 'wolf':[42] thus, in his capacity as surrogate-parent to Jake and Fred, Ralph is to Silvio what the she-wolf was to Silvia.)
(4) 'd'Orangerie' appears to be a deliciously zany pun on Andy's former status as a mandarin. (This may also account for the brothers' fixation with things Chinese (M 7; 73).)

We are told virtually nothing about Silvio d'Orangerie, except that, in Jake's opinion, he is 'an incredibly violent person' (M 44). This detail alone would seem to suggest that the Lieutenant-Colonel ought to be viewed in the same light as other militaristic characters from Pinter's more recent work, such as Nicolas in *One for the Road* and the Sergeant in *Mountain Language*; though there is also an atavistic link with Colonel Roote and his formidable predecessors in *The Hothouse*. Despite his truculent reputation (or perhaps because of it), Silvio is revered by the two brothers in much the same way as the despotic old Commandant had been by the officer in Kafka's 'In the Penal Colony'.

This soldierly motif accentuates an already intriguing parallel between *Moonlight* and *Hamlet*. Indeed Pinter's play contains two direct quotations from Act 1 Scene 2 of Shakespeare's Danish tragedy. Towards the end of the second biblical charade, Fred echoes a line addressed to Hamlet by Horatio: 'I knew your father' (M 59).[43] A few moments later, he says of Jake's father – as Hamlet had said of his recently deceased father: 'He was a man, take him for all in all, I shall not look upon his like again' (M 60).[44] At the close of this scene in *Hamlet*, the eponymous Prince of Denmark, having been told that the ghost of the old king is strutting along the castle ramparts in full battle attire, remarks to himself: 'My father's spirit in arms! All is not well'.[45] Correlatively, in *Moonlight*, the fact that the father stalks the corridors of power in the guise of a man-at-arms also seems to have an ominous significance. This in turn finds a distant resonance in the name 'Andy' – the pet form of Andrew, the first element of which derives from the Greek *andr–*, denoting 'man' and, more particularly, 'warrior'.[46]

The connection between Lieutenant-Colonel Silvio d'Orangerie and the father is insinuated in a number of different ways: firstly, d'Orangerie both conforms to and enlarges upon Andy's description of himself as 'an envied and feared force in the temples of the just' (M 17–18); secondly, Fred claims to have known Silvio from their time together in Torquay (M 44), and this is echoed later when he mentions that he knew Jake's father (M 59); thirdly, like the Lieutenant-Colonel, the father is described as having been 'A leader of men' (M 61); fourthly, d'Orangerie's appointment to 'speak off the record at 7.15 precisely' (M 41) is mirrored to some extent by the father's meeting in the Black Horse at '7.30 sharp' (M 62); fifthly, the memorial service for Silvio – which Jake claims to have attended – is discussed immediately after the scene in which Andy had seemed ready to give up the ghost, and therefore is identified with the father's funeral; sixthly, and most tellingly, Fred pays his own unique tribute to the late lamented d'Orangerie with the words, 'I loved him like a father' (M 79).

* * *

Two of the longest and most extraordinary scenes in *Moonlight* are those in which Jake and Fred fantasize about the glorious character of the father and his legacy. What makes these episodes so remarkable is not just the fact that Pinter employs religious imagery more capriciously and indeed more extensively here than he had done in any of his previous plays, but, more specifically, that he contrives to augment the patri–filial motif with a medley of allusions to the book of Genesis and the history of Jesus Christ: in other words, the dramatist replicates exactly what Kafka had done in both 'The Judgement' and 'The Metamorphosis'.

Let us begin our analysis of the biblical charades in *Moonlight* by pin-pointing the focus of Pinter's references to the Old Testament. In 'The Judgement', Kafka had initially taken his cue from the story of Jacob's embezzlement of the blessing intended for Esau (Genesis 27), and then flashed back to the account of Abraham's readiness to sacrifice Isaac (Genesis 22). Astonishingly, it is this same pair of chapters that Pinter evokes in *Moonlight* to facilitate Jake and Fred in their parodic exaltation of the father. In the course of their disingenuous genuflections, the two brothers strive to present Andy as a great and gracious patriarch who has so affected his sons that they are willing to suffer and even die for him.

The very fact that one of the brothers in *Moonlight* is called Jake – which is of course a familiar abbreviation of Jacob – should alone be sufficient to alert us to the possibility of an allusion to the quasi-homonymous Old Testament hero. Still, the fact that the other brother is called Fred would seem to stop this particular train of thought dead in its tracks. If we consider for a moment, though, that Esau was also known as Edom, meaning 'red', then the name 'Fred' may not sound quite so out of tune with this line of inquiry after all. (Not only was Esau distinctly red when he came out of his mother's womb (Genesis 25:25), but he would later agree to trade his birthright for some red stew (Genesis 25:30–4).) Moreover, it is worth noting that one of the *dramatis personae* in *Party Time* – the play which immediately precedes *Moonlight* in the Pinter canon – is also called Fred. Pinter's decision to depart from his usual convention and ascribe the same monicker to a leading character in two consecutive plays would seem to indicate that this name is especially significant in the second instance.[47]

The story of Jacob and Esau is often cited as the classic illustration of the doctrine of predestination. Even before the twins were born – that is, before either of them had the opportunity to do anything good or evil – their fates had been sealed in accordance with God's sovereign purpose. As the foetal pair struggled together within her, Rebecca was told by the Lord:

> Two nations are in thy womb, and two manner of people shall be separated from thy bowels; and the one people shall be stronger than the other people; and the elder shall serve the younger. (Genesis 25:23)

Like many ancient communities, the Hebrews observed the hereditary tradition of primogeniture. Under normal circumstances, therefore, Esau would automatically have been entitled to inherit the mantle of the patriarchs, since he was the firstborn of Isaac's sons and, what is more, the apple of the old man's eye. On this occasion, however, God chose to turn that custom on its head in order to demonstrate His elective grace. Thus, in Malachi, the last book of the Old Testament, it is written:

> Was not Esau Jacob's brother? saith the LORD: yet I loved Jacob, And I hated Esau, and laid his mountains and his heritage waste for the dragons of the wilderness. (Malachi 1:2–3)

At the heart of the matter here is the issue of paternal favouritism. By virtue of their being providentially conceived, the twins have in effect two fathers – an earthly father in Isaac and a Heavenly Father in Jehovah – each of whom favours a different son. A similar conflict of filial interests is also evident in *Moonlight*, despite there being only one progenitor: for it would seem that Andy has been partial in his attitude to both of his sons. Indeed we are told that even though Fred was Andy's 'most favoured son' (M 60), the old man, in a combination of 'passionate religious fervour, [. . .] bloodtingling spiritual ardour, [and] spellbinding metaphysical chutzpah' (M 12), had elected to bequeath his entire personal fortune to Jake on the very day of that boy's birth. Pinter uses this preferential paradox to highlight the fact that Andy is purported to have a dualistic nature, which alternately reflects both the humanity of Isaac and the divinity of Jehovah. It would seem therefore that Fred was cherished by the human aspect of the father (just as Esau had been the darling of Isaac), while Jake was honoured by the divine aspect of the father (just as Jacob had been the chosen one of Jehovah). This at least is how the sons themselves would have it. As far as Andy is concerned, though, he has never made any distinction between the two boys. On the contrary, he has always despised both of them in equal measure.

If Andy's singular use of 'Jake' and 'the other one' (M 35) is – as I previously surmised – symptomatic of his failure to distinguish between the two brothers, then this represents a further parallel with the Genesis narrative, since the dying Isaac was also confused by the identities of his sons: 'The voice is Jacob's voice, but the hands are the hands of Esau' (Genesis 27:22).[48] Moreover, given that Andy arbitrarily acknowledges the name of Jake and completely disregards that of Fred, it is perhaps not surprising that the Esau-like son should appear so acutely alienated during

Jake's triumphant verbal identifications with the patriarch. It is indeed Jake who provides the main impetus for the unctuous reminiscences about the father and who pledges his allegiance to all that the old man stood for. At one point, he even staunchly defends the father's reputation against what he sees as Fred's 'atrociously biased and illegitimate' (M 56) aspersions. While both lads are happy to affirm their fraternal kinship, it is noticeable that Fred talks only of Jake's sire, not his own. He always prefaces the word 'father' with the possessive adjective 'your'. He never says 'my father', 'our father' or simply 'father'. This would seem to indicate an unusually keen sense of filial estrangement, consistent perhaps with one who, like Esau, had formerly enjoyed 'most favoured' status.[49] Jake, on the other hand, underlines his much more intimate connection with the patriarch by using the endearment 'Dad' (M 56; 61).[50]

The version of the story of Jacob and Esau offered in *Moonlight* departs from the Genesis model in one crucial respect. In the Bible, we are told that Jacob was marginally younger than his fraternal twin, having emerged from his mother's womb clutching Esau's heel (Genesis 25:26). By contrast, in Pinter's play, Jake is actually one year older than his rival sibling. As a result of this thematic discrepancy, the right of primogeniture – which was famously overturned in the book of Genesis – is duly upheld in *Moonlight*. There are two questions which need to be addressed here. The first question is: Why does the dramatist decide to uphold the right of the firstborn? While there is no scriptural basis for the law of primogeniture, the custom would in general seem to have met with God's approval. The case of Esau could indeed be seen as the exception which proves this unwritten rule. What is more, his birthright was only annulled because the outcome would have been contrary to the elective purpose of God; whereas in *Moonlight*, the venerable right of primogeniture is merely contradicted by the sentimental predilection of man. In both these instances, it is the higher authority which prevails; since providence must always take precedence over the vagaries of the human heart. The second question is: Why does Pinter reverse the position of seniority? By deliberately inverting the Genesis paradigm, the playwright draws attention to the subversive tenor of the whole biblical masquerade, and thereby hints at the hidden agenda of the two brothers. Their purpose is not to praise Andy, but to bury the myth of the old man as the ever-loving and all-bountiful

Father. Accordingly, in a splendidly ironic twist, Jake's much-vaunted inheritance turns out to be worth even less than the mess of pottage that Esau received in return for his birthright; because the beneficent patriarch had apparently 'run out of pesetas in a pretty spectacular fashion' (M 14) and was in fact bankrupt. Still, Pinter's perverse insistence on the pre-eminence of Jake's sonship facilitates that character in his attempts to forge a link between himself and the Person of Jesus Christ – whose superlative firstborn status is emphasized throughout the New Testament (for example, Romans 8:29; Colossians 1:15–19). And indeed, as we are now about to see, it is this idea of primogeniture which heralds the play's kaleidoscopic array of Christian symbols.

During the first appearance of the two brothers, Fred opines that their situation would be completely transformed if they could only lay hands on some capital. It comes as quite a surprise to him, therefore, when Jake replies that he has already acquired this talismanic commodity:

> FRED: You've got it?
> JAKE: I've got it.
> FRED: Where did you find it?
> JAKE: Divine right.
> FRED: Christ.
> JAKE: Exactly.
> FRED: You're joking.
> JAKE: No, no, my father weighed it all up carefully the day I was born. (M 9)

The key reference here is to the Divine Right of Kings. Originally expounded in medieval times to safeguard the royal houses of Europe against the growing threat of religious extremism, this political doctrine found its fullest flowering in the seventeenth century, and nowhere more so than at the court of the Sun King, Louis XIV of France. Put simply, the theory maintains that any monarchy based on the principle of primogeniture can legitimately expect to command absolute and unquestioning loyalty from its subjects, since such an institution is ordained by God, in much the same way as the dynastic tradition of the Old Testament patriarchs had been. Thus Jake, by claiming to have received his inheritance through this august prerogative, effectively declares himself to be a divinely anointed king. Furthermore, his is no ordinary kingship – indeed, as the oath uttered by Fred in response would appear to imply, Jake's kingdom may not even be of this world. Certainly, the absence of either a question mark or an exclamation mark after the word 'Christ' is highly significant: the former would have been too obvious, the latter too oblique. As it stands, though, the punctuation achieves a perfect balance between dramatic tension and thematic ambiguity. For his part, Jake is only too eager to apply this Messianic title to himself; just as Georg Bendemann had done with the charwoman's cry of 'Jesus!' (CSS 87) in 'The Judgement'.

At the first mention of Jake's father, Fred somewhat mischievously inquires: 'Oh, your father? Was he the one who was sleeping with your mother?' (M 9). This is just the sort of question that some wag might put to (the actor playing the part of) Jesus in a sacrilegious travesty of the Gospel – *à la* Monty Python's *Life of Brian.* One of the fundamentals of the Christian faith, the issue of the paternal origin of Jesus has simultaneously, and almost from the very moment of His conception, been the focus of intense devotion and bitter controversy. Here, Fred slyly exploits this phenomenon by insinuating that Jake, given his self-styled Messianic status, may also have been sired by supernatural intervention. After all, if Mary had shared a bed with Joseph, and he was not the true progenitor of the Holy Child of Bethlehem (according to St Matthew, their marriage was not actually consummated until after the Virgin Birth (Matthew 1:25)), then it must surely follow that Bel's husband is not necessarily the biological father of the blessed Jake. Ultimately, therefore, it is Andy who turns out to be the butt of this particular joke; since, in the eyes of his sons, he has lost all credibility as either father or God.

The fact that Jake was ostensibly something of a literary prodigy brings to mind the precocious erudition of the boy Jesus, who at the age of twelve had astonished the sages of Jerusalem with His understanding and acumen (Luke 2:46–7):

FRED: You were writing poems when you were a mere child, isn't that right?
JAKE: I was writing poems before I could read.
FRED: Listen. I happen to know that you were writing poems before you could speak.
JAKE: Listen! I was writing poems before I was born. (M 7–8)

What is especially significant about this last remark is that Jake's wondrous pre-natal existence should centre on the idea of the written word. In Chapter 1 of the Gospel according to St John, Jesus is Himself characterized as the Word, who, having existed with God and as God since the very beginning, was made flesh and came to dwell amongst mankind. What is more, it could be said that Christ, as the primordial and pre-incarnate Logos, was also involved in the writing of poetry before He was born – the poetry, that is, of the Old Testament.

This Christological motif also coincides with an idea which is implied in the title of Pinter's play – that of luminosity. At the start of his account of the Gospel, St John tells us two important things about light: the first of these is that 'the light shineth in darkness; and the darkness comprehended it not' (John 1:5); the second is that Jesus Christ is 'the true Light, which lighteth every man that cometh into the world' (John 1:9; cf. 8:12). It is these verses which are assimilated and customized by Jake in *Moonlight*. In the first instance, Jake explains to his benighted brother that special light-meters now exist which 'can test the quality of light down to a fraction of a centimetre, even if it's pitch dark' (M 54). He then goes on to suggest that, 'as a reward for all [his] labour and faith and all [his] concern and care for others', every man shall be entitled to receive 'whatever light is left in the dark' (M 54). This, according to Jake, will thenceforth serve the recipient as his 'own personal light eternal' (M 55).

A further aspect of Jake's Christ-like persona comes to the fore when he appears to wonder whether the bed-bound Fred is suffering from dehydration:

> JAKE: How's your water consumption these days?
> FRED: I've given all that up.
> JAKE: Really?
> FRED: Oh yes. I've decided to eschew the path of purity and abstention and take up a proper theology. (M 49)

From a Christian perspective, water is perhaps most immediately associated with the sacrament of baptism. Here, however, we are concerned specifically with the idea of drinking water – and to discover the symbolic significance of this we must turn once again to St John's Gospel. In Chapter 4 of his narrative, the evangelist describes how Jesus and His disciples, while travelling through a mountainous region of Samaria, had stopped to rest at a well that had been established by Jacob. During their sojourn, a Samaritan woman came to fetch some water from the well, whereupon Jesus asked her to give Him a drink. The woman was amazed that Jesus, being a Jew, should have made such a request of her, since no self-respecting Jew would have anything to do with the Samaritans. Jesus explained to her that if she knew who He was she would have asked Him for, and would have received, the water of life:

> Whosoever drinketh of this water [from Jacob's well] shall thirst again: But whosoever drinketh of the water that I shall give him shall never thirst; but the water that I shall give him shall be in him a well of water springing up into everlasting life. (John 4:13–14)

Correspondingly, the water which Jake offers his brother in *Moonlight* also carries with it the promise of immortality. Citing the tradition of 'the great village elders' (M 50), Jake claims that this seemingly humble liquid had been the nectarean secret of their numinous potency:

> JAKE: [. . .] you know what made them the men they were?
> FRED: What?
> JAKE: They drank water. Sheer, cold, sparkling mountain water.
> FRED: And this made men of them?
> JAKE: And Gods.
> FRED: I'll have some then. I've always wanted to be a God.
> JAKE (*Pouring*): Drink up. (M 51–2)

Perversely, this exchange also echoes the passage in Genesis which recounts how the Tempter had enticed Eve into eating of the fruit of the tree of knowledge of good and evil:

> And the serpent said unto the woman, Ye shall not surely die: For God doth know that in the day ye eat thereof, then your eyes shall be opened, and ye shall be as gods, knowing good and evil. (Genesis 3:4–5)

For Fred, the prospect of becoming divine proves just as irresistible; and not least because it means that he will finally be on a par with the high and mighty father.[51]

At the very heart of the New Testament is the story of a Son who is willing to sacrifice His own life for the love of His Father. During His long prayer on the night before His death, Jesus refers to the glory that He has received from the Father, who, He says, has loved Him from before the foundation of the world (John

17:24). Earlier, the Saviour had revealed the reason for His uniquely beloved status:

> Therefore doth my Father love me, because I lay down my life, that I might take it again. No man taketh it from me, but I lay it down of myself. I have power to lay it down, I have power to take it again. This commandment have I received of my Father. (John 10:17–18)

It is evident from this that the love of the Father is not proffered unconditionally, but rather is predicated on His foreknowledge that the Son will at the appointed hour make the supreme sacrifice. Such a proviso is also insinuated in *Moonlight,* where Jake can boast of a similar calling in his bid for Messianic glory. He too has been specially chosen at a formative stage by an exalted father, who indeed yearned to bestow 'all that was best and most valuable' (M 57) upon his loving son. Moreover, like Jesus, Jake is fully prepared to honour his commitment to the father, regardless of the cost to himself: '[My father] loved me. And one day I shall love him. I shall love him and be happy to pay the full price of that love' (M 57). Two thousand years have not altered the price of that love; which is, as Fred points out and Jake immediately confirms, 'the price of death' (M 57). Truly, this is a dreadful duty for any son of man to have to discharge. The very thought of it was enough to cause even Jesus Himself to waver:

> And he was withdrawn from them about a stone's cast, and kneeled down, and prayed, saying, Father, if thou be willing, remove this cup from me: nevertheless not my will, but thine, be done. And there appeared an angel unto him from heaven, strengthening him. And being in an agony he prayed more earnestly: and his sweat was as it were great drops of blood falling down to the ground. (Luke 22:41–4)

In the passion play within *Moonlight,* the role of the emboldening angel is momentarily assumed by Fred, who stresses that Jake's intended martyrdom is also 'strictly in accordance with the will of God' (M 58). The same sacrifical pattern had of course impressed itself – almost stigmatically – on the imaginations of the paranoid heroes of 'The Judgement' and 'The Metamorphosis'. Yet while Kafka's filial protagonists take up the cross in order to make themselves worthy of a sublime father, the imitations of Christ in *Moonlight* are simply the *reductio ad absurdum* of Andy's theomania.

Fittingly enough, this sequence of misappropriated Christian imagery concludes on an eschatological note. As the brothers continue to discuss the sacrifice of the beloved son, their remarks find a peculiar resonance in the Apocalypse:

> JAKE: It's the first axiom.
> FRED: And the last.
> JAKE: It may well be both tautologous and contradictory.
> FRED: But it nevertheless constitutes a watertight philosophical proposition which will in the final reckoning be seen to be such. (M 58–9)

Three times in the book of Revelation, Christ declares Himself to be 'the first and the last' (Revelation 1:17; 2:8; 22:13). Moreover, on the third of these occasions, He prefaces this claim with the words 'I am the Alpha and the Omega, the beginning and the end [. . .]'. To the uninitiated, such statements do indeed appear to be 'both tautologous and contradictory'. However, as Fred is quick to remind us, the metaphysical truth of all this will be made manifest in 'the final reckoning' – a phrase that would seem to be synonymous with the Last Judgement, which incidentally is also known as the Day of Reckoning.

By synthesizing these various elements from Genesis and the New Testament, Pinter is able to access and exploit a rich vein of scriptural cross-references in much the same way that Kafka had done in 'The Judgement':

(1) Jacob and Jesus both enjoyed the distinction of being specially 'chosen' by God even before they were born.
(2) Jacob and Jesus were both miraculously conceived through the agency of the Holy Spirit. (Isaac's wife, Rebecca, was barren, just as his own mother, Sarah, had been.)
(3) The idea of deception is related to both Jacob and Jesus. Translated literally, the name 'Jacob' means 'he grasps the heel', that is to say, figuratively, 'he deceives'; and, according to St Matthew, the chief priests and the Pharisees referred to Jesus as 'that deceiver' (Matthew 27:63).
(4) Jacob's dream of a ladder to heaven with 'the angels of God ascending and descending' (Genesis 28:12) is alluded to by Jesus in the first chapter of St John's Gospel (John 1:51).
(5) It is widely accepted that the numinous man with whom Jacob had grappled so tenaciously at Peniel (Genesis 32) was actually a manifestation of the pre-incarnate Christ. (After this

incident, Jacob's name was changed to 'Israel', which means 'he struggles with God'.)

(6) The book of Numbers proclaims that 'there shall come a Star out of Jacob, and a Sceptre shall rise out of Israel' (Numbers 24:17); and the fulfilment of this Messianic prophecy is celebrated in the book of Revelation, where (a) Jesus declares Himself to be 'the bright and morning star' (Revelation 22:16), and (b) we are told that He shall rule the nations 'with a rod of iron' (Revelation 2:27; 19:15).

So far we have considered only the verbal dimension of the biblical pageant in *Moonlight*. There is, however, a visual aspect to the brothers' charades. Furthermore, if Jake is the undoubted kingpin in the oral realm, then Fred is very much the cynosure in the optical domain.

At the centre of both *Moonlight* and Genesis 27 is the figure of a bedridden patriarch, uncertain as to how long he has left to live, and thus anxious to confer his testamentary benediction on his progeny. In Pinter's *oeuvre*, this recurrent image of the father on his deathbed is imbued with a mystical, even sacramental significance. The motif is evoked explicitly, and with some solemnity, in three of his other plays: firstly, in *The Birthday Party*, where Goldberg tells McCann about how he knelt beside his dying father and swore on the good book that he would respect the ancestral traditions of hard work and loyalty to his family (I 72); secondly, in *The Homecoming*, where Max claims that his recumbent father exhorted him, in his 'last sacred words' (III 47), to look after his brothers – a charge which he felt duty-bound to obey; thirdly, in *Family Voices*, where the mother reports that her late husband, as he lay *in articulo mortis*, had paradoxically both blessed and cursed their errant son. In all of these instances, the iconic portrait of the father on his deathbed is represented verbally through the particoloured reminiscences of one of the characters. In the case of *Moonlight*, however, the paternal deathbed is actually the focal point of the *mise en scène*; and so, when this shrine-like centre-piece is apparently travestied in an adjacent area, the sacrilegious impact is all the more devastating.

It is no coincidence that the two scenes in which the brothers discuss the legacy of the father should also be those in which we are told that Fred is himself in bed.[52] The parallel here between the dying father and his younger son is, however, not simply a matter of posture. Indeed the fact that Fred is deliberately mimicking Andy's predicament is underlined in several ways:

(1) Fred affirms that he, like Andy, has been 'confined to bed with a mortal disease' (M 77).
(2) Immediately after Andy's clandestine drinking-bout, Fred rejects Jake's tentative offer of water and vows 'to eschew the path of purity and abstention' (perhaps something of an administrative malaprop for 'abstinence'?) (M 49).
(3) Fred echoes Andy's concerns about whether there is light after death (M 54–5; cf. 46).
(4) Only after Andy has apparently given up the ghost is Fred seen to be able to walk about the room.

This exercise in patri–filial identification resembles a rather sardonic variation on the empathetic game which Kafka had liked to play whenever he was about to deal the *coup de grâce* to one of his fictional *alter egos* (DII 102). For his secret amusement, the novelist would also lie on his supposed deathbed and project himself into the personality of a doomed man. But whereas Kafka had simply desired to savour prospectively the moment of his own quietus, Fred's sole purpose is to make a mockery of the real victim's final hours – a sick joke at his father's expense. Moreover, with a truly Machiavellian sense of irony, the ostensible frailty of Fred is then offered as *prima facie* evidence of his having an extraordinarily close affinity with Andy. Consequently, it would seem that the younger son is suffering vicariously with and indeed for the old man. By creating this impression, Fred is able to counterbalance the Messianic claims of Jake and present himself as the very image of an obedient, Christ-like son who is willing to pay the ultimate price for the love of his father.

The two brothers thus engage in a mock contest to prove which of them has the greater claim to being the beloved son in whom the father is well pleased. Just as Fred continually challenges Jake on the question of his inheritance, so Jake tries to persuade Fred to get out of bed. When it is suggested that they might go for a walk around the block, Fred replies:

> Oh no, I'm much happier in bed. Staying in bed suits me. I'd be very unhappy to get out of bed and go out and meet strangers and all that kind of thing. I'd really much prefer to stay in my bed. (M 53)

We are reminded here of Eduard Raban, the hero of Kafka's abortive novel 'Wedding Preparations in the Country', who was similarly determined to stay in bed, and even planned to send his 'clothed body' (CSS 55) out into the world, so that his true self could assume the form of a large beetle and pretend to hibernate. (As previously noted, this last detail prefigures the basic premise of 'The Metamorphosis'; and indeed, in that story, we are told that Gregor Samsa also 'would rather stay in bed' (CSS 93) than subject himself to the possibly traumatic business of getting up.)

As a quasi-religious symbol, the bed itself is highly equivocal. In 'The Judgement', for example, Mr Bendemann's bed initially resembles a place of immolation (upon which Georg attempts to put his father down), but ultimately turns out to be the high seat of justice (from which the old man condemns Georg to death). In the corresponding biblical diorama in *Moonlight*, however, Fred's bed is both these things at the same time. The son's likeness to the bed-bound patriarch is in fact a kind of double exposure. Not only does Fred's recumbent posture imitate that of the aged Isaac in Genesis 27, but it simultaneously recalls the moment when the innocent Isaac had expected to die at the hands of his father in Genesis 22. The pictorial ambiguity of this scene is exploited to bolster the patri–filial fantasies of both young men. Consequently, from Jake's point of view, Fred represents the father who has bestowed his blessing upon him from the theocratic throne; while, from Fred's point of view, Jake represents the father who has laid him upon the sacrifical altar.[53]

In the course of all this heretical hokum, Jake and Fred make a number of parodic references to Andy's quasi-divine status. Typically, the attributes which the brothers choose to highlight are those indicative of a God of judgement. The father, who, like his opposite number in *Family Voices*, appears to have been in existence 'from time immemorial' (M 56; cf. IV 300), is characterized as 'a truly critical force' (M 10). Not only was he 'proud and fiery' (M 61) by nature, but he had also insisted on 'the rule of law' (M 11). As a result, he was forever on the look-out for such mortal sins as 'blasphemy, gluttony and buggery' (M 10). Moreover, Jake recounts how a vicar, on hearing the word of the father at the trustees meeting, was so impressed that he stood up and launched into a special Gloria Patri in his honour (M 12–13).

Throughout the play, Andy himself alludes to the fact that he possesses various qualities which are associated largely, or exclusively, with the Almighty. The attributes in question are:

(1) *Omnipotence*	He portrays himself as the very personification of temporal and spiritual authority (M 17–18);
(2) *Omnipresence*	He claims to have been present the first time that Bel and Maria had lunch together in a restaurant (M 63–6);
(3) *Omniscience*	He claims to have been able to hear the thoughts of Bel and Maria (M 65–6);
(4) *Perpetuity*	He claims to have 'no past' (M 70) – the implication being that, like I AM (Exodus 3:14), he exists in an eternal present;
(5) *Perfection*	He claims to be entirely free from sin or fault (M 4; 17);
(6) *Inspiration*	He claims to have inspired all those under him (M 17);
(7) *Awfulness*	He characterizes himself as a 'feared
(8) *Pneumaticity*	force
(9) *Holiness*	in the temples
(10) *Judgement*	of the just' (M 18).

Yet, for all his theomaniacal insinuations, it has to be said that Andy makes a rather unconvincing Supreme Being. After all, he has even lost whatever vestiges of earthly glory he once possessed, and is no longer in a position to lord it over anyone. On the contrary, he is now a hopeless invalid, precariously perched on the edge of the abyss. Andy's self-deifying braggadocio should therefore be viewed in much the same light as the ostensible apotheoses of the aged and ailing patriarchs in 'The Judgement', 'The Metamorphosis', *The Homecoming* and *Family Voices*. Metaphorically speaking, it could be argued that Andy has been 'stricken' (M 18) precisely because he has had the temerity to equate himself with God. It was of course this same presumption which resulted in Adam being stripped of his nascent immortality and expelled from Paradise. Indeed there are two further connections between the father in *Moonlight* and the biblical prototype of mankind. Firstly, the names 'Andy' and 'Adam' are virtual analogues, since they derive respectively from the Greek and Hebrew words for 'man' – a semasiological circumstance which effectively gives the lie to the divine pretensions of the bearer in each case. Secondly, in an apparent reference to the unhappy consequence of Adam's eating the forbidden fruit, Andy, when informed that he is about to receive an apple from his helpmate, immediately uses the verb 'fall' twice in quick succession (M 34).

Slipping away under the mortal curse of the Fall, Andy hopes that he might live long enough to see the spring and, in particular, 'All the paraphernalia of flowers' (M 19). This ambition suggests a vague yearning to return to the botanic splendour of the Garden of Eden. Nevertheless, Bridget intimates that her father's wish may actually be fulfilled after his journey through life is over. In a speech reminiscent of Shakespeare's Ophelia[54] – another tragic nymph – the daughter describes how she herself is strolling through a lush primeval jungle, in which she is surrounded by all manner of exotic blooms: 'Hibiscus, oleander, bougainvillea, jacaranda' (M 21). Here, in this paradisical place, the weary soul can evidently find shelter, freedom and a sense of belonging.

Moonlight presents us with a reverse image of the situation in 'The Metamorphosis'. In both these works, the central character is represented as an Adamic figure – a deluded victim of his own pride. The difference is, however, that in 'The Metamorphosis', it is the son who is identified with Adam, whereas in *Moonlight*, it is the father. This contradistinction can be related partly to the peculiarities of the respective genres. Kafka's story, although written in the third person, is narrated almost entirely from the paranoid perspective of the son; consequently, the father is represented as the towering and jealous deity against whom the creature dares to rebel. Pinter's play, on the other hand, offers a much more objective and balanced picture of domestic conflict; as a result, the father emerges as a frail and frightened little man, wrestling with delusions of his own grandeur and intimations of his own mortality.

Given the fact that Andy is so closely associated with Adam, it follows that Jake and Fred should bear some resemblance to Cain and Abel – another pair of rival and ultimately 'lost' sons, who indeed were also embroiled in a controversy about sacrifice and favouritism (Genesis 4). This in turn implies that Jake and Fred, in their respective Christological impersonations, are actually having to make atonement for the seminal sin of their earthly father.

There are times in *Moonlight* when the grand strategy against the father begins to merge disconcertingly with the hectic sparring of the brothers themselves. At such moments, Jake and Fred would appear to be transferring their antipathy for Andy on to each other instead. During one exchange, Fred even addresses Jake as 'son' (M 43). Kafka would undoubtedly have approved of this cognate confusion, not least because he himself had contrived to suggest a quasi-fraternal connection between the two combatants in 'The Judgement'. Early on in that story, the decrepit patriarch says to Georg, 'Since the death of *our* dear mother certain things have been done that aren't right' [my italics] (CSS 82); however, as soon as he has established his superiority over the young pretender, Mr Bendemann declares, 'All by myself I might have had to give way, but *your* mother has given me so much of her strength [. . .]' [my italics] (CSS 86).[55] In a letter to Max Brod, Kafka asserted his belief that the patri–filial conflict was in reality a surreptitious form of sibling rivalry:

> the struggle with the father doesn't mean much. After all, he is only an elder brother, also a scapegrace son, who from jealousy is merely pitifully trying to distract his younger brother from the decisive struggle and moreover does so successfully. – But now it is quite dark, as it must be for the final blasphemy. (FFE 251)

The 'final blasphemy' would seem to refer to the fact that the author here has dared to impugn the godhead of the father. It was of course a similar piece of impudence which had hastened the destruction of the son in 'The Judgement'. Moreover, just as Kafka appears to have been instantly troubled by his benighted conscience, so Georg Bendemann – who had the audacity to suggest that his father was no more than a washed-up 'comedian' (CSS 86) with a sideline in conjuring tricks – 'realized at once the harm done and, his eyes starting in his head, bit his tongue back, only too late, till the pain made his knees give' (CSS 86). This in turn reminds us of the moment in *The Homecoming*, when Sam finally plucks up the courage to taunt Max – who is both the *paterfamilias* and his elder brother – with the sordid details of Jessie's adulterous taxi-ride with MacGregor, and then immediately '*croaks and collapses*' (III 86) as if struck down by some judicial thunderbolt for his profane presumption. Blasphemy is, by definition, a wilful offence. In order to commit blasphemy, a man must first acknowledge – at least to some extent – the divinity of the one against whom he blasphemes. Implicit in the sin of blasphemy, therefore, is an element of self-condemnation. (This perhaps was what prompted Salman Rushdie's temporary recantation at the height of the *Satanic Verses* controversy.) The true blasphemer not only fears divine retribution, but also in a sense invites it. It is this combination of angst and awe which ultimately causes the Kafkan challenger to throw in the towel and kowtow to his paternal lord.

In another of his 'blasphemies', Kafka not only contradicts the biblical view of God 'dwelling in the light which no man can approach unto' (1 Timothy 6:16; cf. 1 John 1:5), but goes on to suggest that the remoteness of the Father has more to do with security than sanctity:

> God dwells in [darkness]. And this is a good thing, because without the protecting darkness, we should try to overcome God. That is man's nature. The Son dethrones the Father. So God must remain hidden in darkness. And because man cannot reach him, he attacks at least the darkness which surrounds the divine. He throws burning brands into the icy night. But the night is elastic like rubber. It throws them back. And by doing so it endures. (CK 63–4)

This situation is reflected in 'The Judgement', where the usurping son remarks how the room in which his godlike father abides is 'unbearably dark' (CSS 81). Nevertheless, as a great and terrible being, the Kafkan patriarch is in fact more like the Wizard of Oz than the Lord God of Israel. The dread-inspiring aura with which the father surrounds himself is based not on power and glory, but on bluff and bravado. Behind the smokescreen of his sable Shekinah, there lurks a vain, vulnerable and rather pathetic little dotard, who is simply adept at the jiggery-pokery of pulling all the right levers and the wool over the eyes of his subjects. Evidence of this affinity between the paternal character and the Wizard of Oz can also be found in both *Moonlight* and *Family Voices*. In *Moonlight*, Jake reckons that the oration his father gave at the trustees meeting in the Cotswolds 'was the speech either of a mountebank – a child – a shyster – a fool – a villain –', at which point Fred interjects, 'Or a saint' (M 15); and indeed this miscellany of labels virtually amounts to an Identikit picture of the eponymous magician in L. Frank Baum's classic fairy-tale. Parallels abound between *Family Voices* and *The Wizard of Oz* – or more specifically MGM's celebrated 1939 film version of the story, which starred Judy Garland as Dorothy. Like Dorothy, Voice 1 runs away from home and makes his way to a mysterious metropolis (cf. the Emerald City), encountering a variety of bizarre characters, who are, to some extent, misshapen editions of the people he knew in the world he left behind. (Several of the actors in the film are featured in alternate guises as the action moves between the monochrome reality of Kansas and the Technicolor fantasy of Oz.) At the end of Pinter's epistolary play, the young man even echoes the sentiment of the spell-breaking refrain which finally brings Dorothy back to her folks – 'There's no place like home'.[56] Of most significance, though, at least in relation to the present study, is the fact that the hallowed father in *Family Voices* should confess to being scared out of his wits by a barking dog; since in *The Wizard of Oz*, it is Toto, Dorothy's little terrier, which goes behind the curtain into the *soi-disant* Holy of Holies and exposes 'The Great and Terrible Humbug'[57] (who incidentally is described in the book as 'the Voice'[58]) by frightening him with its bark. Furthermore, just as the harassed Wizard laments that his inviolability would never have been lost if he had kept the visitors outside his Throne Room, so Voice 3 only complains about the Baskervillian hound after his *alter ego*, Mr Withers (who is himself, like the Wizard, 'a little old man, with a bald head and wrinkled face'[59]), has invited the doggishly named Bobo into his private chamber.

In 'Letter to his Father', Kafka relates how there was a 'terrible trial' pending between himself and his father, in which the old man kept on claiming to be the judge, whereas, in reality, he was a party too, just as weak and deluded as his son (WPC 188). Nevertheless, in the legal process of Kafka's fiction, the filial defendants, for all their gestures of contempt, are ultimately bound to recognize the authority of the paternal bench and accept its rulings. In Pinter's drama, there is an analogy with a different kind of court: namely, the household of a king. Pinterian sons are like perfidious princes, waiting – usually in exile – for their autarchical sire to fall off his lofty perch. In *Moonlight*, the princely plot against Andy is advanced not only by Jake's claiming of his divine right, but also by Fred's parroting of the words of Hamlet – arguably the most famous prince in the history of world literature.[60] Moreover, this quote from Hamlet ('He was a man, take him for all in all, I shall not look upon his like again' (M 60)) would seem to have been chosen quite deliberately to underscore the mortality of the majestic patriarch. Thus, as if following the advice of another of Shakespeare's royal tragic heroes, Jake and Fred wile away the time by sitting and telling sad stories of the death of a king.[61]

The crucial factor in all this is the way in which the father's power is perceived by his son(s). In Kafka's writing, the authority of the father appears to emanate from his person; whereas in Pinter's work, the old man's influence is thought to derive from his position. It is indeed highly significant that Jake and Fred should refer to the father as 'The Incumbent' (M 62) – and even more significant that they should do so retrospectively. The word 'incumbent' is generally used to denote one who occupies a position of some prestige. It also implies that the office in question will not be held in perpetuity by the same individual: the tenure is by definition a limited one. In the course of time, the sitting tenant, as it were, must expect to yield his chair to another candidate. Likewise, the father's kingdom could endure only so long as his strength held out against his rivals. 'Uneasy lies the head that wears a crown',[62] says Shakespeare's Henry IV; and while the Incumbent remained on the throne, he must have lived in constant apprehension of the fact that some day his reign would come to an abrupt end. It is no coincidence therefore that the patriarch reportedly made out his last will and testament on the very day that his eldest son was born. The two circumstances were indeed linked by an ineluctable sense of destiny; since the arrival of his natural successor was a portent of the father's own demise.

* * *

The biblical and bureaucratic sequences in *Moonlight* both climax with the revelation that the simulacrum of Andy is deceased. In the first instance, Jake makes explicit reference to the fact of the patriarch's death (M 57); and in the second, Fred is informed about the recently held memorial service for the man whom he 'loved liked a father' (M 79). The Incumbent and Lieutenant-Colonel Silvio d'Orangerie are thus symbolically skewered like voodoo dolls. With the publication of these obituaries, the brothers' secret mission is accomplished. (The way in which their fictitious fathers are dispatched is reminiscent of the scene in Edward Albee's *Who's Afraid of Virginia Woolf?* where George takes his revenge on Martha by announcing the death of their imaginary son.) Through their double-dealing games of devotion and duty, Jake and Fred have in effect assassinated the character of their father.

There are further echoes here of *Hamlet*. Just as the Prince of Denmark must slay Claudius – his ersatz father and counterfeit king – in order to lay to rest the obtrusive ghost of his true progenitor, so Jake and Fred dispose of their paternal bugbears in order to free themselves from the oppressive influence of Andy. What is more, like Hamlet, the two brothers choose to implement their plot against the tyrant through the art of play-acting. (With respect to the other half of the Oedipus complex, Jake and Fred's prickly attitude to their mother is strongly redolent of Hamlet's rough handling of Gertrude.)

In a moment of transcendental euphoria, Andy boasts that he once spied on Bel and Maria in a restaurant from behind a copy of *The Brothers Karamazov* (M 65). It is indeed particularly ironic that the father should have decided to shield himself with a book which so famously combines the themes of fraternal skulduggery and patricide. However, in terms of their *modus operandi,* Jake and Fred appear to have been taking their cues not from Dostoyevsky's characters, but from the two executioners in Kafka's *The Trial.* (It is possible that the same deadly duo had also provided the inspiration for Pinter's other pair of bedchamber hit men – Ben and Gus in *The Dumb Waiter.*) When confronted by the Court lynchers, Joseph K. is immediately struck by their air of cheap theatricality. With their formal attire, pasty complexions and affected demeanour, they give him the impression of 'Tenth-rate old actors' (T 249) or 'tenors' (T 250) from some comic opera: 'What theatre are you playing at?' (T 249) he asks them with a wry touch of superciliousness. Correlatively, in *Moonlight,* Jake and Fred have a special penchant for amateur dramatics, which, as we have seen, they indulge by putting on and starring in a couple of rather tacky yet highly subversive bedroom farces. More remarkably, Kafka's portrayal of the histrionic goons in *The Trial* actually anticipates certain key elements of the biblical and bureaucratic charades in *Moonlight.* In the first instance, the two 'gentlemen' (T 249) simultaneously resemble the other characters involved in the stories in Genesis about the bed-bound Isaac: like Jacob and Esau, they appear to be twins; like a double-minded Abraham, they wield a butcher's knife over an (ostensibly) innocent victim. In the second instance, it is significant that the names of the judicial murderers in *The Trial* and those of the bogus officials in *Moonlight* should both remain something of a mystery: furthermore, like Saunders-alias-Kellaway (Jake) and Macpherson-alias-Gonzalez (Fred), the killers are employed in the service of a sprawling and impenetrable administrative octopus. (Incidentally, Kafka thought it extremely appropriate that in twentieth-century society the executioner should have been accorded the status of a respectable and well-paid bureaucrat. Indeed it seemed to him that there was a hangman lurking in every conscientious civil servant. It was, after all, the function of the administrative executor to transform 'living, changing human beings into dead code numbers, incapable of any change' (CK 19).) Just as the condemned man in *The Trial* had sat waiting apprehensively for the arrival of his exterminating angels, so Andy in his opening words – 'Where are the boys?' (M 2) – may well be making an anxious inquiry about the advent of his nemeses. The phrase 'the boys' is of course a popular euphemism for ruthless underworld thugs, and if Andy were to be using it in that sense, then Jake and Fred would begin to take on the appearance of England's most notorious pair of fraternal 'performers' – the Kray twins.[63] Joseph K.'s not-so-good 'companions' (T 250) perform their lethal turns by the light of the moon and, as already mentioned, there is an obvious resonance here with the title of Pinter's play. Moreover, it is worth noting that the word 'moonlight', when used as a verb, can also have the meaning 'to wound'.[64] Jake and Fred, for their part, might not actually twist a cold steel blade in their father's heart, but they do carry out a kind of vivisection on the old man's personality. The reciprocal manner in which the executioners handle the knife is even imitated by the two brothers during the 'Chinese laundry' scene, where they persist in passing the telephone receiver back and forth to each other, as Bel attempts to apprise them of their father's critical condition.

This urge to kill the father is not peculiar to the sons in *Moonlight*. Patricidal aspirations also surface in both *The Homecoming* and *Family Voices*. Lenny, the arch-usurper in *The Homecoming*, first threatens to dispose of the irascible Max: 'You'll go before me, Dad, if you talk to me in that tone of voice' (III 19); and then exhorts the old man to hasten his own departure: 'Look, why don't you just . . . pop off, eh?' (III 43). Similarly, in *Family Voices*, Voice 3 alleges that his son has been praying for his death 'from time immemorial' (IV 300).[65] Paradoxically, it is to the father himself that these filial orisons have been addressed. It is as if the Eternal were being petitioned to terminate His own existence. Moreover, even when the son's pleas have been granted, they continue to reverberate in the ears of the father, who, as he lies in his crystal mausoleum, is still reluctant to acknowledge his own mortality. Voice 1, for his part, is careful not to incriminate himself on this matter. Later, he even suggests that it was his mother who did away with the old man (IV 302). (The young hero of *Family Voices* might well be said to have anticipated Jake and Fred's attempts to divide and conquer the personality of the father. If, as some have argued, the Withers house and its inhabitants are in fact mere figments of Voice 1's imagination, then the two senior male figures in the tenement could be seen as dissected portions of the paternal character. On the one hand, there is Mr Withers, a crazy old hermit with one foot in the grave; and on the other, there is Riley, who, despite his virile physique, is a homosexual, and thus as 'intellectually incapable of marrying' (WPC 210) as the archetype of the Kafkan son himself. Neither of these demi-fathers could be described as the epitome of patriarchal perfection; yet it is precisely because of their relative impotence that Voice 1 thinks that he can co-exist more easily with them than with the real thing.)

The final appearance of Jake and Fred takes on the colour of a victory parade. Having remained virtually immobile throughout the play, the orphaned pair proceed to swagger around the room, stretching their young and healthy bodies, as if emancipated by the passing of Andy. Yet all is not what it seems. The orbital nature of their motion and the fact that their hands are held fast behind their backs suggest that the boys are caught up in a vacuous circle from which they can do nothing to extricate themselves. Moreover, it is significant that Fred should be wearing shorts – boxer shorts? – since this implies that he is as ill-suited for life in the outside world as the pyjama-clad Stanley Webber had been in *The Birthday Party*. What started out as a parody has now become a prison. The brothers' hugger-mugger efforts to bring the curtain down on the old man's existence have resulted in themselves being hemmed in. It is in fact their own lives that are being frittered away in 'all these enervating charades' (M 46). As for their allusions to *Hamlet*, the truth is that Jake and Fred have much more in common with Rosencrantz and Guildenstern than with the philosophic Prince; not least the fact that they too have been hoist with their own petard.[66] Indeed, what with their confusable names and vaudevillian repartee, the two brothers often remind us of Tom Stoppard's ingenious enlargements of those fey Shakespearean stooges.

* * *

As Michael Billington has suggested in his recent biography of Pinter, there is reason to believe that *Moonlight* was inspired in part by the playwright's less than happy relationship with his own son, Daniel. The only child from Pinter's marriage to Vivien Merchant, Daniel was born in 1958. Throughout his childhood and adolescence, he and his father are reported to have been 'very close',[67] though relations between them became increasingly strained after his parents split up. A highly intelligent and creative young man, Daniel won a scholarship to Oxford University, but while he was there he suffered a nervous breakdown. He subsequently withdrew to the quiet seclusion of the Fens, where he set to work on an ambitious musical project. During the writing of *Moonlight*, the author and his son, while not totally estranged from each other, were living in what amounted to 'a spasmodic state of alienation'.[68] In 1993, the year in which the play received its première, the pair decided that it would be better if they did not see one another. Pinter Snr, while expressing his deep sense of sadness and 'impotence' at the stand-off between himself and his son, later told Billington: 'Daniel's determination to free himself from me has been the source of his alienation'.[69] The most obvious sign of this filial tergiversation had come many years earlier, when, in a bid to establish an identity of his own (or, at least, one distinct from that of his famous father), Daniel had changed his surname to 'Brand' – the maiden name of his maternal grandmother. Now it just so happened that when Harold Pinter himself was a young man, he too had chosen not to use his patronymic, preferring the stage name (David) 'Baron' – which curiously enough had been the maiden name of his paternal grandmother. Ironically, therefore, Daniel, while contriving to distance himself from his father, had actually followed in the old man's footsteps. What is more, the lad even ended up with the same initials that his father had been working under at the time of his birth. (We may recall that in the babel of surnames in *Moonlight* the greatest confusion had surrounded those beginning with B (M 42–3).) However, the very fact that Harold assumed the name of a grandmother from one side of the family and Daniel opted for that of a grandmother from the other side perfectly exemplifies the enantiomorphic opposition between father and son.

In Oscar Wilde's *The Importance of Being Earnest*, one of the characters declares: 'All women become like their mothers. That is their tragedy. No man does. That's his'.[70] The corollary of this thesis – namely, that all men become like their fathers – is insinuated in various ways throughout Pinter's *oeuvre.* Consider, for example, the case of the Italian waiter in *Betrayal,* whose appearance prompts the following exchange between Jerry and Robert:

JERRY: Is he the one who's always been here or is it his son?
ROBERT: You mean has his son always been here?
JERRY: No, is *he* his son? I mean, is he the son of the one who's always been here?
ROBERT: No, he's his father.
JERRY: Ah. Is he? (IV 247)

In each of the patri–filial plays, the similarity between the father and son(s) – if not quite so express – is no less remarkable:

(1) The three lads in *The Homecoming,* for all their itchy individualism, each settle into a role that had previously been associated with their father: Teddy, with his wife and three boys, takes after Max the family man; Lenny, with his entrepreneurial interests, emulates Max the business man; and Joey, with his passion for pugilism, smacks of Max the hard man. At the same time, Max himself still lives under the spectre of his own father, who likewise is reputed to have been a formidable combination of domestic devotion, commercial acumen and gladiatorial brawn.
(2) In *Family Voices,* the young dodger's identification with his father is sealed through his ventriloquial impersonations of Messrs Withers and Riley, who, as we have seen, represent complementary aspects of the paternal character.
(3) Notwithstanding their mutinous intent, the bureaucratic and biblical tableaux of *Moonlight* actually validate the fateful premise of Jake and Fred becoming like their father: in the first instance, the two brothers act as if they have followed their old man into the upper echelons of the Civil Service; and in the second, Fred's demeanour replicates the plight of the bedridden patriarch, while Jake's profession of a Christological oneness with his 'Dad' reminds us of how Jesus Himself had proclaimed: 'he who hath seen me hath seen the Father' (John 14:9).

Moreover, given this pattern of antagonistic assimilation, it is signally appropriate that two of these plays should depict a violent confrontation between a man and his reflection in a mirror (III 45; M 46).

Fundamentally absurd and ultimately self-defeating, the revolt of the son against the father is indeed, as Kafka had concluded, a subject more suited to comedy than to tragedy (CK 68). In this perennial sciamachy between youth and age, the more the son tries to box clever, the more he gets caught on the ropes; the more he struggles to break free, the more he becomes entangled; the more he renounces the father and all his works, the more he resembles a chip off the old block. Regardless of whether the father is a butcher or a bureaucrat, a codger or a colossus, a draper or a dramatist, whether he is nearby or faraway, alive or dead, he remains the standard by which all things must be judged. The son's fixation with the paternal character permeates all of his attitudes and actions, all of his aspirations and achievements: everything he is, has or does is liable to be measured against the imago of his progenitor. The fact of the matter is that the son would find it easier to lose his own shadow than to rid himself of the influence of his father.

Notes and References

1 Descriptions of a Struggle

1. Max Brod, note to 'Letter to his Father' (WPC 441, n. 30).
2. The Czech word *pavlatche* 'signifies a long balcony of the kind which ran round the inner courtyard of many of the more ancient houses in Prague. It was generally shared by several apartments' (WPC 442, n. 34).
3. Two of the elements of this ordeal – the bed and the door – would later become trademarks of Kafka's fiction.
4. In Germanic folklore, the Erl-king is a bearded giant with a golden crown who abducts little children and transports them to the land of death.
5. This notion is perhaps most lyrically expounded in Wordsworth's 'Ode: Intimations of Immortality'.
6. In *The Homecoming*, Teddy, on entering his father's house, immediately recognizes the armchair as the seat of patriarchal authority (III 28).
7. Kafka left instructions for Brod to burn all his writings after his death. Yet Brod had told his friend in advance that, if appointed executor, he would never perform such a holocaust, and instead devoted much of his own life to the preservation and propagation of Kafka's legacy. See Postscript to the first edition of *The Trial* (T 291–6).
8. Max Brod, *Franz Kafka: A Biography* (New York, 1960) p. 24.
9. However, in 1989, sixty-five years after the author's death, Schocken Books published a tetralogy entitled *The Sons*, comprising the three stories originally proposed by Kafka and 'Letter to his Father'.
10. 'The Judgement' carried this inscription on its original publication in the annual *Arkadia*. However, when the story was re-issued three years later in the series *Der jüngste Tag* (October 1916), Kafka had replaced 'the outdated dedication' with an even more discreet homage: 'To F.' (FEL 505).
11. Kafka's first impressions of Felice are recorded in his diary (DI 268–9). He portrays her in such a harsh and clinical light that she emerges as a *belle laide* of rare distinction.
12. On 14 August 1913, Kafka reflected in his diary: 'Conclusion for my case from 'The Judgement'. I am indirectly in her debt for the story. But Georg goes to pieces because of his fiancée' (DI 296).
13. In 'The Urban World', the father blocks a window when he gets to his feet (DI 48); while in 'The Judgement', the father, on rising from his chair, is described by Georg as 'a giant of a man' (CSS 81).
14. In a curious piece of authorial camouflage, the friend in 'The Urban

World' bears the same forename as Kafka himself. This device is also employed in *The Trial*, where one of the warders assigned to Joseph K. is called Franz.

15. Georg has, of course, already assumed the senior executive position in the family business.
16. Heinz Politzer, *Franz Kafka: Parable and Paradox* (Ithaca, N.Y., 1962) p. 291.
17. Herbert Tauber, *Franz Kafka: An Interpretation of his Works* (London, 1948) p. 15.
18. The phrases quoted here are taken from a letter to Robert Klopstock, in which Kafka discusses Kierkegaard's *Fear and Trembling*. I shall touch upon the connection with Kierkegaard in the paragraph after next.
19. See also WPC 117–18; 438–9, n. 22.
20. We are reminded of how Jesus, at the moment of His betrayal, had ironically addressed the perfidious Judas as 'Friend' (Matthew 26:50).
21. Ben Jonson, *Volpone*, or *The Fox*, 4.5.113–14.
22. A charwoman is featured in the latter stages of 'The Judgement' and 'The Metamorphosis'. In both instances, there is evidence to suggest that she is being used to parody Mary Magdalene's visit to the sepulchre on the morning of the Resurrection (John 20:1–18). In 'The Judgement', the charwoman encounters the master as he is going down into Sheol, not after he has risen up from it; while in 'The Metamorphosis', the charwoman – in shades of Mary Magdalene's frantic report to the disciples – has a fit of the giggles as she tells the dead Gregor's family: 'you don't need to bother about how to get rid of the thing next door. It's been seen to already' (CSS 138).
23. This particular old master has inspired a number of literary works, including W.H. Auden's 'Musée des Beaux Arts' and William Carlos Williams' 'Landscape with the Fall of Icarus'.
24. The Greek word *monogenes* ('only begotten son') is applied to both Isaac and Jesus in the New Testament (Hebrews 11:17; John 3:16).
25. Identified in the travel diaries as 'H.', this gentleman – who appeared to have all the answers – came from Silesia and was a land surveyor by profession. In a wry touch, Kafka would later assign the same occupation to the benighted protagonist of *The Castle*.
26. See Coleridge's own explanatory note to the poem. Samuel Taylor Coleridge, *Selected Poems* (London, 1959) pp. 142–3.
27. Elias Canetti has argued that, 'by virtue of some of his stories, Kafka belongs in the annals of Chinese literature' (Elias Canetti, *Kafka's Other Trial* (Harmondsworth, 1982) p. 72). And indeed Kafka himself once proclaimed: 'I am a Chinese' (FEL 594).
28. John Milton, *Paradise Lost*, bk 4, l. 690.
29. Ibid., bk 4, ll. 690–705.
30. There is a clear parallel here with the flamboyantly liveried liftboys at the Hotel Occidental in *America* (A 152–3).
31. Kafka had observed how his own father was often overawed by those who 'were for the most part only seemingly' his social betters (WPC 175–6). Correspondingly, in the course of 'The Metamorphosis',

we witness Mr Samsa cringing – literally with cap in hand at one stage – before such tin gods as the chief clerk and the lodgers.

32. Interestingly, Kafka listed both carpentry and gardening among his own hobbies (DII 198).
33. Whereas Salome, the stepdaughter of Herod Antipas, had requested the head of John the Baptist as a reward for her Terpsichorean turn, Mrs Samsa, having performed her shambolic strip-tease, asks for Gregor's sconce to be spared.
34. The figure of Lilith is mentioned in Talmudic literature. She is said to have been created at the same time as Adam, but refused to recognize his authority over her, and subsequently left him to become the Devil's dam. She is identified with 'the screech owl' in Isaiah 34:14.
35. It was perhaps because the ending of 'The Metamorphosis' dwelt upon events *after* Gregor's death that Kafka found it so 'Unreadable' (DII 12). (The problem was that any post-mortem finale inevitably involved a jarring shift in narrative perspective – since the rest of the story had been told entirely from the insect's point of view.)
36. In the Editor's Note to the first edition of *The Castle,* Max Brod recalls how Kafka had once told him how that novel was to end: 'The ostensible Land-Surveyor [. . .] was not to relax in his struggle, but was to die worn out by it' (C 8). However, Brod's assertion in the Postscript to *America* that Kafka's first novel was to finish with Karl Rossmann and his parents all living happily ever after (A 311) is wholly negated by a diary entry from September 1915, in which Kafka himself reveals that Karl was actually destined to share a similar (but harsher) fate to that which befell the hero of *The Trial*: 'Rossmann and K., the innocent and the guilty, both executed without distinction in the end, the guilty one with a gentler hand [. . .]' (DII 132).
37. Kafka's euphoric conceit of a deathsong that fades 'beautifully and purely away' (DII 102) is echoed with a chilling twist in Pinter's *One for the Road,* where the despotic Nicolas exults:

    > Death. Death. Death. Death. As has been noted by the most respected authorities, it is beautiful. The purest, most harmonious thing there is. (IV 379)

    The difference is that, whereas Kafka is fantasizing about his own quietus, Nicolas is gloating upon the extermination of others.
38. As the translators have noted, the German word for 'atonement' – *Versöhnung* – also means 'reconcilation' (DII 323, n. 53).
39. Note the resonance here with Grete's comment that 'If this were Gregor, [. . .] he'd have gone away on his own accord' (CSS 134).

2 Return to a Father

1. Lawrence M. Bensky, 'Harold Pinter: An Interview', in *Pinter: A Collection of Critical Essays,* edited by Arthur Ganz (Englewood Cliffs, N.J., 1972) pp. 21–2. This interview was originally published in *The Paris Review* 10 (Fall 1966).

2. Ibid., p. 22.
3. Pinter, interviewed by John Sherwood, BBC European Service, 3 March 1960; cited in Martin Esslin, *Pinter: The Playwright* (London, 1982) p. 40.
4. *Beckett at Sixty* (London, 1967) p. 86.
5. The first of Pinter's works to be submitted to Beckett for perusal was *The Homecoming* (CP 28). At the time of his death, Beckett was reading Pinter's screenplay of *The Trial* (CP 144).
6. This term was first applied to Pinter's work by Irving Wardle in an article which appeared in *Encore* in September–October 1958.
7. Ronald Hayman, *Harold Pinter* (London, 1980) p. 1.
8. Not surprisingly, the connection between Pinter and Kafka has been attracting more attention since the dramatist wrote his screenplay of *The Trial*. (See, for example, the articles by Francis Gillen and John L. Kundert-Gibbs listed in Works Cited.) I shall discuss the significance of *The Trial* in the opening section of Chapter 4.
9. However, he did write at least one short play – namely, 'The Warden of the Tomb'; and indeed a number of fragments in dramatic form are to be found in his diaries.
10. In Great Britain, the stories of *Description of a Struggle* were published in an omnibus edition with those of *The Great Wall of China*. The latter selection had been issued separately in 1933.
11. Pinter, cited in ' Two People in a Room', *The New Yorker*, 25 February 1967, p. 35.
12. Pinter, interviewed by Sir Jeremy Isaacs on *Face to Face*, BBC2 TV, 21 January 1997.
13. Ibid.
14. In 1948, Pinter received his call-up papers for National Service and – to the consternation of his parents – promptly declared himself a conscientious objector. As a result, he was twice summoned to appear before a military tribunal and there was a real possibility that he would be sent to prison. However, in each of the two civil trials which followed, he was fortunate enough to encounter an unusually lenient magistrate, who decided that, since the defendant was under twenty-one, a stiff financial penalty would be more appropriate. On both occasions, Pinter Snr just about managed to scrape together the money to pay the fine. See Michael Billington, *The Life and Work of Harold Pinter* (London, 1996) pp. 21–4.
15. Pinter married the non-Jewish actress Vivien Merchant (Ada Thomson) in 1956. They separated in 1975 and were divorced in 1980. (Incidentally, his second wife, the author Antonia Fraser, is also a gentile.) See Billington, pp. 53–4.
16. All four of Pinter's grandparents were Ashkenazic Jews: his maternal grandfather came from Odessa; the other three came from Poland. See Billington, pp. 2–3.
17. Pinter, cited in Esslin, p. 15. The family home was a 'very comfortable', three-storey, terraced house at 19 Thistlewaite Road, near Clapton Pond. Pinter recalls how his mother – Frances (*née* Moskowitz) – was 'a marvellous cook' and always kept the house 'immaculate'.

18. Pinter, cited in 'Two People in a Room', p. 35.
19. The Yiddish word *schochet* denotes a rabbinically appointed ritual slaughterer.
20. MIL, follows p. 75, l. 16; cited in Jiří Gruša, *Franz Kafka of Prague* (New York, 1983) p. 70.
21. Brod, p. 74.
22. Ibid., p. 109.
23. Butcher's hooks, incidentally, are featured prominently in the opening and closing frames of Pinter's screen version of Fred Uhlman's novel *Reunion* (CS 55; 98–9). Evidently, the Nazi authorities also regarded them as 'the classic formula for dealing with troublemakers' (M 62); since those implicated in the plot against Hitler were hanged upon such hooks.
24. Pinter worked closely for about a year on *The Handmaid's Tale* with director Karel Reisz (having previously collaborated with him on the film of *The French Lieutenant's Woman*). However, when Reisz withdrew from the project and was replaced by Volker Schlondorff, the dramatist felt too exhausted to begin redrafting the screenplay. Schlondorff took the script to Margaret Atwood herself and then incorporated suggestions made by members of the cast. In the end, Pinter thought that there was just about enough of his work in the 'hotchpotch' to warrant his name appearing in the credits as the sole scenarist. Significantly, though, he has decided not to publish the screenplay. See Billington, p. 304.
25. Barry Supple, 'Pinter's Homecoming', *The Jewish Chronicle*, 25 June 1965, p. 7.
26. John Lahr, 'An Actor's Approach: An Interview with Paul Rogers', in *A Casebook on Harold Pinter's The Homecoming*, edited by John and Anthea Lahr (London, 1974) p. 160.
27. William Shakespeare, *Hamlet*, 2.2.304–7.
28. James Joyce, *A Portrait of the Artist as a Young Man* (London, 1992) p. 183.
29. Kafka's mother told Max Brod that all her husband's family were 'giants' (Brod, p. 4).
30. There is indeed a rather *louche* analogy between Teddy and the prodigal son. The latter had left his father's house for a far country, where, having wasted his money on harlots, he ended up feeding husks to swine. In *The Homecoming*, the filial 'stinkpig' (III 79) returns from a far country with a harlot in tow.
31. Charles Baudelaire, cited in François Truffaut, *Jules and Jim: A Film by François Truffaut* (London, 1968) p. 37.
32. John Milton, 'A Mask (Comus)', ll. 50–3.
33. It would seem that Ruth – whose triumphant transition from despised outsider to royal dam ironically parallels the history of her Old Testament namesake – has had her eye on Max's seat of power from the very moment she first entered the house:

    TEDDY: That's my father's chair.
    RUTH: That one? (III 28)

There are in fact two large armchairs in the living-room: one at the centre, the other to the right of centre. The first of these is the one that belongs to Max, and is also the one that is occupied by Ruth at the end. See French's acting edition of *The Homecoming* (London, 1965) pp. 1; 8; 40–3.

34. 'Counterparts' appears in Joyce's celebrated collection of short stories *Dubliners*.
35. Erich Heller, *Kafka* (London, 1974) p. 21.
36. Pinter could not have known about these particular details when he was writing *The Homecoming*, since *Letters to Felice* – in which they appear – had not yet been published.
37. According to Gustav Janouch, Kafka had summarized the play thus: 'In [. . .] *The Playboy of the Western World* the son is an adolescent exhibitionist who boasts of having murdered his father. Then along comes the old man and turns the young conqueror of paternal authority into a figure of fun' (CK 69). Although fair enough as far as it goes, this synopsis fails to take account of the final twist in the plot. The play in fact ends with the son asserting himself as 'the master of all fights'. Driving his befuddled father onward, the young fellow departs the stage 'like a gallant captain with his heathen slave'. J.M. Synge, *The Playboy of the Western World* and *Riders to the Sea* (New York, 1993) p. 57.
38. Ibid., p. 34.
39. Ibid., p. 21.
40. Ibid., p. 33.
41. Ibid., p. 27.
42. Ibid., p. 23.
43. This is a paraphrase of the opening lines of both L.P. Hartley's *The Go-Between* and Pinter's screenplay of that novel.
44. Kafka was awarded a doctorate in jurisprudence from the Karl-Ferdinand University in Prague in 1906.
45. Jack Pinter was more sympathetic to his son's nocturnal literary endeavours. The playwright 'recalls with great affection a moment when his father found him, at the age of fourteen, sitting up very late one night in the kitchen tearfully writing some love poetry. Instead of packing him off to bed, his father simply encouraged him to go on writing' (Billington, p. 15).
46. A modified version of this passage appeared under the title 'Bachelor's Ill Luck' (*Das Unglück des Junggesellen*) in Kafka's collection *Meditation* (*Betrachtung*. Leipzig: Rowohlt Verlag, 1913). See CSS 394–5. The author offers a more elaborate treatment of the same theme in 'Blumfeld, an Elderly Bachelor'.
47. Max Brod was told by a mutual acquaintance that the child – a little boy, about whom Kafka knew nothing – had died suddenly at the age of seven in Munich in 1921. See Brod, pp. 240–2. (Brod refers to Grete Bloch cryptically as 'M.M.'.)
48. The Yiddish word *shiksa* is generally used to denote a non-Jewish young woman; though it is sometimes used by Orthodox Jews as a designation for a slatternly Jewess.
49. Billington, pp. 53–4.

3 More Strange Than a Stranger

1. Max Brod, Editor's Note to the first edition of *The Castle* (C 8).
2. This passage is echoed in a letter to Max Brod, dated 25 October 1923 (FFE 387).
3. There is a connection here with Bates in *Silence,* who also lives in a tenement presided over by a landlady with a penchant for alcohol and small talk (III 201).
4. Compare with Proverbs 22:14 and Ecclesiastes 7:26.
5. Brod, p. 9.
6. Teddy is reported to have written several letters to his father – and one to his Uncle Sam – from America (III 70).
7. The poem in question was 'Recognition' by Johann Nepomuk Vogl (1802–66).
8. The idea of a mother and son being unable to communicate is also central to *Mountain Language.*
9. The author gave this parable the title 'Before the Law' (*Vor dem Gesetz*). It was first published in the almanac *Vom jüngsten Tag* (Leipzig: Kurt Wolff Verlag, 1916), and later appeared in Kafka's collection *A Country Doctor* (*Ein Landarzt.* Munich and Leipzig: Kurt Wolff Verlag, 1919).
10. Kafka felt that, on balance, it was probably better if his parents postponed their visit until his condition improved (FFE 414–15); but, instead of improving, it rapidly deteriorated and he died without seeing them again. The date of this letter is given as 19 May 1924 in FFE, though Brod indicates that it was written on 2 June 1924 – just one day before the author's death. See Brod, p. 209.
11. This is arguably another variation on the theme of zoomorphism – as outlined in Chapter 2.
12. The situation in *One for the Road* is rather complicated, because it involves a relationship between an actual father (Victor) and son (Nicky) which is completely overshadowed by the fact that both of them have been subjugated by a professedly theocratic vicegerent (Nicolas).
13. William Shakespeare, *Hamlet,* 1.5.183.
14. References to *Hamlet* are also to be found in Pinter's novel *The Dwarfs* (D 81; 86; 132) and in his screenplays of *The Comfort of Strangers* and *Reunion* (CS 28; 66). Interestingly, Hamlet is characterized in the latter instance as 'a classic example of schizophrenia, of split personality' (CS 66).
15. The wording here is from the New International Version of the Bible.
16. There are in fact a number of intriguing parallels between *The Wizard of Oz* and both *Family Voices* and *Moonlight*. These will be discussed towards the end of the next chapter.
17. The Nephilim – referred to simply as 'giants' in the Authorized Version – were the offspring of the sons of God and the daughters of men. 'They were heroes of old, men of renown' (New International Version, Genesis 6:4; see also Numbers 13:33).
18. There is perhaps a proleptic association here with Riley's namesake

in *Moonlight*, who, we are told, was sometimes 'known under his other hat as the Sheikh of Araby' (M 50).
19. Canetti, pp. 49–52.

4 The Final Blasphemy

1. Pinter, cited in Ronald Knowles, 'Harold Pinter, Citizen', *The Pinter Review* 3 (1989) p. 25.
2. The 20th of June Society – so-named after the date of its first meeting – was a discussion group formed in 1988 by a number of liberal-minded writers who were discontented with the socio-political climate in Britain under the Conservative Government of Margaret Thatcher. Participants – besides Pinter and Antonia Fraser – included John and Penelope Mortimer, Margaret Drabble, Peter Nichols, Germaine Greer, David Hare, Melvyn Bragg, Michael Holroyd, Ian McEwan, Angela Carter and Salman Rushdie. They were frequently ridiculed in the Tory press, which labelled them 'champagne socialists' and 'Bollinger Bolsheviks'. The Society was dissolved in the spring of 1992.
3. Irving Wardle, review of *No Man's Land, The Times*, 25 April 1975, p. 13. (Also cited on the back of Methuen editions of Pinter's collected plays.)
4. Pinter, cited in Matt Wolf, 'Happy 60th Birthday, Harold Pinter', *The Miami Herald*, 7 October 1990, p. 71.
5. Hall's novel was published under the title *The Berlin Memorandum*. 'Quiller' is the name of its central character.
6. Pinter has hinted that some of his supposedly apolitical screenplays do in fact have a political subtext. He points to the example of *The Servant*, which he claims 'is about the English caste system' (CP 72). Presumably, the same could also be said of *The Go-Between*.
7. Louis Marks, 'Producing Pinter', in *Pinter at Sixty*, edited by Katherine H. Burkham and John L. Kundert-Gibbs (Bloomington and Indianapolis, 1993) p. 22.
8. Ibid.
9. In the same week that Pinter's adaptation of *The Trial* opened in UK cinemas, the BBC (the film's co-financiers) screened the Orson Welles version on network television. This eccentric piece of scheduling was seized upon by *The Times*, which ran a factitious story about how Pinter was hopping mad at the BBC for undermining the commercial prospects of the new film. The playwright complained to the Press Council and eventually, after some prevarication, *The Times* issued an apology. See CP 117–18.
10. Pinter, cited in Marks, p. 18.
11. Ibid.
12. Ibid., p. 22.
13. In the interim, Istvan Szabo – the renowned Hungarian director of such films as *Confidence, Mephisto* and *Colonel Redl* – had been signed up to direct *The Trial*. However, it quickly became apparent that he and Pinter had such radically different views about the project that

they could not work together. See Billington, p. 348.
14. Louis Marks, cited in a BBC press release, summer 1989.
15. This scene was devised by Pinter on the advice of Antonia Fraser, who felt that the play needed a sense of Bridget's life together with her brothers (CP 112).
16. Dylan Thomas, 'Do not go gentle into that good night', *Collected Poems, 1934–1953* (London, 1988) p. 148.
17. This circumstance is contradicted by a diary entry from 29 July 1914, in which Kafka relates how Joseph K. had had 'a violent quarrel with his father', a wealthy merchant, who 'had reproached him for his dissipated life and demanded that he put an immediate stop to it' (DII 71). Shades of 'The Urban World' and 'The Judgement'.
18. Kafka worked in the Prague offices of this Italian insurance company for ten months (from October 1907 to July 1908).
19. *The Homecoming* was revived under Sir Peter Hall's direction at London's Comedy Theatre in 1991.
20. Alf Garnett was created by Johnny Speight and first came to life on 22 July 1965 in a pilot programme for BBC TV's 'Comedy Playhouse'. The character made such a sensational impact that the series *Till Death Us Do Part* was immediately commissioned. It ran for fifty-three episodes from June 1966 to December 1975, poking fun at the British Establishment and outraging certain self-appointed guardians of the nation's morals. The series spawned two feature films, as well as a sequel, *In Sickness and in Health*, which appeared in the mid-1980s. Less profane American imitations in the shape of *All in the Family* – with Carroll O'Connor as Archie Bunker – and its sequel, *Archie Bunker's Place*, ran on the CBS network during 1971–78 and 1979–82, respectively.
21. Bensky, p. 31.
22. Ibid.
23. Ibid.
24. We should also include here 'American Football', a seventeen-line poem written in August 1991 as a response to US attitudes to the Gulf War. This scatological psalm was offered to a quintet of leading publications – *The Independent*, *The Observer*, *The Guardian*, *The New York Review of Books* and *The London Review of Books* – all of which considered it unprintable. It was, however, published in the 1991 edition of *The Pinter Review* (p. 41), the annual journal dedicated to the study of the playwright's work (edited by Francis Gillen and Steven H. Gale, University of Tampa Press: Tampa, Florida). Coincidentally, in October 1991, Pet Shop Boys, the ultra-sophisticated British pop duo, released their song 'DJ Culture', a symphonic evocation of the conflict in the Gulf and the public reactions to it, which also uses the metaphor of a football game.
25. Shortly before his powers of censorship were due to be abolished under the Theatres Act (1968), the Lord Chamberlain refused to grant a licence to Pinter's *Landscape*, because it contained a couple of 'objectionable' words. Rather than agree to bowdlerize his own text, Pinter decided to postpone the stage production until the following year.

In the meantime, the play was premièred uncut on BBC radio, over which the Lord Chamberlain had no authority.

26. A late addition to this short list of 'exceptions' is Rebecca in *Ashes to Ashes*. See AA 9.
27. *Mountain Language* was inspired by Pinter's visit to Turkey in March 1985, during which he became acquainted with the plight of the Kurds, who had been forbidden to speak their own language by the Turkish military regime.
28. Henrik Ibsen, *A Doll's House* (London, 1991) p. 53.
29. There is also a connection here with the name of the inventor of the telephone – Alexander Graham Bell (1847–1922).
30. 'Problem' appears in Pinter's *Collected Poems and Prose* (London, 1986) p. 101. The notion that a telephone could be an accessory – if not an accessary – to murder brings to mind the opening scene of *The Quiller Memorandum*, where a man is shot dead while making a call from a telephone box.
31. Josef von Sternberg, *Fun in a Chinese Laundry* (London, 1987) p. 241.
32. In Celtic mythology, Bridget is the name of a fire goddess.
33. Rudyard Kipling, 'The Ladies', *A Choice of Kipling's Verse* (London, 1941) p. 213.
34. William Shakespeare, *King Lear*, 5.3.
35. Samuel Beckett, *The Unnamable* (London, 1975) p. 13.
36. The posture of Fred is not always stated clearly in the text. The relevant stage directions for the seven scenes in which he appears are as follows:

    (1) 'FRED *in bed*' (M 6);
    (2) 'FRED *and* JAKE, *sitting at a table*' (M 23)
    (3) 'BRIDGET *and* FRED *on the floor*' (M 29);
    (4) 'FRED *and* JAKE, *at the table*' (M 41);
    (5) 'FRED *in bed*' (M 49);
    (6) No position specified (M 73);
    (7) 'FRED *is out of bed*' (M 77).

    We can see from the above information that Fred is definitely in bed in (1) and (5), and definitely out of bed in (3) and (7). However, in (2) and (4), two scenes where Fred's position is evidently the same, the presence of the comma in the stage direction is confusing; and all the more so when we consider the absence of a comma from the analogous construction in (3). Are we to understand from this that Fred and Jake are both sitting at a table, or that Fred is still in bed and Jake is at the table? The key to resolving this ambiguity would seem to lie in (5). Indeed the only reason for us to be told in (5) that Fred is in bed is that he must have been out of bed in (4) – and likewise in (2). Finally, the fact that no details are given in (6) would suggest that the situation here is the same as (5); and this is effectively confirmed when we are told quite categorically in (7) that 'FRED *is out of bed*'.
37. Franz Kafka, *The Trial* (Harmondsworth, 1953) p. 168. This sentence – a translation of *Es ist das eine Stellung, die sich immer vererbt* – appears

in the earlier English editions of the novel, but has been truncated in the 'definitive' edition to 'It's a hereditary post' (T 169).

38. In *The Trial*, for example, Joseph K. is interviewed by the Inspector in Fräulein Bürstner's bedroom, consults with a bedridden advocate, and even enters the Law-Court offices by clambering over the bed of the artist Titorelli. Similarly, at various points in *The Castle*, K. discusses his case with the Village Superintendent, Gardana and Burgel as they recline on their respective beds. Most striking, though, as far as *Moonlight* is concerned, is the situation in 'The Married Couple', where the bedroom of a sick son becomes the forum for an impromtu business meeting.
39. Written by Jonathan Lynn and Antony Jay, this satirical saga of British parliamentary politics ran on BBC TV throughout the 1980s. In the original series, the central character, Jim Hacker (played by Paul Eddington), was an inept 'Minister for Administrative Affairs' manipulated by double-talking civil servants, the most crafty being his Permanent Under-Secretary, Sir Humphrey Appleby (played by Nigel Hawthorne). In the sequel, Hacker's wirepullers had managed to get him installed in 10 Downing Street.
40. One possible explanation for this discrepancy is that in most administrative organizations females have traditionally been the flunkeys – typists, receptionists, canteen workers, cleaners and so on – and, as such, the male staff have tended to address them, often quite patronizingly, by their first names.
41. Ivor H. Evans, ed., *Brewer's Dictionary of Phrase and Fable* (London, 1981) p. 257.
42. Patrick Hanks and Flavia Hodges, *A Dictionary of First Names* (London, 1990) p. 275.
43. William Shakespeare, *Hamlet*, 1.2.211.
44. Ibid., 1.2.186–7.
45. Ibid., 1.2.254.
46. Hanks and Hodges, p. 18.
47. Interestingly, in *Ashes to Ashes*, the play which followed *Moonlight*, the heroine (whose maternal status is something of a moot point) is called Rebecca – the name of the mother of Jacob and Esau.
48. This Bible story, in which the patriarch is disorientated by his failing eyesight, is also adumbrated in *Tea Party*, where the dazed protagonist (Disson) is himself a visually-impaired father of two sons.
49. Note how Fred obligingly dissociates himself from the father here in order to facilitate Jake's 'loving son' spiel.
50. This not only recalls the sardonic use of the vocative 'Dad' in *The Homecoming* and *Family Voices*, but also – in the context of Jake's (soon to be discussed) impersonation of Christ – Jesus's extraordinary use of the Aramaic equivalent, *Abba*, in Mark 14:36.
51. In declaring, 'I've always wanted to be a God', Fred is ironically giving voice to the Adamic hubris of Andy himself. Both Fred's mimicry of Andy and Andy's association with Adam will be discussed later.
52. See n. 36.

53. Just as, in Jake, Pinter capitalizes on links between Jacob and Jesus, so, in Fred, he draws on connections between Isaac and Jesus. A full list of the latter is given towards the end of the discussion of 'The Judgement' in Chapter 1.
54. William Shakespeare, *Hamlet*, 4.5.
55. In the original German text, the change is from *unserer* to *die*.
56. Noel Langley, Florence Ryerson and Edgar Allen Wolfe, *The Wizard of Oz* (London, 1991) p. 129.
57. L. Frank Baum, *The Wizard of Oz* (London, 1982) p. 142.
58. Ibid., p. 132.
59. Ibid., p. 134.
60. Hamlet himself had been living away from home prior to the death of his father.
61. William Shakespeare, *Richard II*, 3.2.152.
62. William Shakespeare, *Henry IV, Part 2*, 3.1.31.
63. Born in 1933, the Kray twins – Ronnie and Reggie – were violent criminals who ran a Mafia-style operation in the East End of London during the 1960s. Lionized by some and feared by many, the pair were eventually convicted of the murders of two rival gang members and sentenced to life imprisonment. The idea that London gangsters could be perceived as charismatic 'performers' is explored by Donald Cammell and Nicolas Roeg in their brutal and Byzantine feature film *Performance*, where the personae of a holed-up hoodlum (James Fox) and a fading pop star (Mick Jagger) are gradually interfused.
64. R.W. Holder, *The Faber Dictionary of Euphemisms* (London, 1989) p. 214.
65. This is echoed in *Moonlight*, where Jake claims that his father 'has been from time immemorial pursued by a malignant force' (M 56), and asserts that Fred will ultimately have to account for that force.
66. William Shakespeare, *Hamlet*, 3.4.206.
67. Billington, p. 346.
68. Ibid.
69. Ibid.
70. Oscar Wilde, *The Importance of Being Earnest* (Harlow, Essex, 1983) p. 20.

Works Cited

Albee, Edward. *Who's Afraid of Virginia Woolf?* Harmondsworth: Penguin, 1965.

Atwood, Margaret. *The Handmaid's Tale*. London: Virago, 1987.

Auden, W.H. *Collected Poems*. Edited by Edward Mendelson. London: Faber & Faber, 1976.

Baker, William, and Stephen E. Tabachnik. *Harold Pinter*. Edinburgh: Oliver & Boyd, 1973.

Baum, L. Frank. *The Wizard of Oz*. London: Puffin, 1982.

Beckett, Samuel. *Endgame*. London: Faber & Faber, 1958.

——. *Mercier and Camier*. London: Calder & Boyars, 1974.

——. *The Unnamable*. London: Calder & Boyars, 1975.

——. *Waiting for Godot*. London: Faber & Faber, 1965.

Beckett at Sixty: A Festschrift. London: Calder & Boyars, 1967.

Bensky, Lawrence M. 'Harold Pinter: An Interview'. *Pinter: A Collection of Critical Essays*. Edited by Arthur Ganz. Englewood Cliffs, N.J.: Prentice-Hall, 1972. pp. 19–33.

Billington, Michael. *The Life and Work of Harold Pinter*. London: Faber & Faber, 1996.

Bowen, Elizabeth. *The Heat of the Day*. London: Jonathan Cape, 1949.

Brod, Max. *Franz Kafka: A Biography*. Second, enlarged edition. Translated by G. Humphreys Roberts and Richard Winston. New York: Schocken, 1960.

Burkham, Katherine H. *The Dramatic World of Harold Pinter: Its Basis in Ritual*. Columbus: Ohio State University Press, 1971.

Canetti, Elias. *Kafka's Other Trial*. Translated by Christopher Middleton. Harmondsworth: Penguin, 1982.

Coleridge, Samuel Taylor. *Selected Poems*. Edited and with an introduction and notes by James Reeves. London: Heinemann, 1959.

Dostoyevsky, Fyodor. *The Brothers Karamazov*. 2 vols. Translated and with an introduction by David Magarshack. Harmondsworth: Penguin, 1958.

Esslin, Martin. *Pinter: The Playwright*. London: Methuen, 1982.

Evans, Ivor H., ed. *Brewer's Dictionary of Phrase and Fable*. Revised edition. London: Cassell, 1981.

Fowles, John. *The French Lieutenant's Woman*. London: Picador, 1992.

Gillen, Francis. 'From Novel to Film: Harold Pinter's Adaptation of *The Trial*'. *Pinter at Sixty*. Edited by Katherine H. Burkham and John L. Kundert-Gibbs. Bloomington and Indianapolis: Indiana University Press, 1993. pp. 137–48.

Gruša, Jiří. *Franz Kafka of Prague*. Translated by Eric Mosbacher. New York: Schocken, 1983.

Gussow, Mel. *Conversations with Pinter*. London: Nick Hern, 1994.

Hall, Adam. *The Berlin Memorandum*. London: Collins, 1965.
Hanks, Patrick, and Flavia Hodges. *A Dictionary of First Names*. London: Guild Publishing, 1990.
Hartley, L.P. *The Go-Between*. London: Hamish Hamilton, 1953.
Hayman, Ronald. *Harold Pinter*. Fourth edition. London: Heinemann, 1980.
——. *K: A Biography of Kafka*. London: Weidenfeld & Nicolson, 1981.
Heller, Erich. *Kafka*. London: Fontana, 1974.
Higgins, Aidan. *Langrishe, Go Down*. London: John Calder, 1966.
Holder, R.W. *The Faber Dictionary of Euphemisms*. London: Faber & Faber, 1989.
The Holy Bible. Authorized Version. London: Oxford University Press.
——. New International Version. London: Hodder & Stoughton, 1986.
Homer. *The Odyssey*. Translated by E.V. Rieu. Harmondsworth: Penguin, 1946.
Ibsen, Henrik. *A Doll's House*. Translated by Michael Meyer. Commentary and notes by Non Worrall. London: Methuen, 1991.
Janouch, Gustav. *Conversations with Kafka*. Revised and enlarged edition. Translated by Goronwy Rees. Introduction by Hugh Haughton. London: Quartet, 1985.
Jonson, Ben. *Three Comedies*. Edited and with an introduction by Michael Jamieson. Harmondsworth: Penguin, 1966.
Joyce, James. *Dubliners*. Introduction and notes by Terence Brown. London: Penguin, 1992.
——. *A Portrait of the Artist as a Young Man*. Introduction by Anthony Burgess. London: Minerva, 1992.
Kafka, Franz. *America*. Definitive edition. Translated by Willa and Edwin Muir. Introduction by Edwin Muir. Postscript by Max Brod. London: Secker & Warburg, 1949.
——. *The Castle*. Definitive edition. Translated by Willa and Edwin Muir. Additional material translated by Eithne Wilkins and Ernst Kaiser. London: Secker & Warburg, 1953.
——. *The Complete Short Stories*. Edited by Nahum N. Glatzer. London: Minerva, 1992.
——. *Description of a Struggle* and *The Great Wall of China*. Translated by Tania and James Stern, and Willa and Edwin Muir. London: Secker & Warburg, 1960.
——. *Diaries, 1910–1913*. Edited by Max Brod. Translated by Joseph Kresh. London: Secker & Warburg, 1948.
——. *Diaries, 1914–1923*. Edited by Max Brod. Translated by Martin Greenberg, with the co-operation of Hannah Arendt. London: Secker & Warburg, 1949.
——. *Gesammelte Werke* [Collected Works]. Herausgegeben von Max Brod [Edited by Max Brod]. Frankfurt am Main: S. Fischer Verlag, 1976.
——. *The Great Wall of China and Other Short Works*. Translated and edited bv Malcolm Pasley. London: Penguin, 1991.
——. *In the Penal Settlement: Tales and Short Prose Works*. Translated by Willia and Edwin Muir. London: Secker & Warburg, 1948.
——. *Letters to Felice*. Edited by Erich Heller and Jürgen Born. Trans-

lated by James Stern and Elizabeth Duckworth. London: Secker & Warburg, 1974.
——. *Letters to Friends, Family and Editors*. Translated by Richard and Clara Winston. London: John Calder, 1978.
——. *Letters to Milena*. Edited by Willy Haas. Translated by Tania and James Stern. London: Secker & Warburg, 1953.
——. *Letters to Ottla and the Family*. Translated by Richard and Clara Winston. Edited by N.N. Glatzer. New York: Schocken, 1982.
——. *The Transformation and Other Stories*. Translated and edited by Malcolm Pasley. London: Penguin, 1992.
——. *The Trial*. Translated by Willa and Edwin Muir. Harmondsworth: Penguin, 1953.
——. *The Trial*. Definitive edition. Translated by Willa and Edwin Muir. Revised, and with additional material translated by E.M. Butler. London: Secker & Warburg, 1956.
——. *Wedding Preparations in the Country, and Other Posthumous Prose Writings*. Translated by Eithne Wilkins and Ernst Kaiser. Notes by Max Brod. London: Secker & Warburg, 1954.
Kierkegaard, Søren. *Fear and Trembling*, and *The Sickness unto Death*. Translated by Walter Lowrie. Princeton, N.J.: Princeton University Press, 1954.
Kipling, Rudyard. *A Choice of Kipling's Verse*. Made by T.S. Eliot, with an essay on Rudyard Kipling. London: Faber & Faber, 1941.
Knowles, Ronald. 'Harold Pinter, Citizen'. *The Pinter Review* 3 (1989): pp. 24–33.
Koestler, Arthur. *Darkness at Noon*. Translated by Daphne Hardy. London: Jonathan Cape, 1940.
Kundert-Gibbs, John L. '"I am powerful . . . and I am only the lowest doorkeeper": Power Play in Kafka's *The Trial* and Pinter's *Victoria Station*'. *Pinter at Sixty*. Edited by Katherine H. Burkham and John L. Kundert-Gibbs. Bloomington and Indianapolis: Indiana University Press, 1993. pp. 149–60.
Lahr, John. 'An Actor's Approach: An Interview with Paul Rogers'. *A Casebook on Harold Pinter's The Homecoming*. Edited by John and Anthea Lahr. London: Davis-Poynter, 1974. pp. 151–73.
Langley, Noel, Florence Ryerson and Edgar Allen Woolf. *The Wizard of Oz*. Edited and with an introduction by Andrew Patrick Hearn. London: Faber & Faber, 1991.
Malory, Sir Thomas. *Le Morte D'Arthur*. 2 vols. Edited by Janet Cowen. Introduction by John Lawlor. Harmondsworth: Penguin, 1969.
Mamet, David. *Glengarry Glen Ross*. London: Methuen, 1990.
Marks, Louis. 'Producing Pinter'. *Pinter at Sixty*. Edited by Katherine H. Burkham and John L. Kundert-Gibbs. Bloomington and Indianapolis: Indiana University Press, 1993. pp. 18–23.
Maugham, Robin. *The Servant*. London: Falcon Press, 1948.
McEwan, Ian. *The Comfort of Strangers*. London: Jonathan Cape, 1981.
Miller, Arthur. *Death of a Salesman*. Harmondsworth: Penguin, 1961.
Milton, John. *Poetical Works*. Edited by Douglas Bush. London: Oxford University Press, 1966.

Orwell, George. *Nineteen Eighty-Four*. London: Secker & Warburg, 1949.
Page, Malcolm. *File on Pinter*. London: Methuen, 1993.
Pinter, Harold. 'American Football'. *The Pinter Review* 5 (1991): p. 41.
——. *Ashes to Ashes*. London: Faber & Faber, 1996.
——. *Collected Poems and Prose*. London: Methuen, 1986.
——. *The Comfort of Strangers and Other Screenplays*. London: Faber & Faber, 1990. Also contains: *Reunion; Turtle Diary; Victory*.
——. *The Dwarfs* (a novel). London: Faber & Faber, 1990.
——. *Five Screenplays*. London: Eyre Methuen, 1971. Contains: *The Servant; The Pumpkin Eater; The Quiller Memorandum; Accident; The Go-Between*.
——. *The French Lieutenant's Woman and Other Screenplays*. London: Methuen, 1982. Also contains: *Langrishe, Go Down; The Last Tycoon*.
——. *The Handmaid's Tale*. Film released in 1990. Screenplay unpublished.
——. *The Heat of the Day*. London: Faber & Faber, 1989.
——. *The Homecoming*. Acting edition. London: Samuel French, 1965.
——. *Moonlight*. London: Faber & Faber, 1993.
——. *Party Time*. London: Faber & Faber, 1991.
——. *Plays One*. London: Faber & Faber, 1991. Contains: 'Writing for the Theatre'; *The Birthday Party; The Room; The Dumb Waiter; A Slight Ache; The Hothouse; A Night Out; The Black and White; The Examination*.
——. *Plays Two*. London: Faber & Faber, 1991. Contains: 'Writing for Myself'; *The Caretaker; The Dwarfs; The Collection; The Lover; Night School; Trouble in the Works; The Black and White; Request Stop; Last to Go; Special Offer*.
——. *Plays Three*. London: Faber & Faber, 1991. Contains: 'Mac'; *The Homecoming; Tea Party; The Basement; Landscape; Silence; Night; That's Your Trouble; That's All; Applicant; Interview; Dialogue for Three*; 'Tea Party' (short story).
——. *Plays Four*. Revised edition. London: Faber & Faber, 1993. Contains: 'Speech at Hamburg'; *Old Times; No Man's Land; Betrayal; Monologue; Family Voices; A Kind of Alaska; Victoria Station; Precisely; One for the Road; Mountain Language; The New World Order*.
——. *The Proust Screenplay – À la Recherche du Temps Perdu*. London: Eyre Methuen, 1978.
——. *The Trial*. London: Faber & Faber, 1993.
——. *Twelve Early Poems*. London: Greville Press Pamphlets, 1992.
Politzer, Heinz. *Franz Kafka: Parable and Paradox*. Ithaca, N.Y.: Cornell University Press, 1962.
Rushdie, Salman. *The Satanic Verses*. London: Viking, 1988.
Shaffer, Peter. *Equus*. London: Andre Deutsch, 1973.
Shakespeare, William. *The Complete Oxford Shakespeare*. 3 vols. General editors: Stanley Wells and Gary Taylor. London: Guild Publishing, 1989.
Sophocles. *The Theban Plays*. Translated by E.F. Watling. Harmondsworth: Penguin, 1947.
Stoppard, Tom. *Rosencrantz and Guildenstern are Dead*. London: Faber & Faber, 1967.
Supple, Barry. 'Pinter's Homecoming'. *The Jewish Chronicle*, 25 June 1965: pp. 7; 31.

Sykes, J.B., ed. *The Concise Oxford Dictionary of Current English*. Sixth edition. Oxford: Oxford University Press, 1977.
Synge, J.M. *The Playboy of the Western World* and *Riders to the Sea*. New York: Dover, 1993.
Tauber, Herbert. *Franz Kafka: An Interpretation of his Works*. Translated by G. Humphreys Roberts and Roger Senhouse. London: Secker & Warburg, 1948.
Thomas, Dylan. *Collected Poems, 1934–1953*. Edited by Walford Davies and Ralph Maud. London: Dent, 1988.
Truffaut, François. *Jules and Jim: A Film by François Truffaut*. Translated by Nicholas Fry. London: Lorrimer, 1968.
'Two People in a Room'. *The New Yorker*, 25 February 1967: pp. 34–6.
Uhlman, Fred. *Reunion*. London: Collins, 1971.
Von Sternberg, Josef. *Fun in a Chinese Laundry*. London: Columbus, 1987.
Wardle, Irving. 'Comedy of Menace'. *Encore* 5 (September–October 1958): pp. 28–33.
——. Review of *No Man's Land*. *The Times*, 25 April 1975: p. 13.
Welles, Orson. *The Trial: A Film by Orson Welles*. Translated by Nicholas Fry. London: Lorrimer, 1984.
Wilde, Oscar. *The Importance of Being Earnest*. Edited by Robert Wilson, and with a personal essay by Michael Billington. Harlow, Essex: Longman, 1983.
Williams, William Carlos. *Selected Poems*. Edited and with an introduction by Charles Tomlinson. Harmondsworth: Penguin, 1976.
Wolf, Matt. 'Happy 60th Birthday, Harold Pinter'. *The Miami Herald*, 7 October 1990: p. 71.
Wordsworth, William. *The Poetical Works of Wordsworth*. Edited by Thomas Hutchinson. Revised by Ernest De Selincourt. London: Oxford University Press, 1950.

Index